MW01106724

LBJ AND GRASSROOTS FEDERALISM

NUMBER 122

Centennial Series of the Association of Former Students

TEXAS A&M UNIVERSITY

LBJ

and GRASSROOTS FEDERALISM

CONGRESSMAN BOB POAGE, RACE, AND CHANGE IN TEXAS

Robert Harold Duke

*For Jennis + Joyce —
We could write a book about
our long friendship.
Bob
8/14/14*

TEXAS A&M UNIVERSITY PRESS
College Station

FRONTISPIECE: (*Left*) Southern congressmen, including Texans Johnson and Poage, posed at the White House after President Roosevelt's signing of cotton legislation in August 1937. This photo opportunity came early in the first terms of congressmen Poage and Johnson. *Courtesy Lyndon Baines Johnson Library and Museum.* (*Center and right*) Poage and Johnson, speaking in White House Cabinet Room, October 9, 1967. *Courtesy Lyndon Baines Johnson Library and Museum.*

LIBRARY OF CONGRESS CATALOGING-IN-PUBLICATION DATA

Library of Congress Cataloging-in-Publication Data

Duke, Robert Harold, author.
   LBJ and grassroots federalism : Congressman Bob Poage, race, and change in Texas / Robert Harold Duke. — First edition.
      pages cm — (Centennial series of the Association of Former Students, Texas A&M University ; Number 122)
   Includes bibliographical references and index.
   ISBN 978-1-62349-172-7 (cloth : alk. paper) —
   ISBN 978-1-62349-185-7 (ebook)
   1. Federal government—United States—History—20th century—Case studies. 2. Central-local government relations—United States—History—20th century—Case studies. 3. Johnson, Lyndon B. (Lyndon Baines), 1908-1973. 4. Poage, W. R. (William Robert), 1899-1987. 5. Economic assistance, Domestic—Texas—History—20th century. 6. United States. National Youth Administration in Texas—History. 7. Federal aid to water resources development—Texas—History—20th century. 8. Federal aid to community development—Texas—Waco—History—20th century. 9. Texas--Ethnic relations—History—20th century. 10. Mexican-Americans—Texas—Politics and government—20th century. 11. Waco (Tex.)—Politics and government—20th century. 12. Texas—Politics and government—1865-1950. 13. Texas—Politics and government—1951– I. Title. II. Series: Centennial series of the Association of Former Students, Texas A&M University; no. 122.
   JK325.D85 2014
   320.609764'284—dc23
   2014000844

This book is dedicated to

my family, to my teachers,

to my students, and to Sandy.

CONTENTS

ACKNOWLEDGMENTS

THE WRITERS FOR THE *Smothers Brothers Comedy Hour*, a staple of Sunday night television viewing at my home for the few years the CBS censors could corral them, spurred my interest in Lyndon Baines Johnson. A share of the credit goes to David Frye, an incredibly gifted mimic whose uncanny impressions of all the political figures of the day—except Eugene McCarthy, who somehow rose above impersonation—made the often-terrible news somehow more tolerable. My father, seven years younger than LBJ, grew up in Central Texas picking cotton and raising turkeys on his parents' tenant farm. Although he migrated north during the Depression to find work and did not return until retirement in 1971, the sound of Central Texas remained in his voice, and my young ears heard it in Johnson's voice as well.

For the ceramics project in my eighth grade art class in 1967, I sculpted a bust (head, mostly) of LBJ. Previous issues with firing my work in the kiln, according to Mrs. Schultz, the teacher, meant that this particular piece would remain unfinished. The ears would not have survived, I know. A snippet of wire from a coat hanger served well for some glasses propped on the prominent proboscis. A clay Stetson completed the look, and my statue of Lyndon followed me well into my teaching career, only to be lost somehow. It was a great conversation starter, because my clay caricature caught enough of the Texan's persona that students and other visitors would see him perched (or placed, because he had no feet) on my desk and say things like, "Hey, that looks like LBJ!" Usually this would be followed with, "Not many people . . ." and I would use it as a teachable moment by sharing some bit of Lyndotrivia.

Perhaps I discarded the clay LBJ when I left the classroom after twelve years to become an administrator. I taught ten years longer than he did, but the fact that a teacher became president of the United States captivated me. I'd learned enough about federal education policies to know that his finger-prints were all over them. When the time came to retire from K–12 education as a superintendent to return to school to pursue my doctorate in history at Western Michigan University and teach again, I knew I wanted to write about Johnson.

Under the patient direction of the late Nora Faires, I began my quest for a topic. Early in my doctoral studies, her seminar on migration introduced a potential lens for analysis of how race, ethnicity, and class shaped the po-litical culture of Central Texas. Spurred by scholars from Donald Meinig to Neil Foley, I sought my own path to understanding the interplay between the cultural geography of LBJ's Hill Country, of Austin, and of Bob Poage's blackland prairie cotton-based society of Waco. Superb biographies of LBJ by Robert Caro, Robert Dallek, and Randall Wood, among many others, established that the Pedernales flowed in his veins, but because of Nora's influence, I knew I wanted this study of Johnson's enduring, productive re-lationship with his Waco colleague to demonstrate that we must also see the Brazos flowing—under control—in Poage's.

By that stage of her career, Nora specialized in the US-Canadian border-lands. My interest in the emergence of white integrationists in the South merged with her field in the form of readings on German migration to Cen-tral Texas in the 1840s. As I made the connections between Johnson's youth in the Hill Country, thick with German Texans, and the antislavery values of those migrating families, I saw my project take shape.

A school architect I worked with connected me with the godmother of his daughter, who happened to be the director of the Texas Historical Com-mission in Austin. When I made my first research trip there in 2004, I in-troduced myself to Cynthia Beeman, who in turn introduced me to her col-league, chief historian Dan K. Utley. Their invaluable, unselfish, downright friendly assistance sustained me on multiple trips over the next several years.

Both have since retired, joining forces to write critically acclaimed books about Texas history for Texas A&M University Press.[1]

More readings about transatlantic migration, assimilation, cultural retention, and cultural diffusion led me to reflect on the impact of LBJ's first year as a teacher, when he worked with children from Spanish-speaking homes in Cotulla, Texas, on his thinking about education policy later in his political career. Consistent with the trend at that time in US schools, LBJ's classroom in Cotulla was English only. One of the last major pieces of education legislation in the Great Society era was the Title VII amendment to the Elementary and Secondary Education Act, also known as the Bilingual Education Act, signed into law by Johnson in January 1968. My adviser, Nora, reminded me that she did not want to supervise a doctoral student working on a history of education policy project.

A seminar in labor history with WMU professor Bill Warren opened more doors. During my teaching career, I was an activist in the Michigan Education Association, so I arranged with Bill to do a literature review about the scholarship on K–12 teachers' unions and their influence on education policy. The Walter Reuther Library at Wayne State University in Detroit, Michigan, awarded me a research grant, the Albert Shanker Fellowship, in 2006 that enabled me to dig deeply into the archives of the American Federation of Teachers (AFT) housed at the Reuther with valuable help from Daniel Golodner, the AFT archivist. I am grateful to the North American Labor History Association for giving me the opportunity to present some of my work on teachers' unions at their conference in Detroit in October 2009.

In the course of my readings on teachers' unions, I naturally came upon education historian Wayne Urban's *Gender, Race, and the National Education Association* (NEA).[2] There, on page 234, like a vision of the Holy Grail to a member of the Monty Python troupe, appeared my dissertation topic. Urban concisely stated that the NEA promoted bilingual education funding at the federal level and the AFT opposed it. Johnson, it turned out, felt no enthusiasm for the bill, but at that beleaguered stage of his term, it was no time to get in the way of legislation popular with a most loyal constituency, the Mexican Americans.

Unknown to most educators today, as well as to the general public, the Bilingual Education Act did not mandate anything. It began as a grant program, whereby school districts wishing to train teachers, develop curriculum, and implement programs could get a boost in the form of federal funds.

True to the way Johnson had done things since he served as state director of the Texas National Youth Administration in 1935–37, schools had a long leash in terms of the range of strategies they could employ. Those decisions needed to be tailored to the needs of the students and of the teachers. It turned out there were fewer applicants than budgeted for, and the federal government only spent two-thirds of the $321 million allotted to Title VII for FY1969. Some communities applied, and some did not. Why?

I point this out because this became the heart of my research question: In communities that sought Title VII bilingual education funds, where did the leadership come from to actually pursue the grant funds. Teachers? Community-based organizations? I decided to compare Waco, Texas, with Kalamazoo, Michigan—two similar-sized cities familiar to me. And Nora approved, because my research concentrated on the agency of the unions and of community-based organizations and activists, not on the policy itself. Thanks to funding from Western Michigan University, I was able to present some of my findings at the Texas State Historical Association meeting in Corpus Christi in 2007, in a session attended by one-time US secretary of education Lauro Cavazos. The paper I delivered, titled "Beyond Sandtown," became the basis of one of the chapters of this book.

Along the way I learned more about the ruin that befell downtown Waco in May 1953. My dad's mother lived on Fifth Street at the time, directly across the street from the Carroll Science Library on the Baylor campus. Divorced, she cooked in one of the dormitories and ran a boardinghouse. I learned about the ruinous storm as a part of family folklore. No one spoke of the slum housing along the riverfront a few blocks away, routinely subject to the floods on the Brazos, but now obliterated by the tornado. The Mexican Americans concentrated in that area, known as Sandtown, dispersed across the city, but many moved to the south end of town. The schools there suddenly faced a reality they had not encountered. Nature caused a diaspora of the city's Spanish-speaking children.

I read about plans to build a new dam that would prevent the devastating floods on the Brazos. Lyndon Johnson's name started to come up—and Bob Poage's—and I decided that I wanted to know more about those two and how their careers changed Waco. Ben Rogers at the W. R. Poage Legislative Library at Baylor spent many hours helping me to flesh out the relationship between Johnson and the far lesser known Poage. Just a short walk through the lovely Baylor campus, lined with live oaks, the incredibly helpful staff at the Texas Collection and the Baylor Institute for Oral History guided me through vast holdings, some of which, like the files of the Waco Alliance of Mexican Americans, had not been accessed by any researcher before me. Ellen Suniyuki Brown, Elinor Maze, Tom Charlton, and Becky Shulda provided ongoing support throughout the project.

Beginning in 2004 I made periodic visits to the LBJ Presidential Library in Austin, where the outstanding professionalism of the staff would make Johnson proud. Among the highlights of those trips to the Reading Room was an elevator ride with Robert A. Caro, who impressed me as a most gracious fellow. Even more impressive were his work habits. As I thought about the years going by since I began *LBJ and Grassroots Federalism*, it was somehow comforting to know that after more than thirty years, Caro finally got to 1964, in his fourth installment.

I am grateful to my colleagues at Western Michigan University and at Eastern Michigan University for their interest and support over the life of this endeavor. Finally, a Texas-sized hug for Sandy Duke, who keeps it all together for me, as she has since Bob Poage's last term in Congress.

LBJ AND GRASSROOTS FEDERALISM

Introduction

DEEP IN THE HEART OF LYNDON

UNLIKE ABRAHAM LINCOLN at Gettysburg, Lyndon Johnson could have correctly observed that the "world will not long remember what we say here" as he addressed members of the audience gathered at the groundbreaking ceremony for the construction of a new dam in Waco, Texas, on July 5, 1958. LBJ claimed legislative victories far greater than securing federal funding for this flood control project, but close ties to Central Texas made the event a priority on the Senate Majority Leader's crowded calendar. The upcoming Texas Democratic primary in August meant local and state-level office seekers would savor the chance for a photo opportunity and a handshake. The Waco Chamber of Commerce lobbied ceaselessly for the new dam since the 1930s, so ol' Lyndon, nearly fifty years of age, with a major heart attack behind him, slapped backs, flattered faces, and swapped stories with the likes of newspaper publisher Harlan Fentress, his *Waco Tribune-Herald* editor in chief Harry Provence, and a local Ford dealer, Jack Kultgen. A keen sensitivity to the egos of political friends and rivals, and how these might be massaged or bruised to his advantage, always served Lyndon Baines Johnson well.

The most important of these Waco friends, congressman W. R. "Bob" Poage (D-Eleventh District), called for federal funding for a new dam while campaigning unsuccessfully for the House in 1934.[1] Unlike Johnson, who coaxed a commitment from FDR for a dam in Austin shortly after winning a special election in 1937, Poage could not garner sufficient support to initiate the Waco project, even in an era when it seemed the Army Corps of Engineers would leave no river undammed. Poage's long association with the ambitious senator proved the key to ultimate success, because the Flood Control Act of 1954 (Public Act 780) opened the spillway of the US Treasury for Waco—again.

A total of $2.4 million in requested federal disaster relief had poured in from Washington the previous year following a catastrophic tornado that destroyed much of downtown Waco on May 11, 1953, and took 114 lives.[2] The need to rebuild the leveled business district, along with the planned new dam that enabled the city to reclaim a previously risky floodplain along the Brazos River, meant economic opportunity for private investors. The teamwork of Lyndon Johnson in the Senate and Bob Poage in the House assured local officials federal funds would keep flowing at the most pivotal time in the city's history since railroads connected Waco with Houston and Dallas in the 1870s. What they did not foresee was the newfound prominence of brown and black faces in the civic life of the new Waco.

When Johnson stepped to the podium in a hastily modified setting in a hangar at nearby Waco Air Field, a change of venue caused by an ill-timed, rare summer deluge, he did so as a politician at the top of his game. Invited by his longtime Waco ally to address the festive, though somewhat drenched, crowd, the future president from the Hill Country one hundred miles southwest (and politically to the left) of Waco, kept his remarks brief.[3] Although given to platitudes in formal appearances since his days as a high school debater, LBJ downplayed his own role in cutting the deal, emphasizing how the entire endeavor demonstrated "strength in unity" by harnessing the will and the resources of citizens and their elected officials across all levels of government. After decades of disappointment, the coalition of private and public interests in Waco celebrated success. The system worked, even if, as Poage put it when he took his turn at the improvised dais, "The mills of God grind slowly—so it sometimes seems does the federal government."[4]

Throughout his career, LBJ's brand of federalism advanced a progressive agenda by directing use of the nation's resources to implement the deferred goals of local officials in a manner that simultaneously empowered community leaders and secured loyalty to him. The "Master of the Senate," so vividly depicted in noted LBJ biographer Robert A. Caro's monumental portrait, played variations on this theme as state director of the National Youth

Bob Poage, JFK, and LBJ combined forces to handily win over Central Texas voters in the 1960 election, with the assistance of Viva Kennedy! campaign organizations formed by Mexican Americans in Waco, Austin, and other Texas cities. *Courtesy W. R. Poage Legislative Library.*

Administration (NYA) in Texas in 1935–37, and later in Washington at both ends of Pennsylvania Avenue.[5] Four decades after Johnson's death, as citizens and their elected representatives search for the lost keys to the engines of government, Lyndon Johnson's interactions with community leaders in Waco, Texas, offer intriguing alternatives to the stalled state of affairs among policy makers in Washington, DC, in the Obama era.

Although she may not have led a chorus of "Happy Birthday, Dear Lyndon," Hillary Clinton uttered his name during her 2008 presidential campaign, a rarity in Democratic politics since 1968. Clinton's assertion that the Civil Rights Act of 1964 and the Voting Rights Act of 1965 became law due to Johnson's mastery of the legislative process inadvertently stirred old passions, however, as some African American leaders interpreted her remarks as diminishing the role of Dr. King and the civil rights movement.[6] As the campaign continued, Obama and his Democratic rivals evoked Johnson's memory again as they reflected on the enactment of Medicare in 1965. These echoes of an era defined by action, not by political gridlock, make today a fertile time for inquiry into a host of issues connecting the evolution of federalism since the New Deal to what Barack Obama referred to in his first inaugural address as the "era of responsibility." When it appeared President Obama might not steer health care legislation through Congress successfully, pundits jumped on the call by one of their own urging the new president to "get in touch with his inner LBJ."[7]

If Obama sought a handbook on the "Johnson treatment," he could look to virtually every one of LBJ's biographers; each offers rich examples of the cajolery, hyperbole, and shamelessness of his quest for votes. Knowledge of the people whose votes he sought, not persuasive technique, held the key to Johnson's success. The lifelong student of politics believed that when you look someone in the eye to get their vote, you must know who they are, where they are from, and what they need. On a larger level, familiarity with the community or city affected by legislation made Johnson more effective in garnering support for the legislation's passage. The significance of place in LBJ's worldview showed as he agonized over specific bombing targets in Vietnam, handpicking them by some calculus his conscience could live with, perhaps. People and the places they come from matter, in politics and war. Absent from the body of scholarship on LBJ up to this point, however, is a study of the impact of his political career on a place. Examining the work Lyndon Johnson and Bob Poage did that affected Waco, an untouched vein of lore lies waiting to expose federalism literally at work on the infrastructure of Central Texas and the nation. Therein resides a testimonial to a functioning system of government, "with the bark off," as LBJ might put it.[8]

For several decades after the Johnson administration ended in January 1969, historians marveled at or denigrated Johnson's approach to acquiring and exercising sufficient power to enact policies he favored. One cannot set aside the Vietnam debacle, but this investigation does not call upon the reader to consider foreign policy matters. Nor does it focus on the presidency. Instead, *LBJ and Grassroots Federalism* locates Johnson entirely in a domestic policy context for the purpose of using his entire political career to illustrate the evolving nature of federalism in the mid-twentieth century.

To these ends this book spotlights the political culture of Central Texas during a transformative period in the twentieth century when the federal government altered landscapes, broke down barriers, and opened doors to the engagement of African Americans and Mexican Americans in community planning processes. It locates the struggle for civil rights, often presented in terms of voting booths and classrooms alone, along a transition from the stark reality of segregated NYA advisory councils in Waco during the 1930s to the significant roles played by historically underrepresented groups in planning federal urban renewal and various other Great Society programs a generation later.

Consequently, rather than another traditional biographical treatment of LBJ, this book presents a place-based portrait of LBJ's interactions with his colleague from the neighboring Eleventh District. These key figures, sculpted by the distinctive environments they experienced within Central Texas, brought about monumental changes in the physical landscape of Waco that had a domino effect on the economy, the demographics, and on the political culture of the city. The challenge one faces when writing about LBJ lies in shining a light in places unexamined, while with Poage, the problem lies in writing about a largely forgotten public figure.

Spurred by his formative NYA experience, Lyndon Baines Johnson believed federalism in the American political system guaranteed that the government and the people, like the states in the nation, were indivisible and interdependent. Indeed, attitudes and values about education, politics, tolerance, and countless other matters rooted in the environment of his youth, woven together in the tapestry of experience, informed Johnson's vision of the role the federal government played in the daily lives of not only Texans but of all Americans. From his bear-hug embrace of Franklin Roosevelt's New Deal through the Great Society programs like Medicare and Head Start that steer national public policy debates in health care and education even a half-century later, LBJ's life cast a longer shadow and shone a brighter light than most.

Collaborating on ways to ease the hard lives of their constituents, New Dealers Johnson and Poage applied their shared philosophy, seeking to renegotiate the terrain between the federal government and the citizen. These two white Texans, eager to influence the course of life in a segregated society, accomplished many shared policy objectives. With very few exceptions in their long careers, Poage and LBJ held similar positions on the issues of the day, aligning themselves with Truman and the national party when its irreconcilable paths of human dignity and racial bigotry parted at the 1948 convention in Philadelphia. Neither walked with the Dixiecrats, but neither risked excessive exposure to the "bright sunshine of human rights" that Minneapolis mayor Hubert Humphrey invoked in his breakout speech there.[9]

Despite his traditionalist views on matters of race, Poage the New Dealer remained a staunch advocate of combining federal resources with state and local funds to "prime the pump." He supported urban renewal projects and dozens of federal investments in the Eleventh Congressional District that clearly targeted low-income minority citizens, but he consistently opposed the use of federal power to override local norms with regard to race relations.

Johnson, however, would spend the last quarter of his life figuring out how to use the power of the federal government to wash away the stains of Jim Crow laws and customs. He supported states' rights arguments and opposed federal lynching laws representing the Tenth District from 1937 to 1949, and for most of his Senate career. As his perspective broadened during his years as Senate Majority Leader, and as his presidential ambitions stirred after recovery from the heart attack in 1955, Johnson distanced himself from the extremes in the Democratic Party. He staked out a centrist position that threaded the political needle by retaining conservative credentials in Texas while endorsing moderate policies that could make the southerner one of few who might be considered for a national slate.

Caro's superbly told tale of the evolution of Senator Johnson's thinking on how to move civil rights legislation through the chamber in 1957 revealed the complex calculus of compassion and nominating conventions. Later, as vice president and president, Johnson's deeply held convictions about the relationship between the economic plight of the rural South, the urban North, and the wall of racism crystallized in the form of the most progressive package of domestic policy changes the nation had ever seen. When he grabbed southern senators or House members by the arm and made his case, he appealed to them by citing the damage done to the prosperity of everyday people due to the walls of segregation.[10] These remarkable developments in the passions that drove Lyndon Johnson certainly strained the long alliance with Poage to the breaking point. By the time LBJ occupied the White House, the pro–civil rights coalition of moderate Republicans and nonsouthern Democrats in the House of Representatives rendered Poage's vote inconsequential. There is little evidence Poage regretted this stance on civil rights later in life.[11] And there is little reason to believe LBJ had much respect for Poage for not standing up for equality after being elected overwhelmingly for fourteen straight terms of office. Later that year, Johnson closed the Twelfth Air Force Base at Waco and moved its operations to Austin, represented by Jake Pickle (D-Tenth District), one of five southern Democrats in the House who voted for the Civil Rights Act of 1964. LBJ was in touch with his inner LBJ.

This study strives to illuminate the workings of federalism in Central Texas during the careers of Lyndon Johnson and Bob Poage, highlighting instances when key issues faced citizens of Waco that local officials could not fully address without federal resources. Doing so illustrates more than political acumen on the part of elected officials, because so much of the interaction hinges on the agency of the citizens themselves, advocating their needs and expectations. The sophisticated lobbying skills evidenced by the internal and external communications of the Waco contingent demonstrated extraordinary levels of preparation. For example, letters from Ford dealer Jack Kultgen, who became the president of the Brazos River Authority (BRA), reveal a level of political insight worthy of the obvious respect Poage and Johnson had for him. Johnson and Poage shared a commitment to constituent service, as evidenced by the volume of letters on file in their respective papers. Both men earned reputations as guides familiar with the swamp of bureaucracy, equipped with machetes to slash the vines of red tape, knowledgeable about avoiding quicksand, and keen on detecting potential ambushes by Republicans, or other hostiles.

As more federal programs came to Waco, including Model Cities, the federal requirements for inclusiveness among community representatives meant more seats at the proverbial table for the previously excluded African Americans and Mexican Americans. Tokenism existed, but that game gets played across color lines as representative categories are filled: a clergy member, a teacher, or a "homemaker," for example. Boards of this kind vary widely in terms of effectiveness with truly advocating for the needs of the people they purportedly represent. For many who were given the opportunity to serve on various federal advisory boards, like Robert Aguilar of Waco, their desire to serve their community intensified, leading many to careers in public service. Aguilar and Ernest Calderon applied lessons learned from their experiences as they organized the influential Waco Alliance of Mexican American Citizens in 1967. The advisory councils mandated by various federal agencies served as indispensable training grounds for the next generation of community leaders.

The first manuscript of this book carried the title *Strength in Unity* because the phrase from the groundbreaking ceremony in July 1958 concisely captured Johnson's governing philosophy. The same wording takes on another important dimension, however, when applied to his political partnership with Bob Poage, whose forty-two years in the House now seem largely forgotten. The roles LBJ and Poage played in transforming the "Heart of Texas" (as Waco boosters dubbed their city) merit further investigation because these Texans modeled patterns of effective grassroots engagement with the federal government. As activist Democrats, they did so fully aware of being steeped most of their lives in a whites-only political culture characterized by decades of widespread sensitivity among those whites, regardless of social class, to federal encroachment on state sovereignty. The model used for the Selective Service System, whereby local citizens would carry out a draft board's federally mandated responsibilities with a modicum of real discretion, seemed to satisfy public sensibilities.

Fittingly, the first encounter between these two men as public officials involved the establishment of a citizen advisory council to propose projects for the National Youth Administration in Waco in 1935, when LBJ, the state director, called upon then state senator Bob Poage to recruit members—all white. Ten years in the Texas Senate provided him with an ample list of possible nominees, so Poage moved quickly with his invitations, and the Waco Advisory Council for the NYA undertook its duties that fall. New Deal federalism did not cut out the state altogether, as evidenced by this nomination process carried out by a state senator at the request of the Texas state NYA director, but the centers of gravity moved to county seats, urban centers, to Washington, DC, and away from state capitol buildings.

Swept up to Congress from the state senate with the surge of Franklin Roosevelt's electoral tsunami in 1936, Poage represented Waco (and surrounding rural areas in the Eleventh District) in the House of Representatives for twenty-one terms. Johnson, whom Poage already knew from their NYA correspondence, took the oath of office five months later, following victory in the special election called after the passing of James "Buck" Buchanan, who held the Tenth District seat.[12] Significantly, across the corridor from the office assigned to LBJ sat Bob Poage, who recalled the arrival of the newest member:

When he came to Washington, as was customary with new Congressmen, he had to take what was available in the way of office space. Congressman Albert Thomas had come from Houston the same time I did. We had offices on the fourth floor of the old building about as far from the front as you could get, over on the east side; and there was an inside office across the hall from us. Lyndon got that office.... As I recall it, he stayed there until the next January probably. And beginning the next January, I moved a little closer—I moved on the same floor, but around a little closer to the front door and save about a two-block walk. I believe that at the same time that he moved up on the fifth floor into what became his Congressional office for some time. Of course, he finally got three rooms up there, sort of an attic space, but he recognized the need of space and recognized it before we did and got the extra space.[13]

For the next three decades Poage's interactions with that ambitious man from the Hill Country placed Waco in a highly favorable position to enjoy the fruits of the federal system during times of scarcity and plenty.

Farm prices for livestock and grain rivaled the weather as the most frequent topic of discussion in Central Texas. Johnson and Poage, like many of their constituents, knew the rigors of farm life and drew from the well of goodwill represented by their efforts to expand existing federal programs such as the Rural Electrification Act and to create new ones like the Rural Telephone Act. These and other examples of applied political philosophy derived from experiences in community survival common to rural environments. They grew up where instincts for individualism gave way to exercises in barn raising, where the need for collective action spoke for itself—whatever the language. Both men developed a strong belief that the resources of the federal government could be put to use on projects for the common good. Despite the privileged contacts they encountered, they believed common sense would tell anyone but a damn fool, rich or poor, when a situation required help from Washington. Of course, the big boys knew this, too. Along the way, Johnson and Poage became attached to political interests and constituencies that led to excesses such as those described by Linda Scarbrough in *Road, River, and Ol' Boy Politics*.[14]

Scarbrough, a newspaper publisher and historian, included Johnson and Poage among the players in her study of the juggernaut of interests behind excessive construction of dams and highways that transformed her beloved Williamson County, located north of Austin (Travis County). As she documented the passing of rich traditions of family farms and ranches spurring the livelihoods of small towns between Austin and Waco, Scarbrough portrayed a political culture addicted to the use of huge federal contracts to enrich campaign war chests with Texas-sized contributions from the likes of the Brown and Root firm.[15] The recounting of how a plausible argument for one dam ended up with the construction of three represents a victim's deposition documenting how landscape and lifestyle became pawns in the chess game among players distant and near.

The cautionary tale about the waste products of abuse of power represents a familiar setting for LBJ, but far less so for Bob Poage, portrayed by Scarbrough as captive to the construction industry–political complex in

Texas closely linked to Johnson's career ladder.[16] Poage's role in securing federal funding for a flood control dam on the Brazos River system to protect Waco, his crusade for a quarter-century, seemed motivated by loftier goals than the circumstances Scarbrough described. *LBJ and Grassroots Federalism* takes place earlier in his career, accounting, perhaps, for differences in the ratio of idealism to cynicism and comparing his responsiveness to citizen input in Waco to the debacle Scarbrough described on the San Gabriel system.

The Johnson portrayed in *Road, River, and Ol' Boy Politics* has his finger to the wind, seeking the best political lift if the warm winds of public opinion blew his way. LBJ earned a reputation for being utilitarian in his maintenance of relationships. Robert A. Caro, whose probing, provocative four volumes (and counting) in *The Years of Lyndon Johnson* series essentially framed the academic and public discussion of LBJ since the publication of *The Path to Power* in 1982 brought attention to Johnson's cultivation of relationships with political "daddies." These mentors included FDR, Speaker of the House Sam Rayburn, and Georgia senator Richard Russell. Caro's portrayal of the interactions between Johnson and these imposing figures revealed how the Texan used deference to achieve his goals, as warranted by the status of those involved. Subordinates, on the other hand, such as his aides, routinely experienced withering insults and bullying tactics at stressful times. Bob Poage, almost nine years older than LBJ, fell in between. Poage and Johnson began their relationship essentially as peers, offering a different perspective for historians to explore. Although a major player in the House of Representatives for many years, Poage never achieved the stature of a Rayburn or a Russell in the Senate and has been nearly lost to history. When he does appear in an article, monograph, or biography, typically Johnson or agriculture policy is the main subject.

After leaving Congress in 1979, Poage devoted time to writing about Texas and his family. His memoir, *My First 85 Years*, a story "worthy of recording only because it is so typical of the period," manages to avoid any direct reference to African Americans, civil rights, or anything specific about his own record with regard to those matters.[17] Extensive oral history interviews conducted with Poage between 1968 and 1983 reveal, sadly, the effects of aging over that fifteen-year span. Confronted with blunt questions about his relationship with LBJ and his voting record on civil rights, Poage faced some accountability, but in the memoir, under no apparent editorial pressure to reflect on race relations, his family's use of African American domestics, attending segregated schools in Throckmorton County and Waco, his reaction to lynching in Central Texas, voting rights—none of these garnered a single comment. Was Bob Poage's life typical of the period? No, perhaps his preference to discuss other matters made for polite conversation among good white Christians in Waco, but Poage's modesty was unwarranted.

By the time *My First 85 Years* appeared in print in 1985, Lyndon Johnson had been dead for twelve years. Liberated to speak his mind, but at a stage of life when a number of factors could color the tone and content of his remarks, Poage's analysis of the most important political ally of his career makes their accomplishments together in Waco even more fascinating. His profile of LBJ began:

> Lyndon Johnson was my friend. I admired much of his vigorous approach to those practices he considered wrong. I admired his repeated efforts to help those who he saw as oppressed, even though I disagreed with his methods. . . . He tried to reform our entire social system too fast.[18]

"Was my friend," said it all. Their relationship broke in the 1960s as the United States observed the centennial of the insurrection Texas children learned to call the "War between the States." Brother against brother. The eventual rupture in the long, productive Poage-Johnson relationship reveals the tragic collateral damage of the aftermath of the Civil War. Five score years later, white Americans faced a time of reckoning.

The brief biography of Poage appearing in the *Handbook of Texas* contains this statement that captured the problematic nature of placing him on the ideological spectrum:

> Since the Eleventh District was then primarily dependent on agriculture for its livelihood, Poage kept his focus on the needs of his constituents. Known to some as "Mr. Agriculture," this conservative Democrat spent his career trying to improve life in rural America. He consistently supported government programs protecting farm prices through federal subsidy.[19]

The *Handbook* then lists a series of legislative accomplishments showing Poage's political philosophy quite consistent with mainstream, if not progressive impulses when it came to the role of the federal government in the economy in the mid-twentieth century. Support for federal subsidies as a means of dealing with fluctuations on the commodities market could be explained away as political expedience, but to describe Poage's achievements as a leader in rural utilities, the establishment of wastewater systems from the New Deal to the Nixon era, as simply "conservative" misleads. If one measures Poage's career solely on the basis of his voting record on issues affecting race relations, the term fits as well as any. In his memoir, Poage labeled himself "conservative," while recognizing "political names mean very little," and "we must use new policies to deal with new problems."[20]

The Democrats who decided to include Poage in the purge of House dinosaurs in January 1975 certainly viewed him as unacceptably conservative and tied to agribusiness interests.[21] Massive Republican losses in the Watergate-tinged 1974 election changed the balance of power within the House, leaving longtime southerners like Poage, whose seniority once made him a respected powerhouse on key matters like school lunches, farm subsidies, and food stamps, humiliated on the party's compost pile. He lost the chairmanship by a vote of 144–141 shortly after the House convened in January 1975. His voting record on civil rights came back to haunt him again, because surely at least two of those "no" votes were cast for more reasons than a revolt against seniority within the Democratic Party.[22]

Indicative of the complexity of their long political relationship, even though as president Lyndon Johnson used every persuasive technique in his vast arsenal to win the votes of House members and senators to gain passage of the Civil Rights Act of 1964, he never asked Bob Poage to support the landmark legislation. Poage voted against it, as Johnson knew he would. Glaring differences between Poage and Johnson on civil rights did not emerge publicly until the late 1950s. It stands as the most significant parting of the ways on policy matters between these two strong advocates of utilizing federal funds to transform life in Central Texas from the ground up.[23]

In the first two volumes of *The Years of Lyndon Johnson*, Caro mentioned Poage solely to characterize him as "unassertive" not once, but twice, identifying the Waco congressman as one of the "very few" of LBJ's contemporaries tolerant of the demanding Johnson, whose efforts to "dominate other men succeeded with one or two fellow Texans (most notably, quiet, unassertive Representative Robert Poage of Waco)."[24] Poage barely reached the status of bit player, without even a single mention in Caro's third volume, *Master of the Senate*, despite six years (1955–61) when Johnson led Senate Democrats and Poage wielded clout on the House Agriculture Committee. *The Passage of Power*, the fourth volume in the series, takes LBJ into the early months of his presidency, omitting any reference to Poage, who continued to be a power broker on agriculture policy but whose contacts with the new president decreased considerably from what they had known since the early days.[25]

Historian Robert Dallek's biographies characterized LBJ as a "lone star rising" who became a "flawed giant." Among other faults, Johnson consistently placed his political ambitions ahead of relationships with everyone from Lady Bird to Robert Kennedy. A wagonload of evidence of how LBJ treated friends and foes, sufficient to fill both volumes of Dallek's study, does not mention Poage.[26] To date, the body of scholarly literature about LBJ gives the Wacoan the status of an obscure pawn in the Texas congressional delegation. Certainly none of the dozens of Johnson biographies or memoirs of cabinet officials devoted any real attention to him.

There are several intriguing, though brief, references to Poage in *Gaining Access: Congress and the Farm Lobby, 1919–1981*, by political scientist John Mark Hansen, in the context of the relationship between agribusiness interests and members of Congress. Hansen points to evidence of Poage's clout dealing with agriculture issues during the Johnson presidency.[27] An "insider" memoir by Fowler West, Poage's longtime congressional aide, titled *He Ain't No Lawyer: Memories of My Years with Congressman Bob Poage*, offers anecdotal glimpses from the author's service from 1963 to 1979.[28] Poage's role in shaping federal agriculture policy received considerable attention, with West offering an intriguing, but undocumented, report that Poage declined JFK's invitation to serve as Secretary of Agriculture, leaving Kennedy to appoint Orville Freeman, instead.[29] A snafu over such a matter might seem unlikely until one considers the clumsiness the Kennedys showed with informing Johnson of his vice-presidential nomination at the convention in 1960, a story LBJ relished in recounting, replete with his RFK imitation, for historical accuracy.[30] If Poage had sought the cabinet post under Kennedy or Johnson, he threw away any conceivable chance when he opposed the Civil Rights Act of 1964.

Deftly steering his recollection of this volatile era away from Poage's opposition to Johnson's civil rights agenda, the account by Poage's aide offered a constituent service success story involving the assistance provided to an elderly African American man experiencing problems with documenting his age for the Social Security Administration.[31] Poage's appreciation for the traditional social order would not prejudice service of that kind. Dating back to his interactions with the NYA, the federal agency LBJ used to expand opportunities for youths of all ethnicities in Texas, Poage's opposition to federal civil rights legislation did not mean he would have blocked access to students of color to NYA opportunities. Perhaps if he had to serve a broader constituency than the historically segregationist-leaning Eleventh District, Bob Poage's views of race relations might have followed Johnson's, but Poage never caught the Senate strain of Potomac fever.

Poage stated in multiple interviews that LBJ thought he should have set his sights on a run for the US Senate in 1941, but noted Johnson probably said the same to "two hundred people in Texas" as part of his own calculations. Recalling Johnson's pitch, Poage stated,

[He] picked me up at 6th and Congress and we rode around for two hours. He was rubbing his nose against mine trying to convince me.[32]

Poage told the man earning a national reputation for his persuasive skills that he simply didn't want to "pay that price." Frances Poage read the situation differently. According to her husband, she "always more or less thought that he was disparaging my ability. Well, he said if I was—energetic wasn't the word, but if I was as determined as he was, that I could do these things."[33]

In an era distinguished by an intractable Cold War and an unstoppable civil rights movement, one could choose a pulpit more bully than preaching to the cotton choir, but Poage allied himself with those interests. The *Encyclopedia of American Agricultural History* identified Poage as "an ardent champion of high price supports . . . an inveterate foe of Ezra Taft Benson while being one of the chief formulators of farm programs as they emerged from Congress."[34] If one engaged in racial profiling, the pattern fits the white southern New Deal Democrat who gradually became more and more conservative, especially on issues of farm labor. The House was full of these after the 1938 elections proved Roosevelt's high-water mark of popularity receded sharply after the court-packing mess and the steep recession that spiked unemployment to disturbing levels. The Roosevelt bandwagon slowed considerably, and the administration's support for labor unions did not play well in a region where the Southern Tenant Farmers' Union dared to conduct surreptitious integrated meetings.

As Neil Foley documented in his study of the Central Texas cotton culture, *The White Scourge*, no daylight existed between issues of labor rights and race when it came to farm labor. To be an organizer appeared tantamount to being a race mixer in the eyes of owners. A high percentage of the population remained landless and poor, and landowners did not want to see tenants or sharecroppers organizing, certainly not across racial lines.[35] Meanwhile, Poage acquired seniority and prime acreage. In this context, Poage seemed to fit the caricature of the gentleman rancher who used his political station to maintain the status quo once the symptoms of the agricultural depression had been treated to his satisfaction. One can see him marching in lockstep with like-minded southern Democrats, including those Dixiecrats who bolted in 1948, but there is a problem—he did not.

W. R. Poage lacked a necessary trait of a conformist. He failed to conform. In a study of southerners who did not affix their signatures to the post-*Brown* decision obstructionism represented by the Southern Manifesto in 1956, historian Tony Badger characterized Poage as one of four "stalwart conservative senior figures" in the Texas congressional delegation choosing not to sign it, along with thirteen other members, including Rayburn and one Republican, Bruce Alger.[36] Poage's decision to withhold his signature raises intriguing questions about the political calculus involved in reaching that conclusion.

Was he "going along to get along," as Mr. Sam's political primer taught in the Texas delegation deemed by Badger the "the most cohesive and powerful in the South?" Wright Patman's district in the "piney woods" of northeast Texas contained similar demographics in terms of race as Poage's Eleventh, but Patman signed. Badger stated, "even someone as conservative as Bob Poage" viewed another colleague who did sign the manifesto as a "perfectly honest and sincere reactionary."[37] At that point, the Republican Party in Texas, and across the South, stood nearly invisible, so Democrats had the advantages and disadvantages of a very, very wide tent in terms of member ideology. The research conducted for this inquiry into his career suggests Poage responded to pressure from an emerging force in the Democratic camp—racial moderates. These influences were not academic "lefties" but Texans whose worldview after World War II tended more toward inclusion and less toward exclusion. They remained somewhat closeted, but they tended to be educated, skilled communicators in the business community who were needed by and admired by Bob Poage.

Bob Poage had no need to establish his conservative bona fides within the extensive network of supporters he established since he ran for state senate in 1924 as a twenty-four-year-old graduate of Baylor. When casting his net again and again for votes for the Civil Rights Act of 1964, LBJ wasted no time asking for Poage's vote, because he did not need it. Research into the circle of friends and advisers who had Poage's ear in the 1950s, however, suggests that overt racism, such as the defiant white supremacy voiced by the Southern

Manifesto, would not advance his standing. Jim Crow social policies grew problematic as business interests faced crises of conscience and of bottom line. Bob Poage did not sign the Southern Manifesto because it would have hurt him more than it helped him. This analysis, informed by oral histories and correspondence, shows another facet of the kaleidoscope of race relations: a relatively moderate cohort of elites tempering the voting behavior of a staunch segregationist.

Why has Bob Poage's tenure in the House of Representatives, spanning the New Deal through Watergate, received such limited scholarly attention? One factor to consider would be that for the first twenty-four years as a member in the Texas delegation of House Democrats he operated under the strict tutelage of Sam Rayburn.[38] Perhaps his chosen area of specialization, agriculture policy, lacked the perceived gravitas that accompanies a seat on the House Intelligence or Ways and Means Committee. Although he compiled a solid record of achievement, Poage's name is not associated with legislation that makes it into survey textbooks, perhaps because his focus, not that of most historians, remained on rural affairs.

The portrait of the partnership between the two men that emerges from my analysis of hundreds of letters and telegrams exchanged from 1935 to 1969 contributes to existing Johnson scholarship by offering a longitudinal study of a peer relationship and its impact on public policy in a selected place. "Core samples" of collaborations between Congressman Bob Poage and Johnson illuminated LBJ's legendary political skills in a collegial context by mining the rich archival veins in the W. R. Poage Legislative Library and the Texas Collection at Baylor University. LBJ's biographers naturally discuss his interactions with major power brokers but seldom address his conduct with figures whose personalities needed and thereby attracted less attention, like his colleague from Waco. Extensive interviews with midwestern transplant Jack Kultgen, Robert Aguilar, and many more whose experiences informed this book added considerable context and perspective to the body of work on LBJ and on the political culture of Central Texas.

Poage's consistent role as a conduit between LBJ and citizen activists in Waco as Johnson moved up the political ladder affirms the significance of grassroots engagement during an era often associated with centralization. Neither of these veteran New Dealers forgot lessons learned in seeing federal programs implemented in a states' rights political culture.

LBJ and Grassroots Federalism accentuates the dynamics of federal-state-local interactions during a transformational period in the political culture of the United States in the setting of a region undergoing great change due to internal and external forces. As president, Johnson's ability to enact policies on race, health care, education, and the environment brought millions of Americans into day-to-day contact with the federal government far beyond the scope of the New Deal. The life and times of Lyndon Baines Johnson inspired dozens of valuable scholarly studies informing this one, and the field remains vibrant. Yet there are still aspects of Johnson's political philosophy and method worthy of illumination, especially by considering the corresponding career of Bob Poage, a fellow Democrat who represented Waco in Congress for more than forty years. Far less celebrated or vilified in the rich folklore of Texas, but arguably one of Johnson's staunchest allies in Congress, Bob Poage lived in a political climate decidedly more conservative in Waco than in LBJ's beloved Hill Country base, as discussed in chapter 1, "The Texas They Knew."

For Johnson biographers, abundant stories of LBJ's interactions with opponents and allies alike demonstrate how his appeal to "reason together" varied from one senator or member of Congress to the next, but the notion that it all represented an exercise in self-aggrandizement has faded in the weight of evidence to the contrary, even in Caro's assessment. For a time, Caro believed, the dominant feature of LBJ's character was a "hunger for power in its most naked form, for power not to improve the lives of others but to manipulate and dominate them, to bend them to his will."[39] Twenty years after that provocative assessment of the roots of Johnson's gargantuan ambitions, a more complex portrait emerged in Caro's *Master of the Senate*. Seeking and maintaining political power comprised one major component of the life force of LBJ, but as Caro found, the quest for results comprised another.

An analysis of LBJ's relationship with Tom Miller, a legend of Austin politics, by historian L. Patrick Hughes, reinforces the image of Johnson as a force of nature unto himself, but still operating by the laws of politics. Johnson proved fully capable of "working within the system." In the words of Austin mayor Tom Miller, an iconic Texan in his own right:

> Lyndon, I believe you are pretty near as good as you recommended yourself to me one day at the City Hall . . . you gave a pretty glowing account of your ability and experience in Washington. . . . While you made some broad statements of what you could do, I have just about come to the conclusion that they were not hyperbolic and that you have made good.[40]

The characterization by historian L. Patrick Hughes leads to a distinctly different conclusion than those scholars more inclined to see LBJ as manipulating the system to selfish ends. More recent biographers of LBJ, notably Randall Woods, inevitably influenced by their own contemporary political context, approach Johnson's domestic record not unlike sports fans considering the on-the-playing-field accomplishments of "heroes" with personal failings.[41] Historian James T. Patterson portrayed LBJ in *Freedom Is Not Enough* as a passionate crusader who fought for his vision of human rights, but became puzzled and hurt by race-related violence from Watts to Newark that Johnson knew would solidify white resentment of his affirmative action initiatives.[42] To Bob Poage, still a segregationist at heart, Lyndon Johnson acted more and more like a race radical. Johnson died wishing he had done more, dreading that conservative forces would roll back all he had done.[43]

One-half century later, the results of those efforts give pause, for Johnson's orchestration of the legislative drama surrounding civil rights, voting rights, Medicare, and so many other initiatives evoked Shakespeare for reasons far nobler than the snarky satire of the time, *MacBird*.[44] The release of various documents from the papers of Martin Luther King Jr., along with White House tape transcripts, enabled journalist Nick Kotz to analyze the relationship between the civil rights leader and the president in *Judgment Days* (2005), revealing the fascinating machinations of high stakes politics between giants.[45] The drama so palpable, the players so iconic, so mindful of destiny—but public policy makers do not come down from the mountaintop. They come from Main Street, or just down the road some, and they deal with the varied consequences of bigotry as down-to-earth issues.

The daunting nature of their task must have been even more imposing for Johnson because of his working knowledge of the intractability of institutions, and how to work within them or around them, as the situation dictates. As we can see from the provocative *When Affirmative Action Was White*, by political historian Ira Katznelson, who traced discriminatory practices in several New Deal agencies, a racist culture replicates and reinforces itself in its social systems. Katznelson recognized the subtleties of distinctive approaches states used to employ Jim Crow practices to limit access by African Americans, factors the Roosevelt administration weighed carefully in drafting federal policy. The significance of this sensitivity to local practices resides in the pattern it established for voluntary models of federal-state-local partnerships, wherein states would be responsible for establishing mechanisms to link citizens with federal personnel in a local setting to facilitate access to federal resources.[46] *LBJ and Grassroots Federalism* comes to somewhat different conclusions.

When the BRA and similar agencies were established in the 1930s, there were no suspicions that leveraging federal funding would be countered by federal intrusion in the form of forced integration. This fear soon developed, however. In the context of his study of the continued expansion of federal agencies, Gareth Davies observed, "Southern Democrats worried that federal involvement would hasten racial integration." Davies also offered a broader, national perspective, stating, "traditional patterns of American federalism had been utterly upended by the successive traumas of the Great Depression and the second world war."[47]

These direct exchanges between federal personnel and citizens, however, increasingly circumvented local and state elected officials. In *The Challenge to Urban Liberalism*, Philip Funigiello described the withering of state governments as a consequence of mushrooming New Deal and World War II home front bureaucracies.[48] In rural communities and urban neighborhoods, federal offices opened where shuttered storefronts or empty office buildings stood. Like the post office, local people staffed these. Federal monies passed through state capitals, and reports compiled from submissions by local agencies carried the signatures of governors, but even in his role as state director of the Texas NYA agency, Johnson carried out federal policies at the local level by helping them customize projects to suit their needs.[49]

Thirty years later one of the most controversial of the Great Society initiatives, the Community Action Program (CAP), upset Democratic mayors by providing federal resources to nongovernmental organizations. According to political scientist Richard Flanagan, CAP "is the idea that innovation, administration, and coordination of programs—power, really—should reside with the people in the communities whose lives are touched by the programs."[50] Flanagan assessed motives in the context of the evolving political movements of the 1960s, but could Johnson's experience as NYA director be somewhat predictive of the CAP model? This investigation of Johnson, Poage, and the NYA in Central Texas suggests this to be the case. While he did call upon political elites, like state senator Poage, to name appointees to local advisory councils that would determine how federal funds would be spent, he did so knowing their inclination would be to direct the federal monies toward whites, not to those on the margin. Historian Mitchell Lerner recently conducted a comparative study of the involvement of African American and Mexican American youth in NYA programs across the South, quantifying higher rates of engagement in Texas than elsewhere.[51] So LBJ worked around elites, or he found ways to create new circles of elites to nurture. Those NYA councils were, in a real sense, the CAPs of their day.

This use of alternative channels should come as no surprise, because it fits within a broader pattern. LBJ's handling of campaign funds, audited exhaustively and conclusively by Robert A. Caro in *The Means of Ascent*, the second volume of his biography, demonstrated a sense of how to exercise power in the meanest sense. Yet given the repeated use of stakeholders to drive decision-making processes from the bottom up indicates less craven purposes, and certainly reinforces the outlines of a remarkably radical sense of empowering citizens with resources made available by the taxing authority of the federal government.

Each of the three public policy matters within LBJ's expansive sphere of influence discussed in *LBJ and Grassroots Federalism* draws upon distinctive circumstances in Waco. These include the establishment in 1935–37 of National Youth Administration (NYA) programs serving high school and college students from segregated schools, securing federal funding to relieve lives along the ravaged Brazos River floodplain, and engaging previously marginalized Mexican American citizens in the urban renewal process triggered by a devastating tornado. Following this path through time, from 1935 to the end of the Johnson era, one can trace growing federal engagement in the local affairs, with an increasing emphasis on community engagement as part of the formula. Johnson's grasp of the technologies of power in Washington and Texas made him a central figure in determining the fate of federal projects for cities like Waco. If the Johnson presidency represents the "high tide of liberalism," then mapping the evolution of Johnson's governing philosophy prior to the White House involves a journey through the expanding role of the federal government throughout the mid-twentieth century.[52]

Why locate a study of federalism in the Johnson era in Central Texas? Near the end of the first term of President George W. Bush, political historian James McEnteer criticized the disproportionate influence of a "cowboy mentality" in public affairs. In *Deep in the Heart: The Texas Tendency in American Politics*, he asserted that beginning with the Wilson administration (1913–21), "Texas gained a prominent, permanent place at the apex of federal power."[53] McEnteer cited growing opposition to FDR's programs, stating "a number of power Texans, including some in government, indicted government itself as the enemy." The Texas grip on Washington, comparable to that of Virginia in the early days of the Republic, according to McEnteer,

The essential waters of the Brazos and Colorado Rivers defined the Central Texas cities that grew along their banks, especially in terms of housing patterns and land values. As Waco and Austin grew, managing those arteries challenged local and state governments beyond their capacity, a reality that contributed to close working relationships with federal officials. *Courtesy Perry-Castañeda Library Map Collection, University of Texas Libraries.*

grew stronger by the 1950s, when Rayburn and Johnson "rode herd," setting policies with "special attention to Texas oil interests."[54] The presidencies of Johnson, George H. W. Bush, and George W. Bush speak to the power of "establishment" Texans in Washington, and the curious flirtation Governor Rick Perry pursued with the notion of seceding if federal-state relations deteriorated further might indicate the "powerful reactionary movement" observed in Texas in the late 1930s still occupies real space within the political culture. Most recently, Senator Ted Cruz, elected in 2012, successfully mined this vein.

The Central Texas setting for these two congressional districts comprises varied terrain, with the Eleventh District more disposed to a cotton-based economy in the nineteenth and early twentieth centuries than the drier, rockier Tenth District. Many of the counties in the Tenth District (Gillespie, Blanco, Travis, and Bastrop) voted against secession, while the blackland prairie cotton counties like McLennan and Falls joined the majority by breaking away in March 1861. Travis County would record no lynching as society reconstructed, but images of Waco seared into the broader American consciousness that made the city something of a symbol of this nation's struggle to define the boundaries of federal authority.

The infamous "Waco Horror" of 1916 involved the extralegal execution of an African American named Jesse Washington on May 15 before thousands of spectators.[55] In an era notorious for lynching, this killing stood as the starkest evidence of local control taken to a hideous extreme. Bob Poage, fifteen years old at the time, attended high school in the city. If 10,000 white people observed the atrocity, or as other estimates state, one-half of the city's white men, it is reasonable to speculate that Poage himself may have witnessed it.[56] W. E. B. Du Bois published a detailed account of the grizzly event in *The Crisis*, with imagery so vivid that his use of the phrase the "Waco Horror" became the proper noun for the event. Despite widespread outrage outside the South at the news of the awful fate of Jesse Washington, antilynching legislation went nowhere in Washington, DC. As determined by the Compromise of 1877 ending Reconstruction, states protectively retained jurisdiction in such matters, resulting in laissez-faire civil rights policies from the nation's capital. During the Wilson administration, at a time when poor relations with Mexico led to serious conflicts at the border and along the Gulf of Mexico, Texas did not oppose a strong federal presence.

The other notorious and relevant "public" memory of Waco, burned into the consciousness, came from the conflagration at the Branch Davidian compound in 1993, sparked when federal agents confronted leader David Koresh and his followers.[57] Zealous conservatives argued that federal encroachment on the rights of citizens threatened not only cherished liberties but also life itself. Rhetorical references to "jackbooted" federal police rang through emerging new media known as the "Internet." Hard-line conservatives railed against a pattern of abuses and usurpations by the FBI and the Clintons.

The common tension running through these tragic events in Waco derives from a political system seeking an elusive equilibrium that satisfies a community's sense of empowerment while yielding to the expectations of policy makers at the federal level. Considering the killing of Jesse Washington with the force threatened against David Koresh, one weighs the legacy of too little federal authority to deal with lynching, while heavy-handed federal force in the case of Koresh pressed down on the other end of this conceptual scale. This book concentrates on a span of time between these notorious extremes, beginning in the New Deal era when the immoderate political ambitions of Lyndon Johnson found a valuable moderate ally in Bob Poage. Their odd-couple alliance changed Waco. Working with community members committed to economic development for altruistic reasons and for self-interest, they demonstrated that the federal system piloted during the New Deal successfully linked citizens with their national government without undermining local control. For states' rights advocates (unreformed confederates, in a sense), the New Deal model undermined the role of the state. The use of advisory boards comprised of community stakeholders representative of the population as a standard requirement for municipalities seeking desirable federal funding created a problem for the local political establishment. As evident through the interactions among Waco community leaders, Lyndon Johnson, and Bob Poage, the promise of money produced extraordinary leverage in both directions. It may not be what James Madison had in mind.

Much of this inquiry derived from some elementary questions involving people and civil society in twenty-first-century America: This political system used to work—what happened to the ability of elected officials to govern? How did business get done with Lyndon Johnson involved? Almost unimaginable, but true—Lyndon Johnson has emerged from the wilderness of memory and discourse. Despite his legendary skills as a legislator, which Johnson later channeled into an imposing list of pivotal changes in domestic policy as chief executive, this fascinating individual forever wears a scarlet V for the needless bloodshed in Vietnam. A series of disastrous decisions

concerning US military strategy in Southeast Asia far too familiar and complex to relate here relegated him to the status of the Great Unmentionable for
Democrats from the moment he left the White House until recent years. A
confluence of factors, including the anniversary in 2008 of his one hundredth
birthday, account for his partial rehabilitation as the Kennedy-Johnson ad-
ministrations recede to the half-century mark in fading public memory.

As evident from the discussion of marvelous biographies by Caro, Dallek,
and other historians who have influenced this book, researchers kept the ar-
chivists at the LBJ Presidential Library occupied all these years, even if no
Democrat candidates spoke of him until 2008. In the monologues with historian Doris Kearns Goodwin that became *Lyndon Johnson and the American Dream*, Johnson expressed his belief historians would always discuss his
legacy in terms of that of John F. Kennedy.[58] Now, Kennedy appears quite
mortal, to the extent that an unflattering reassessment of JFK's civil rights
records by BBC correspondent Nick Bryant in *The Bystander: John F. Kennedy and the Struggle for Black Equality* passed without a ripple.[59] Perhaps
Kennedy had to become less mythic for Johnson to become more human, or
maybe the morass of wars of Iraq and Afghanistan put misguided Vietnam
policies in a new light. In the gridlocked environment that has characterized
Washington, DC, in recent times, Johnson's legislative record appears nothing less than remarkable.

In a recent biography, *Lyndon B. Johnson*, journalist and former West Virginia legislator Charles Peters distilled current thinking on the Texan, noting, "History has gradually taken a kinder view."[60] From the perspective of
Kevin J. Fernlund, a historian of the American West, Johnson was the last
truly western president, so his *Lyndon Johnson and Modern America* presents
a distinctly regional perspective on LBJ.[61] Fernlund counters conventional
wisdom by criticizing Johnson for withdrawing from the 1968 presidential
campaign, suggesting his self-imposed lame duck status weakened his hand
in negotiations with Ho Chi Minh. Had LBJ run, he would have beaten
Nixon and been in position to end the war sooner than his successor, in the
scenario Fernlund conceived.[62]

Johnson spoke openly in his retirement years at the ranch in Stonewall,
Texas, about his certainty that the "bitch of a war" eroded the coalition for
progressive domestic policy that he had cultivated since his arrival in Washington in the 1930s.[63] It did, and George Orwell's Big Brother could not have
airbrushed Winston Smith from Oceania more thoroughly than Democrats
excised LBJ for forty years. His image apparently banned from convention

halls, no applause line used in the past forty-five years included a reference to Lyndon Baines Johnson, except at receptions featuring Lady Bird, Lynda, or Luci.

If some applause comes his way, so be it, but I wrote *LBJ and Grassroots Federalism* to find out how the federal system functioned so effectively in a place that over the years has come to be associated with some resentment toward the federal government. To sum it up, my book posits that over the course of three decades in the mid-twentieth century, Lyndon Johnson's engagement with Eleventh District representative W. R. "Bob" Poage fostered a level of collaboration between the federal government and local leaders illustrative of Central Texas political culture in that era and instructive beyond the region in today's political climate. Poage, in my estimation, played a more significant role in this phase of the history of Texas and the nation than historians to date have reflected in their studies.

In support of this argument, my analysis concentrates on three examples to illustrate how public policy questions facing diverse elements of the Waco citizenry were resolved as an outgrowth of federal action. I conclude that the use of advisory councils became a central part of LBJ's governing philosophy beginning in his NYA years, and they provided access and leverage for community stakeholders beyond his own legislative career. With these purposes in mind, I have organized the book into four chapters, followed by a conclusion.

As mentioned earlier in this introduction, chapter 1, "The Texas They Knew," analyzes the setting by delineating the similarities and differences of Johnson's roots in the Hill Country and his political base in Austin, with those of neighboring state senator (later congressman) Bob Poage in Waco. Johnson's background is surely better known to the reader than Poage's background. These Texans knew the privileges of whiteness in a segregated society, and they witnessed the resurgence of the KKK in the 1920s. While the Waco of Poage's adolescence epitomized the culture of lynching, the settlement patterns and social conditions of the Hill Country did not produce domestic terrorism in that extreme form. *LBJ and Grassroots Federalism* built upon the contributions of Neil Foley, Dan K. Utley, Thad Sitton, and James Conrad to the scholarship of race and ethnicity in the political culture of rural Central Texas, on the seam where the Confederacy meets the Southwest. The formative years of Johnson and Poage offer a window on subtle and overt aspects of the tensions among Anglos, African Americans, and Mexican Americans within that pivotal portion of the state.

Significantly, Johnson's perspective on civil rights evolved as he set his sights on the Senate and White House, but Poage's views during forty-two years representing Waco and surrounding communities remained more parochial. My examination of the role of race and ethnicity in shaping the political realities these two individuals knew in their formative years lays groundwork essential to establishing the significance of Johnson's call for "strength in unity" in Waco in 1958, amid growing alarm among traditionalists that the direction of federal power pointed to the demise of white supremacy.

Chapter 2, "The National Youth Administration, the State Director, and the State Senator," brings LBJ and Poage together as they learned how to integrate grassroots politics with federal agencies by working with the New Deal's NYA programs. This shaped their understanding of how to use federal programs for the mutual benefit of citizens and for the reinforcement of their growing political networks. The career paths of these two major figures in the political culture of Texas intersected when the NYA came to Waco. Both would use advisory councils comprised of carefully recruited stakeholders to identify local priorities for federal projects, a cornerstone of the architecture of New Deal (and Great Society) federalism that cemented the reputations of these very different men. During this time, Johnson's actions clearly demonstrate the intent to use the system to advance the interests of African Americans and Mexican Americans beyond existing norms in Central Texas.

Chapter 3, "Flood Control, Federalism, and a Ford Dealer," blends environmental with political history by directing the reader's attention to how Johnson and Poage established long-term relationships with members of the business community in Waco who viewed engagement with the federal government as essential to economic development. Poage and Johnson conducted a careful massaging of egos and interests of Waco VIPs, but this chapter offers a new interpretation on the emergence of the New South by positing that the influence of business leaders had the cumulative result of moderating the voting behavior of the segregationist Poage.

While chapter 3 illustrates the vital role of elite whites in advocating and cultivating support for federal initiatives Johnson and Poage favored, chapter 4, "Beyond Sandtown," demonstrates how members of the previously voiceless Mexican American community gained influence in public affairs in Waco through the gateway of federal programming. The focus of the chapter remains on the citizens themselves. In a pivotal moment in the city's history, the massive destruction wrought by the tornado that hit downtown Waco in 1953 triggered the infusion of federal disaster relief funds that amounted to a preview of urban renewal programs. Johnson and Poage used their influence to maximize those federal resources, with eligibility requirements for grantees that called for engagement of community representatives, thereby opening the door for those previously excluded. Although these urban development monies clearly had implications for all of Waco, including the African American community, I concentrate on the impact of federal programming on the future leaders of an influential Latino organization established in the 1960s, the Waco Alliance of Mexican Americans. I do so in recognition of dynamic demographic changes in subsequent decades that demand increased scholarly attention. The availability of untapped primary sources at the Texas Collection at Baylor University, including transcripts of interviews at their Institute for Oral History, makes it possible to further illuminate key developments in the agency of the Mexican American community in the political culture of Central Texas.

The conclusion of the book reprises the main themes and findings, naturally, but also serves as an epilogue. The breach in the relationship between LBJ and Bob Poage over the closing of the air base evidently did not heal prior to Johnson's death in early 1973. The city of Waco benefited enormously from the direct and indirect effects of the new dam, which due to construction delays did not see a dedication ceremony for seven years from the groundbreaking ceremony when LBJ spoke of "strength in unity," beginning operation in 1965. "Strength in diversity" might be just as appropriate for Waco today, where the population is roughly one-third Anglo, one-third African American, and one-third Mexican American. The Texas they knew had changed, as had their relationship.

The Texas They Knew

THE POLITICS OF RACE IN CENTRAL TEXAS,
1916–29

A LITTLE HORSE NAMED REBEL clip-clopped his way through Austin, drawing a wagon with two passengers: a Texas legislator and a future president of the United States. Edward Joseph, a longtime retailer, recognized Sam Ealy Johnson and his boy, Lyndon. Mr. Joseph knew Sam never bought much. Behind the store, a tack room offered cots for travelers to pass the night before taking the long, slow trip back home to Johnson City, or Dripping Springs, or Driftwood. The length of the legislative session determined the extent of Sam Johnson's stay in Austin during those years he represented the Eighty-Ninth District in the House.[1]

Despite the vastness of the state and the spaciousness of the House and Senate chambers in the capitol building, lawmakers numbered just ninety and thirty-one, respectively, when convened.[2] At one desk, William Allen Poage, senator from Waco, served concurrently with the father of the future president during the Thirty-Sixth Legislature, a two-year term beginning in 1918. Senator Poage's health problems ended his engagement in civic affairs prematurely, but his eldest son, Bob, acquired a healthy appetite for politics at this father's side, and would soon reclaim that seat.[3] As they arrived from Waco, the Poages may have recognized ten-year-old Lyndon accompanying his garrulous father. Despite this easily imagined scenario, neither correspondence nor public remarks at any time in their careers referred to such an early acquaintance. These experiences at their father's sides, nonetheless, surely contributed to the vow each boy made to one day have his own desk in the legislature.

One might derive a sense of how Texans felt about the role of state government by the part-time nature of its legislative branch that convened officially once every two years for a few months. When the public's business required, or as the more cynical observers might say, when the promise of earning five dollars a day for special sessions (known as special calls) made it worth the trip, the sound of the Speaker's gavel might be heard more often.[4] The Thirty-Sixth Legislature met for its regular session January 12 through March 19, 1918. A very brief special call found them in session again in early May. Convened once more between June 23 and July 22, 1919, legislators like Sam Ealy Johnson of rural central Texas dealt with routine business. Johnson, for example, sponsored HB 158, a bill providing for more road construction in Blanco County as horse drawn wagons yielded to

State Representative Sam Ealy Johnson, ca. 1905.
Courtesy Lyndon Baines Johnson Library and Museum.

automobiles. Meanwhile, white supremacists, stubborn as mules, yielded to no one.[5]

It is not clear whether Lyndon accompanied his father to Austin for this second special call.[6] "The President used to go to the floor with his father and sit and listen and observe. He liked to hear these grownups talk," recalled LBJ's secretary, Juanita Roberts.[7] Lyndon did not need to be there to hear about the issues, however. A childhood friend remembered, "It seemed like Mr. Johnson was in politics as a representative, a Texas legislator, he would gather the kids in the community area. They would gather at his house, and he loved to have them come. We'd gather around the fireplace in the winter time and he'd start arguments about different things. We argued mostly over political candidates."[8]

W. A. Poage represented Waco and McLennan County in the state senate, then his son's legislative career took him to Austin for two terms in the House (1925–29), followed by three more in the Senate (1931–37); all this before his son's forty-two years representing the Eleventh Congressional District in the US House of Representatives. Sam Johnson served a total of four terms in the Texas House between 1905 and 1923, and Lyndon spent twenty-four years in the US House and Senate from 1937 to 1961. The fact that Bob Poage or his father represented Waco in either Austin or Washington, DC, for all but seven years between 1917 and 1979 is a remarkable story in and of itself.[9] Adding Lyndon Johnson to the cast of characters could hardly detract from its telling.

Along with these aspects of Poage's formative years, which in many ways ran parallel to LBJ's, significant distinctions existed. The lives of Poage and LBJ first intersected in that capitol building through the careers of their fathers. There, steeped in the bourbon, branch water, and spittoons brimming with Texas politics, they would learn the smell LBJ associated with power. He spoke of it later in life, when few knew its seductive scent better.[10] Tracing the roots of their political persuasions leads back to Austin during the racially charged era of World War I and its aftermath. For Poage, it also evoked power redolent of the acrid smoke of burned crosses or the charred, hanging remains of another lynching victim in McLennan County. The trail one needs to follow back to the distinctive cultural geography of the places they called home passed through some dark places.

This chapter explores facets of the political culture of the Central Texas that bred Bob Poage and Lyndon Johnson, with an emphasis on their formative years from 1916 to 1929—a period when Waco and Austin, like much of America, came to terms with segregation in the post–World War I era in distinctive ways.[11] Questions about public policy regarding race relations ultimately divided the future politicians, but during the time they came to know Austin, segregation knew little opposition. At a time in the nation's history when internal and external migration flared nativist nostrils, and economic conditions encountered shortages in tolerance, the federal government stood at ease while race riots rocked East Saint Louis, Chicago, Tulsa, and other cities across the nation, including several in Texas.

Waco and Austin did not experience riots, but like harrowing survival stories of bad weather narrowly missed, stories of violent racial storms passing through Longview, Killeen, and Brownsville circulated in the breeze of daily conversation. In those times, sheriffs, mayors, or governors quashed unrest—sometimes after they had provoked it.

At that time, Longview, a city of approximately 5,000 people located 250 miles northeast of Austin, counted 30 percent of its population as African American. The fuse ignited when a local teacher at a school for African American children, Samuel L. Jones, stood accused by a white mob for contributing an article to the *Chicago Defender* about a lynching that took place in East Texas months earlier. Jones's association with Dr. C. P. Davis, organizer of the Negro Businessmen's League in Longview, further inflamed tempers. Jones was beaten with iron rods and ordered by white authorities to leave Longview. The local police took no action. Several hours later, mobs of angry whites set fire to Jones's and Davis's homes. Longview police arrested six members of the Negro Businessmen's Association for rioting.[12]

The mayor of Longview contacted Governor William P. Hobby to request assistance. Hobby promptly dispatched the Texas Rangers and "several hundred" National Guardsmen, who restored order by July 12. Authorities charged seventeen whites with attempted murder. In addition, nine white men faced arson charges, but all of the accused whites made bail and went home. Citing the need for safety, the African Americans were moved to Austin, where no lynching had ever been recorded. Representatives of NAACP chapters from Austin to San Antonio met with the assistant adjutant general in Austin on July 25 to review the handling of the crisis. By mid-August, all of the African Americans had been released. No trials took place.[13]

Meanwhile, leaders of the white and African American establishment in Austin engaged in rumor control. On August 3, the *Austin American* editorialized:

Without detailing all the rumors and "confidential tips" and many "I know it to be a fact," the net result is that the rumors have created a certain amount of apprehension in some quarters of both whites and negroes, but there is no special reason for alarm or uneasiness, unless, of course, some excitable, hairbrained person would start trouble.

A reporter interviewed city official Jake Plott, who assured citizens by saying, "I have made arrangements to have the city whistle give five blasts to call together all of Austin's thirty policemen and detectives in case they were needed."[14]

From the perspective of the security-conscious twenty-first century, we see that Mr. Plott described a sophisticated early warning system developed to head off the mass rebellion white supremacists saw as inevitable. The contingency plan required careful coordination, honed to local officials and their sense of who represented potential threats. Outsiders, invariably viewed with suspicion by conspiracy-minded whites, could be recognized readily. For matters of this kind, the notion of using federal troops for any disturbance in post-Reconstruction Texas seemed unimaginable, but intermittent cross-border pursuits of Mexicans with varying agendas carried out during the Wilson administration continued for years.

As historian Benjamin Heber Johnson brought to light in *Revolution in Texas*, a secessionist movement of a very different kind kindled in the tense years when unrest in Mexico rippled into Texas, sometimes flaring in the form of pockets of nationalist or separatist movements.[15] Side by side, then, federal and state officials in Texas aligned in their views of the proper role of the federal government. For border issues, federal troops were a necessary evil, but the status of freed slaves and their descendants fell to the states. State capitols often have one foot in a revolutionary past and the other seeking the most stable footing possible.

Engaging Mexico in a series of military incidents from 1913 to 1919 inevitably contributed to an existing problem of negative stereotyping of people of Mexican heritage by "Anglos" at a time when the Spanish-speaking population in Texas and across the southwestern United States grew rapidly.[16] Under Wilson, whose Lone Star connections, notably "Colonel" House, have received considerable scholarly attention, Washington mobilized the nation to a level of regimentation unknown to previous generations of Americans.[17] Wartime conditions led to the most expansive footprint ever trod by Uncle Sam under the War Industries Board and agencies dealing with everything from war gardens at local schools to war bonds parades on Main Street. Matters of race, however, fell to state and local discretion.

Even as segregationists dominated the government at local, state, and federal levels, stifling debate about integration until well after World War II, prominent African Americans openly examined their status (and their future) in American society one-half century after slavery ended. Opinions and strategies varied. Accommodationists continued to counsel patience and self-reliance long after Booker T. Washington's passing in 1915. After World War I, the Harlem Renaissance spurred enormous interest among intellectuals in African culture and art forms. The Twenties would also see the rise and fall of Marcus Garvey and the Universal Negro Improvement Association (UNIA). Within the NAACP, internal divisions about social equality, voluntary segregation, and integration simmered throughout the 1920s, exploding in a heated airing in the pages of *The Crisis* in January 1934 when W. E. B. Du Bois declared integration a futile pursuit.[18] In many ways, the African American community seemed to be engaged in a more open debate about the future of race relations than whites permitted among themselves.

Wilson's Republican successor, Ohioan Warren G. Harding, also endorsed segregation as the best strategy for the nation. The two dominant political parties, whatever other differences divided them, reached consensus on how to keep African Americans in their place. The dread of miscegenation, job loss, and radicalism served as brick and mortar for white supremacists across the country. As the walls of segregation grew taller and stronger, African Americans faced the most hostile social and political climate since the abolition of slavery.[19] The Ku Klux Klan raised its hooded head again, cobra-like, as if the full faith and credit of the political establishment somehow offered insufficient assurance of white supremacy. When riots erupted in several states, fears of revolution and race war incited by radicals internal and external exacerbated the tension. Writing of the standoff, historian John Hope Franklin stated, "whites had steeled themselves against the day when black soldiers would return and make demands for first-class citizenship, and they were ready to put the machinery they had perfected into operation."[20]

Within this national context, whites of varying ethnicities, African Americans, and Mexican Americans of Austin, Texas, conducted their daily lives, earning a living, educating their children, worshipping in accordance with their faith. No matter how self-congratulatory local officials postured about the progressiveness and tolerance of their city, a very resistant strain of contagious fear came knocking. The racialized violence of 1919 and the subsequent rise of the Ku Klux Klan sharply divided the city—perhaps as much as any time since the Civil War.

The postwar atmosphere of paranoia in the United States, with fear of radicalism reinforced by the international headlines, grew stronger from the changes in the makeup of urban neighborhoods. Wartime migration created new realities in terms of housing and school integration for neighborhoods in northern cities that had previously considered the question of integration as an academic exercise, not as the matter of zoning law pending before dozens of councils and boards in cities and suburbs of the industrial Midwest.[21] Restrictive covenants, redlining, and a host of strategies effectively segregated many cities for generations. The reaction by conservative whites, notably through the resurgent Ku Klux Klan, effectively terrorized a significant segment of the targeted communities, as well as many whites. Across the Midwest, as in Central Texas, the Klan and the political establishment often, but not always, became one, until scandals that rocked the Klan in 1925 led to rounds of renunciations. Despite the tactics of the Klan, voices of tolerance could still be heard, as this chapter demonstrates. Significantly, white Democrats opposed to the Klan did so out of concern that a shadow government could ultimately challenge the sovereignty of the state.

In order to get a better sense of the political culture Johnson and Poage came to know in Central Texas, we need to ask how civic life in segregated society played out, because even in the absence of the full rights of citizenship, politics happens. How did the KKK become a dominant factor in the realpolitik of life in a segregated society? Considering the KKK success in Central Texas with an emphasis on its immersion into the mainstream, rather than the kind of terror and violence so closely associated with the organization, one can come closer to seeing it as it appeared to most whites. Like the rest of the old Confederacy and the increasingly segregated North, the Texas LBJ and Bob Poage knew bowed to no federal mandates governing race relations. With no accountability to African American taxpayers through the ballot box, what strategies did community leaders employ to secure essential needs? During their careers in Washington, Johnson and Poage could justifiably take pride in extending public utilities to segments of the population previously deprived of electricity, potable water, sewage disposal, and telephone service, but all of these determinations of who could access the services of modern life and who could not have resided with the jurisdiction of local and state authorities before the New Deal.

To illustrate how whites and African Americans negotiated the landscape of segregation, we will consider the strategies and experiences of two African American power brokers in Austin, the Reverend L. L. Campbell and Dr. Everett Givens.[22] Under segregation, contacts with African American opinion leaders kept whites informed of potential issues. As we will see in the next chapter, Johnson first established his strong political network with the African American community while state director of the National Youth Administration (NYA), creating opportunities for enhancing organizational and leadership skills for establishment figures and for young men and women. Nurturing the latter accelerated as federal programs multiplied, each calling for local stakeholders. Community-based organizations flourished, and sometimes they collaborated with churches and traditional centers of power in the African American community. But competing interests arose as well, with their own leaders seeking places at the table. When federal programs multiplied, traditional leaders in the community needed to adapt.

By the 1960s individuals like Reverend Campbell and Dr. Givens might be derisively accused of being an "Uncle Tom" by activists in the civil rights movement because of their tacit acknowledgment that white superiority within the political system necessitated bargaining from a position of weakness. Effective leaders secure whatever gains are possible with the resources available, and the critics of Campbell and Givens who joined the struggle in the 1950s or 1960s could access the system through means unavailable to an African American community leader in the atmosphere following World War I. Compared to Waco and to many other southern cities, Austin formalized interactions with citizens of color, particularly when the citizens organized. The agency of local African American leaders in both cities cannot be overstated, considering the choices facing members of the African American community in the 1920s. The level of intimidation created in Waco, however, forced much of that agency into the shadows of black and white interaction. William Carrigan argued persuasively in *Making of a Lynching Culture* that the racially motivated murder of Jesse Thomas of Waco (unlike Jesse Washington of nearby Robinson) in 1922 disturbed the city's African American residents more than the far more notorious Waco Horror of 1916, because so many people knew Thomas. "The fire never died," Kneeland Clemons told William Carrigan in an interview.[23] In Waco, the local leaders kept the flame low enough that the whites could not detect the black smoke.

Shades of gray existed within the South's version of apartheid, and even within a region the size of Central Texas significant variations in local history dictated how the political culture around black/white collaboration existed within the larger, intolerant system, illustrating how the process referred to often as "constructive engagement" worked. Absent the blatant, repeated use of terror by local whites, the agency of African American leaders in Austin offers a better opportunity to study American civics, segregation style.

Settlement Patterns, Race, and Ethnicity in Central Texas

In *Sketches from the Five States of Texas*, folklorist A. C. Greene presented anecdotes conveying distinctions of North, South, East, West, and Central Texas.[24] Greene cautioned against seeing all of East Texas as pine forests, or all of South Texas as grasslands. For example, the prime cotton country of the blackland prairie described in historian Neil Foley's *The White Scourge* extends from North Central into South Central Texas.[25] With traditions and attitudes about race closely tied to the slaveholding Deep South, the cotton country around Waco cultivated patterns of racial interaction and isolation characteristic of the Jim Crow South. Just to the southwest of the region Foley examined, rocky terrain wooded chiefly by drought-tolerant cedars and mesquites marks the geologically, agriculturally, and socially transformative Balcones Escarpment near Austin. Greene called this rugged land a "state within a state."[26]

Peering out from the vantage point of the capitol building's second floor, one gets a sense of being at a crossroads. Austin rose on the north bank of the Colorado River in South Central Texas, where the rich soil of the blackland prairie that surrounds Waco ends and the Hill Country of the Balcones Escarpment begins. In *Imperial Texas: An Interpretative Essay in Cultural Geography*, noted historian D. W Meinig asserted, "this part of Texas best displays together the several cultures which have been the most important in the heritage of Texas and thereby also best displays the full range of intercultural tensions which are so important a part of Texas life."[27]

Since its independence from Mexico in 1836, Texas settlers included various white ethnic groups from Europe, largely opposed to slavery, notably Germans, as well as "native" Virginians, like the Poages, who embraced the institution of slavery. The African American population of Central Texas arrived in bondage, with few exceptions, and resided in rural, plantation settings through the Civil War. The postwar model of sharecropping still bound the former slaves to the earth and to a white person holding title to the rows they hoed. Some African American farmers acquired land over time, but migration to urban settings increased through the late nineteenth century through World War I.[28] The political cultures of the congressional districts Bob Poage and Lyndon Johnson represented reflected those historic trends, but the Great War and its aftermath shifted migration patterns, with a sharp reduction in the arrival of Europeans and a rapid increase in migrants from Mexico.

To those unfamiliar with Texas, its appeal to Europeans in the nineteenth century may seem inconceivable today. The Central Texas region encompassing Waco and Austin experienced the heaviest streams of German migrants in the mid-nineteenth century. These highly literate families came via transatlantic ships bound for Galveston at a time of political turmoil in the Vaterland. The greater the concentration of the "Forty-Eighters," as those in the first big wave were known, the more liberal the local political culture in terms of matters of race, alcohol, or women's suffrage. From a political science perspective, V. O. Key's classic study of regional politics, *Southern Politics in State and Nation,* affirmed the influential role played by Germans who "took democracy literally."[29]

Historian Dale Baum substantiated this perspective in his study of the 1861 secession referendum in Texas. Discussing voting trends in five of the eighteen counties rejecting withdrawal in March 1861, Baum mentioned Blanco County, with four other outliers (Gillespie, Medina, Williamson, and Travis) where voters' support for the Union cause prevailed. Baum determined that two of the major reasons for support for the Union cause were European immigrants opposed to slavery and the fact the slavery was "not important to the local economy."[30]

The potential alliance between Texas Populists and these new citizens collapsed under the weight of pressure from the prohibitionists who came to dominate the Populist movement. As Key put it, the German Texans considered such public policy "illiberal." One indication of the role of ethnicity and faith in shaping aspects of the political culture of Central Texas can be seen in the "local option" elections conducted in November 1914. Voters in McLennan County chose "dry," while Austin voters rejected a similar municipal ban on alcohol.[31]

Few issues from that time better enunciate the pronounced role ethnicity played within the world of white politicians than the debate over the teaching of German to students in the public schools that erupted in April 1917 with the declaration of war. The controversy over making English the sole language of instruction in public schools fomented across the nation, but anti-German hysteria proved most divisive wherever German people had concentrated in the United States since the 1840s. The debate in Texas aroused special interest in the teaching of the German language in high school. Representative Sam Johnson argued as passionately for tolerance on this issue as W. A. Poage advocated against it.[32]

The elder Poage's determination to ban the teaching of German can be seen in at least two separate efforts reported in the *Dallas Morning News*, the first resolution being defeated in March 1918. Notable about the second attempt is the timing: W. A. Poage proposed banning the teaching of German in Texas schools in January 1919, more than two months after the Armistice. As LBJ came to terms with his own stance on civil rights later in his life, he often spoke of his father's courageous defense of his beleaguered German-speaking constituency. Even after the anti-German hysteria set wildfires of intolerance across the United States, an adolescent Lyndon Johnson

Rebekah Johnson, 1917. *Courtesy Lyndon Baines Johnson Library and Museum.*

attended ninth grade at a school in the neighboring community of Albert while confronting two issues. For each four-mile commute, Johnson rode his donkey, much to the amusement of other students, apparently. Biographer Robert Caro reported that Johnson's poor command of German also set him apart from other students, despite the enjoyment his mother, Rebekah Johnson, derived from tutoring the local German-speaking children in English. Perhaps young Lyndon's taste of being the "other" stayed with him and grew into empathy, and ultimately into relentless political action.

To a substantial degree, the Texas Johnson knew as a youth differed from that Poage knew. LBJ's beloved Hill Country, the center of his world at the bookends of his life, was largely populated during his boyhood by people from Johnson City or the surrounding German and Scotch Irish (by way of Tennessee) communities. Coming out of the Hill Country to the capitol meant leaving a virtually all-white zone and entering the most diverse urban landscape he would know until he went to Houston to teach in 1929. Trips to Austin exposed him directly to another world, a netherworld he would come to know in Texas, where a virtual caste system stratified the culture by perceived race.

As a twenty-year-old teacher, reliant upon worn copies of state-approved textbooks such as *Geography of Texas*, Lyndon Baines Johnson conducted lessons for his Mexican American students entirely in English, as required by state law, at the Welhausen school in Cotulla, Texas.[33] Ability, ambition, and opportunity took him into the world of national politics as a congressional aide after just two years in the classroom.[34] Neither admirers nor critics doubt the indelible imprints of the impoverished human landscape of Cotulla on his character and worldview. The Hill Country offered its own form of hardscrabble subsistence, and trips to Austin with his father exposed him to urban poverty, so young Lyndon Johnson knew of people living hand to mouth prior to Cotulla.

Johnson's teaching experience affected him like a Peace Corps volunteer immersed in the lives of third world villagers. The young teacher's letters to family members show that the wellspring of the controversial War on Poverty can be traced to the culture shock of moving from the turquoise tranquility of the Pedernales or the cozy familiarity of Johnson City to the leveling poverty of the border country for that school year in Cotulla. In 1960, campaigning in the poorest hollows of West Virginia deeply moved the Kennedy family. Soon after, social activist Michael Harrington's book *The Other America* awakened more Americans to the issue of poverty by depicting the chasm of opportunity between children of Appalachia and those of a broadly affluent society.[35] LBJ needed no awakening. These issues made him sleepless. Encounters with those Mexican American children infused his unquenchable political ambition with a sense of purpose that drove a significant portion of Johnson's career. LBJ, like V. O. Key's Germans, wanted people to take their democracy literally.

The political culture of Central Texas derived from, and power resided in, the hands of "native" Texans and the descendants of a variety of European immigrants, but the region experienced a steadily increasing presence of African Americans and Mexican Americans by mid-twentieth century that challenged that hegemony.[36] Chattel slavery did not take root in the Hill Country west of Austin, but the Brazos bottomlands below Waco knew the institution well. Two generations after the first Juneteenth celebration, nearly one-half of Waco's population in 1910 was African American, whereas nonwhites made up less than 2 percent of the population in the Johnson City/Stonewall area of the Hill Country when Johnson was born in 1908.[37]

By Texas standards, Austin in the early twentieth century may have seemed to African Americans, and to the rapidly increasing Mexican population, a less oppressive city for nonwhites than Waco. Still, in both cities, the factions of Anglo political culture during this era, even with essentially one-party rule under the heading of "Democrats," divided and subdivided on issues along a host of fault lines, but remained seemingly solid as limestone on the sanctity of white supremacy. As monolithic as whites likely appeared to African Americans and Mexican Americans, among whites, national origin mattered a great deal in terms of social status.

Consequently, the influence of Germans on the political culture of the Hill Country and on the lives of Rebekah and Sam Ealy Johnson launched many an LBJ biography. The origins of Bob Poage's worldview did not attract the scholarly attention a president receives. Yet Poage came of age in Waco, Texas, at a time when it gained the reputation as one of the most racially hateful cities in the world—a fascinating counterpoint to the lessons of tolerance LBJ absorbed through his parents and from the months he spent teaching Mexican American children in Cotulla, Texas, in 1928.

Students of LBJ's passion for politics learn of the formative role many Hill Country nights spent on the porch swing, listening to his hero, his father, played.[38] Biographers invariably direct attention to the high expectations Rebekah Johnson held for her first son.[39] His devotion to both parents, especially to his mother, permeated *LBJ and the American Dream*, distilled

Bob and Helen Conger Poage, 1964. *Courtesy W. R.* *Poage Legislative Library.*

William Allen Poage, ca. 1918. *Courtesy W. R. Poage Legislative Library.*

from Doris Kearns Goodwin's work on his memoir, *The Vantage Point.*[40] The newly elected congressman kissed his beloved daddy goodbye on the lips while boarding the train for Washington, DC, in April 1937, bearing witness to a deep bond between an aging father in failing health and a son in a culture not given to physical manifestations of familial love between males. Sam died that October, leaving Lyndon treasured childhood memories of touring the countryside, not even 10 years old, while campaigning at his daddy's side for another term in the Texas legislature. Sam's opponent in that 1918 election, August Benner, would carry a large percentage of the German voters, the largest bloc in Gillespie County at the time. There was more than one way to be a minority in the Hill Country.[41]

Bob Poage, however, spent much of his youth witnessing the Jim Crow system in operation on a day-to-day basis when white families, including his, routinely used African American labor for domestic and farm work. Within a year of his birth in December 1899, his parents left Waco to pursue ranching in North Central Texas, then returned to city life after thirteen years for the dual purposes of W. A.'s career interests and educating a growing family. In their home at 1411 North Sixth Street in Waco, according to data from the US Census of 1900, the three white Poages barely outnumbered the two African American residents of their home: a forty-eight-year-old cook named Ellie (or possibly Ellen) Lenard and a "nurse" for the infant Bob, just nine years of age, named Lottie George.[42] No other census records for W. A. Poage, Helen Conger Poage, Bob Poage, or his brothers Conger and Scott, show any live-in

CHAPTER ONE

domestic labor except in 1900, but that neither confirms nor denies nonresidential workers they may have employed. Bob Poage did not mention this aspect of his family life in *My First 85 Years*.

At the time of LBJ's birth in the Hill Country, the eight-and-a-half-year-old Poage, whom future supporters would dub "Mr. Agriculture," developed his lifelong interest in the rural economy as he learned the ropes on the family's Lazy 'Leven Ranch straddling the Throckmorton and Shackelford County lines. When the family returned to Waco in 1913, however, Poage witnessed a highly segregated system of de facto and de jure interactions governing acceptable conduct between the races. A comment in Poage's memoir, *My First 85 Years*, about his youth, suggested that the Lost Cause lived in the Poage household.

> I never knew how I became such a violent Confederate in my childhood, but at one time I sought to change my name to "Robert Lee Poage." Both my parents and my grandmother all humored me and while I consider Lee and Jackson to probably have done more with less than any military leaders, I think I now have a much better perspective of this era of our history.[43]

Removed from the longtime family estate in Virginia known as Merrifield, where George Poage decided to join Jeb Stuart's cavalry against the Yankees, W. A. Poage built a reputation as a stockman: buying, breeding, and butchering cattle.[44] He married Helen Conger, the daughter of another prominent rancher who was nearly fifteen years younger than her new husband. The rolling acreage of the Lazy 'Leven pastured beef animals on land west of the cotton country in the time before irrigation systems moved cotton farming beyond historian Walter Prescott Webb's famous line of demarcation.[45] Located along the Clear Fork of the Brazos, just above the historic river's mainstream, the land held by the Poages tied them to another Virginian. This was the site of Camp Cooper, where Lieutenant Colonel Robert E. Lee served in 1856, so the Poage's cattle grazed on land that briefly served as a reservation for approximately 450 Penateka Comanches from 1855 to 1859. Only 124 people, all recorded as "White" in the census rolls, were counted in the entire county in 1860.[46]

By the post-Reconstruction era, ranchers dominated the local economy, with sixty-eight such enterprises counted in the 1880 census. Cotton, virtually nonexistent as a crop in Throckmorton County in 1880, took up 3,000 acres of land in 1900 then increased by 700 percent in ten years. The number of farms and ranches quadrupled to over 270 between 1880 and 1900, and more than doubled by 1910, with census records showing 694 families raising crops and livestock. The move from Waco to the ranch near Throckmorton in 1900 occurred at an opportune time during this upswing in the agricultural economy.[47]

The elder Poage's motivations for the move back to the city included his own political ambition and educational goals for the children. The youngest of three sons, Bob Poage would experience life in the racially diverse but heavily segregated city for the first time in his memory. Growing up in the virtually 100 percent white environment of Throckmorton County, he learned about the varied living conditions Anglos experienced in rural Texas by observation, though his family prospered.[48] Bob graduated from Waco High School in 1918; he then had a brief stint in the navy before the Armistice caused a rapid drawdown in US forces. Upon his return to Waco, he studied geology, then law, at Baylor University.[49]

As his family grew, W. A. Poage resumed activity in city politics. Progressive Democrats, followers of Woodrow Wilson advocating "good government" in 1916, did well in the whites-only party primary customary in Waco during the World War I era. Before succumbing to cancer in late 1920, he would serve two terms in the state senate representing Waco and McLennan County. The elder Poage's record shows some progressive inclinations, notably on women's suffrage and federal aid for flood relief.

Like Johnson, Bob Poage flexed his young political muscles at college, where he organized a debate club known as the "Senate." As LBJ's senior by more than eight years, Bob Poage finished Baylor Law School and began teaching law classes there in 1924. There are indications that W. A. Poage's voting record in other areas could have had some bearing on his son's political outlook. For example, as a terrible drought ("drouth" the preferred term in Texas at the time) wore on through the summer of 1918, Representative Poage called upon the federal government to provide relief to victims. The following spring he voted in favor of the federal suffrage amendment; Texas had become one of its earliest adopters among the old Confederacy. The relatively brief voting record of this very successful cattleman who represented a city highly dependent on the agricultural economy reveals a high degree of pragmatism, given the widespread resistance to any perceived overreaching by the federal government. The concurrence of that extended drought with the significantly expanded federal footprint during World War I may point to a temporary softening of antifederal sentiments. The cycles of drought and flooding in Central Texas produced life-and-death struggles that plagued its occupants long before statehood.

In addition to contributions by his parents to shaping Bob Poage's sense of the functioning of civic life, the influences of the cotton culture on Waco remained strong when he came to know the city as a thirteen-year-old. Just three years later, the Jesse Washington incident, arguably the ghastliest public spectacle of barbarism by human beings since the Inquisition, or before, would brand Waco with a reputation for intolerance that would prove difficult to erase. The savage execution by mob of Jesse Washington in 1916, an event certainly critical if not central to reinforcing attitudes toward race during Poage's formative years, led historian William Carrigan to advance the argument that a "lynching culture" developed over eighty years of settlement in Central Texas, with the tacit support of the power structure in Waco.[50] In Central Texas, as in much of the nation in that era, outrage to the incident derived from the extraordinary size of the mob that hijacked the legal system, rather than the systematic denial of basic human rights underlying the situation. Working from Carrigan's thesis, Cynthia Skove Nevels probed the demographics of South Central Texas, particularly the lower Brazos Valley. Cutting through the notion of a monolithic white culture, Nevels's study of lynching led her to conclude that some first- or second-generation immigrants, especially those from southern Europe, participated in lynching "to belong."[51] Austin certainly contained its share of European immigrants, but the lynching culture did not take hold in Travis County, leaving those outsiders to find another assimilation strategy.

Although a lynching culture remained in Waco for a considerable time to come, a segment of the white population stood aghast at the bloodlust. At Baylor University, the flagship institution of the Baptist faith, hints of change could be seen in a strongly worded condemnation from the faculty published in the *Waco Semi-Weekly Tribune*. Baylor dean J. L. Kesler penned a letter to *The Nation* after growing weary of the portrayal of the city (and the university, unfortunately) as standing by idly. He described speaking passionately to hundreds of students about the need to reject violence. Several local white ministers sermonized against the evils of mob rule, but it appears uncertain as to how many actually did so, since the passage of time motivated some to commit the sin of rewriting the past as it became advantageous to do so.[52]

The veils preventing the nonwhite populace of the cities from enjoying the full sunshine of human rights were not cut out of the same cloth.

Emancipation came on June 19, 1865, soon known among African Americans as "Juneteenth," a virtual state holiday for many Texans to this day. Promising indicators of a more tolerant approach to the new social reality evaporated. A Travis County official named Frank Brown, a resident of Austin for many years, wrote about how Austin would fare in meeting the needs of the free. Acknowledging worries in other parts of the state that they "would become an intolerable burden on the public," Brown reported in Travis County "a large proportion went to work with a will [on contract] . . . and proved to be laborious, thrifty, and faithful."[53]

From the end of Reconstruction through the Progressive Era, a marked regression took place in the status of the descendants of slaves and "free people of color" across the South, and in the North, as well, due to the Great Migration. Race relations across the United States continued to deteriorate, but as the distinctive developments in race relations in Waco and Austin between World War I and the end of the 1920s demonstrated, formal and informal racism was local. Based on Johnson's and Poage's future records, perhaps these distinctions in what they experienced as youths need to be given greater weight.

In Waco, the lingering stench of the burned bodies of two generations of post-Reconstruction African American men led to a steep reduction due to out-migration, as Carrigan demonstrated in *Lynching Culture*. Fear of victimization at the hands of white mobs hung like fog over people of color, but especially African Americans.[54] And although voices of white integrationists fell mute by supremacists, sharp divisions among whites were evident when the Klan nearly took over the Democratic Party in Texas. Compared to the overall population of Waco, African Americans declined by 50 percent between 1880 and 1930, from 34 percent to 17 percent.[55] The effects of intimidation through physical violence, or the threat of it, may be at play, but several thousand people of Mexican origin came to Waco from 1910 to 1930, more than in any previous period.[56] The Spanish-speaking population grew from just a few hundred to over four thousand in that span of time, creating enormous pressure on the value of labor, since so many people needed work.

Transitioning from the tense segregation of a biracial society to a less clearly articulated set of social norms for what rapidly became a triracial demographic in Central Texas produced distinctive challenges amid others occurring nationally, such as the reemergence of the Ku Klux Klan. The continuing violence of the era, from the sadistic mob that killed Jesse Washington in Waco in 1916 to the psychological terror generated by burning crosses

CHAPTER ONE

and ghostly robes, aimed to preserve the social order by an ever-evolving system of de jure and de facto codes of behavior for those sorted by the colors white, black, and brown.

What one historian has described as a "great folk movement" took place in Texas as Lyndon Johnson and Bob Poage came of age.[57] Growing up in Central Texas in the first quarter of the twentieth century exposed the sons of white landowners like Sam Johnson and W. A. Poage to Tejanos and to more recent arrivals from Mexico. Tens of thousands of Mexicans crossed the Rio Grande in this period. As early as 1927, sociologist Charles S. Johnson had identified the pattern: "The Negroes from the South have filled the gaps by the receding Europeans, and the Mexicans have filled the gaps created by the Negroes."[58] In 1900, after all, there were fewer ethnic Mexicans than Germans. Yet after 1900 more Mexicans crossed the Rio Grande each year than had come into Texas in all the generations of Spanish rule. Between 1910 and 1920, 264,503 arrivals were counted, followed by more than 165,000 in the next decade. Paradoxically, Mexican Americans played the role of newcomers in Austin and Waco. Prior to World War I, relatively few Mexican Americans resided in Austin or Waco, but that would change quickly, with a substantially greater presence during the decade, only to be reversed in the deportations of the 1930s. In fact, the most significant development in Austin's population between 1900 and 1930 was the increased presence of Mexican Americans and recent arrivals from Mexico.

Limited housing options, kinship networks, and the presence of Spanish-language retailers made East Austin a practical choice for migrants from Mexico. The Catholic dioceses faced some challenging decisions about the future of a church to be named Our Lady of the Guadalupe. By July 10, 1926, the *Austin American* could report the new church would be built in East Austin, with a school attached. By 1929, this school would have over four hundred students enrolled. As Jason McDonald found in his study, several religious and charitable organizations whose missions emphasized service to Mexican Americans and recently arrived migrants from Mexico had to seriously consider moving to East Austin during the 1920s.[59] From a few hundred to nearly five thousand, or almost 10 percent of the community, these new Austinites would make important contributions to the city, not only in terms of the labor market and southwestern cuisine but also in the arts, fashion, language, and in countless other ways.

The Mexican presence in Blanco County was almost nonexistent when LBJ was growing up, based on the recollections of his friend from Johnson

City, Emmette S. Redford. "There were no Mexicans in town, except for a brief time," Redford told an interviewer in March 1982. "While we still lived down on the main street, there was a Mexican-American who set up a restaurant next door to our house, and after a time, the boys or young men rocked him out of town one night. Well, they threw rocks into his restaurant and damaged the place enough that he left."[60]

Historian Emilio Zamora identified several reasons for this upsurge in migration, attributing the increase to traditional push-pull explanations and to turbulence along the border at the time of the 1910 Mexican Revolution and in subsequent struggles among varied interested parties. The economic expansion of the United States during and after World War I created a demand for labor in the Southwest. Zamora also emphasized the impact of improved transportation, increased information, and rural violence and instability in Mexico.[61]

Back in McLennan County, increasing numbers of Spanish-speaking families settled in Waco, especially in the area near the Brazos River, discussed further in chapter 4, known as Sandtown. Whites and African Americans surely noticed the trend, but the reign of terror characterized by mob violence perpetrated by whites on blacks dominated any discussion of race relations. Waco offered a dismal model, a dystopian vision of the aftermath of slavery in the form of a preemptive race war. Patricia Bernstein and William Carrigan documented this with such graphic power that further examination of the awful travails of African Americans in Waco risks redundancy.

Housing options for the African Americans moving into Austin from rural areas were limited by income, and this was true for all new arrivals to some degree. No city zoning regulations served to segregate housing, so this was accomplished by less formal mechanisms. Prior to the 1920s, however, African Americans lived on the north, south, and west sides of the city as well as the east. Each of these districts took on its own name and identity within the larger Austin community, names such as Wheatville, Masontown, and Clarksville. The neighborhood outside East Austin with the most "enduring residential stability" was Clarksville, located on property E. M. Pease donated. In 1907, in a move "widely considered to be a deliberate effort to promote segregation," city and school officials in Austin located the first secondary school for African American students, L. C. Anderson High School, across the deepening color line in East Austin, near the intersection of Pennsylvania and Eleventh Street on Comal

Avenue. African American families in West Austin faced difficult circumstances as public and private service providers followed suit and moved across town.[62] By the end of the 1920s, the African American community leadership grew so focused on improving the infrastructure and business climate in East Austin that the enclave in West Austin became virtually voiceless in the give-and-take of Jim Crow politics between whites and blacks.

Coming of age awash in the political culture of the worlds their parents introduced them to as youths, Bob Poage and Lyndon Johnson observed how whites navigated complex currents in the increasingly racialized environment of Central Texas. Perhaps the most challenging development came in the form of a revitalized Ku Klux Klan.

The Ku Klux Klan and Its White Opponents

The rise of the Klan needs to be seen in the context of the existing racial climate in Austin and Waco, cities where citizens sensed temperatures rising. A portion of the success of the KKK must be ascribed to public relations and pageantry, in addition to physical and psychological violence. The diversity within racial and ethnic groups, then, calls for a textured view of brown, black, and white on the canvas of these Central Texas cities where Poage's and Johnson's political antennas picked up every nuance of distinctive constituencies. The Austin Lyndon Johnson experienced from youth to adulthood revealed differing levels of success and status among African Americans and Mexican Americans that led, in turn, to different strategies for accommodation.

Carl Phinney, chief clerk in the Texas House of Representatives in the early 1920s, recalled the rise of the Klan in an interview conducted in 1968:

> One of the interesting things about President Johnson's father was that he made a speech one day to the House of Representatives against the Ku Klux Klan. At that time, I would say the body was made up of 65 to 70 percent people who were favorable to the Klan. I would say it was really an unpopular time to make this speech. But he had a mind of his own and he never hesitated about speaking on those issues. Following him, another member of the House of Representatives named Wright Patman, who is now a Congressman from the Texarkana District, also

made a speech. I would say Mr. Sam Johnson's attack on the Klan was the entering wedge of the fight that eventually destroyed them.[63]

The dominance of white supremacists in the 1920s is unquestioned, but if Phinney's estimate was correct, there was a significant basis of white opposition to the Klan. This deserves more attention, because the coalitions and alliances around these issues would influence votes on poll taxes, immigration restrictions, and antilynching legislation.

On July 25, 1921, representative Wright Patman introduced a resolution against the Klan in the Texas House. According to Patman's recollection more than fifty years later, someone had made arrangements for a "preacher from Atlanta" to address those present after adjournment. Patman recalled: "But the differences between me and the preacher is that he is a Ku Kluxer and I'm not a Ku Kluxer. I'm against the Ku Klux and I don't want them in this hall. Sam Johnson took my side, too. He was up ready to speak. That's when the Ku Klux issue started in the legislature in Texas."[64]

According to an article in the *Washington Post* on April 1, 1965, Patman's efforts to denounce the Klan, a move Sam Johnson supported, was defeated on July 25, 1921, by a margin of 69 to 54. Patman then switched tactics, removing specific mention of the Klan from his proposal. Instead, the wording would make it illegal "for two or more persons to conspire together for the purpose of injuring, oppressing, threatening or intimidating any person" and to "go in disguise upon public highways." Reported to the House Judiciary Committee in a parliamentary move by the leadership, the bill languished and died.[65] If these memories are accurate, it is all the more unfortunate that no transcript of the Johnson anti-Klan speech has surfaced. Scholars of this period who are inclined to accept Patman's and Phinney's versions point to the prominence of the German American constituency in Sam Johnson's Hill Country district, a voting bloc opposed to the Klan's xenophobic message.

The Klan did not flourish around Johnson City in Blanco County. Longtime Johnson friend Welly K. Hopkins said, "I don't believe those people, as I knew them, were very quick to embrace such ideology and I'm quite sure that the Klan would not have had a stronghold there, for instance, that they had down in my area."[66] Another LBJ contemporary, the aforementioned Emmette Redford, also minimized the Klan's strength when he said, "And I'm just certain that the people I knew in Johnson City who were the leaders of the Protestant religious community were not Ku Klux members. I don't believe there was a single Catholic family in the city."[67]

The Klan's strategy for achieving their goals was multifaceted, with marches, cross burnings, and intimidation, as well as emphasis on more traditional methods of political outreach for good public relations. Local Klan leaders operated the way one would expect from a ward boss in Chicago's Democratic machine in its heyday. Since many members of the KKK in Texas and across the United States did hold elective office, the organization could claim some political sophistication. For example, at three forty-five in the afternoon of August 30, 1921, a representative of the Knights of the Ku Klux Klan dropped by the Children's House on East Eleventh Street. The *Austin Statesman* reported the next day that this "unidentified stranger" gave $100 to Bessie Magee, the "matron" of the home, along with "two letters she was instructed to deliver to the newspapers."[68] A week later, Miss Magee received a load of kindling. Perhaps Ms. Magee spent the $100 on sheets for the beds for the boys and girls.

As in the African American community, the members of congregations of white churches could serve as points of access to wider distribution of a political message. Wright Patman recalled the tactics the Klan used in his hometown of Weatherford, near Dallas:

And the only entertainment you had in Weatherford was going to church all day Sunday and Wednesday night and any other time that anything was going on but they stopped right in the middle of the service and the Ku Klux Klan came right down in a "V." The altar had aisles coming from either side on a slant and they just filled that whole thing. Of course I don't remember the message, but can see now those white robes standing there. They just took over the church service.[69]

The front page of the *Austin Statesman* on September 3, 1921, captured the fascist pageantry of the Klan's dramatic reentry into Austin. After a number of preliminary steps to establish a presence in the city between early July and the end of August, they staged a parade. The specially called legislative session, the Thirty-Seventh Texas Legislature, adjourned on August 25. The Thirty-Eighth Legislature did not convene until January 9, 1923. The Klan leadership negotiated the political landscape of Texas like the insiders they were, so the timing of the parade could be seen as further evidence of a strategic approach to accomplishing their agenda.

The *Statesman* estimated twenty thousand spectators watched as five hundred white-robed Klansmen from Austin and San Antonio "marched in semi-darkness, as all the streetlights on Congress Avenue and East Sixth were extinguished before the beginning of the parade."[70] The article mentioned that the decision to extinguish the lights was "on instruction from Commissioner Eyres."[71] The choreography of the parade showed the attention to spectacle and majesty characteristic of the Klan. Brought in on a special train, the San Antonio contingent filed in as the parade passed the depot. Despite the spectacular display of the strength of unified whites, the Ku Klux Klan played a divisive force within the white community. There were two synagogues in Austin serving congregations totaling 490 members in 1926. Three Roman Catholic churches counted parishioners in excess of 4,400 that same year.[72] It was not just the African American and Mexican American population that feared Klan tactics. Welly K. Hopkins recollected the impact the Klan had on families:

I know I almost got involved in it myself when I was a youngster. And it was a Klan and an anti-Klan thing. It was family against family and brother against brother to the degree they tarred and feathered one man and threw him out the public square in my town . . . but the Klan invaded our courthouse, elected some county officials, and thoroughly divided families I knew, brother against brother, in one instance.[73]

With an estimated membership of 170,000 in Texas by 1924, the Klan was pervasive in a state with a population of 4,663,228 in 1920.[74] Approximately 75 percent, or 3.5 million, of the total population were non-Mexican whites of either native or immigrant stock. Depending on sources consulted, membership figures may include the WKKK ("W" for women), but when one subtracts the Jews, Catholics, Italians, Syrians, and others who would not meet the membership profile, it conveys a sense of the scope of the viral growth of the "secret" organization.

Circumstances suggest that the first KKK-related violence Bob Poage heard about in Waco involved a prominent young local Democrat, Westwood Bowden Hays Jr. Five years after he served as one of six attorneys on Jesse Washington's defense team, while Poage attended Baylor, the KKK tarred and feathered a white man suspected of trafficking in "dope" on the Baylor campus.[75] Witnesses implicated Hays, but no consequences came his way. The single instance brings into focus the extent to which the Klan compromised the legal and judicial systems. Mr. Hays, or whoever befeathered the suspected drug dealer, clearly targeted whites who violated the organization's sense of 100 percent Americanism, providing another reason for moderate whites to oppose the extremists. Carrigan and Bernstein, the historians whose work has illuminated so much about the nature of race relations in Central Texas in the first quarter of the twentieth century, both addressed the tendency of local historians to move right past these issues, but they also point to an important story to be told about the negative reaction to the Klan among whites.

Bob Poage's view of the KKK as it gained strength is not something this research confirmed, but by the time he voted on the "antimask" bill, "the Klan was already a 'dead horse.'" Poage said the action came five years too late.[76] One important clue to how establishment figures like Poage felt earlier can be seen in the Waco Bar Association's strong condemnation to a lynching in December 1921. A progressive element existed within the legal profession in Waco, undoubtedly alongside barely closeted KKK members. Poage's father died from cancer in 1920, before the reemergence of the Klan in Waco, so that son of a Confederate cavalryman could not advise his own son on the matter. Significantly, actively opposing the Klan did not equate to opposing Jim Crow segregation. The Klan challenged the existing power structure in both cities, eliciting reactions based on turf and tactics rather than outrage against racial discrimination.

Lyndon Johnson's exposure to the Klan came from Austin, where their tactics generated enough concern about possible corruption that Judge James R. Hamilton of the Austin Criminal District Court called for a special grand jury in early October 1921. John Shelton, an Austin attorney, used an effective technique to deal with the Klan's penchant for anonymity. He monitored attendance at meetings held in a building owned by a Klan member, producing a list of names of some of those regularly in attendance.[77] Assistance of this kind indicated Judge Hamilton's investigation tapped valuable sources of information about Klan membership, little more than open secrets, perhaps, in a city of approximately 35,000. One of the most dramatic moments came with the confirmation of Sheriff Miller's membership. Among the exhibits presented was evidence that Miller, the chief of police, had paid a membership fee of $16.50 to Capitol City Klan #81.[78]

By December 1921, little more than two years after the Austin NAACP chapter was suspended and effectively neutralized, the Klan found itself on the receiving end of a stern rebuke from Judge Hamilton. As the *Austin Statesman* reported on December 11: "That members of the Ku Klux Klan have only themselves to blame if they suffer from violence against them by opposing organizations was the substance of a warning to the retiring grand jury by James R. Hamilton."[79] The tone of the judge's remarks may have been the result of public pressure regarding Klan-sponsored violence, associated with three whippings, a reported tarring and feathering, and one murder in 1921. The *Austin American* reported on December 17, 1921, that two of the whipping victims were African American porters who were accused of involvement in the procurement of women, presumably for interracial sex.[80]

Johnson and Poage witnessed the Klan's political influence on a statewide level for the first time when Earle B. Mayfield of East Texas, a former state legislator, avowed prohibitionist, and Klan member, was elected to the US Senate in 1922. His chief opponent was former governor James Ferguson, who had been impeached over a scandal involving governance of the University of Texas and resigned from office in September 1917. As the power struggle for control of the Democratic Party played out, the only common platform plank would be support for Jim Crow segregation. However, the Klan proved to be the focal point of the gubernatorial campaign in 1924.

One of the key figures in prosecuting James Ferguson's impeachment, Marian McNulty Crane, found himself in a classic example of strange bedfellows joined by political ambitions. Ferguson's wife, Miriam, forever remembered as "Ma" Ferguson, was in the runoff election for the Democratic nomination for governor against the Klan-sponsored Felix D. Robertson. A former attorney general and lieutenant governor, Crane's opposition to the Klan was so strong that it overcame his reservations about the Fergusons, and he supported Ma.

One of the arguments used against Robertson was the possible fate of the beloved University of Texas. In a letter to Judge Victor Brooks of Austin dated August 12, 1924, Crane wrote:

> If they are laboring under the disillusion that if the candidate of the Ku Klux leaders shall be elected, that the University is going to be free and unhampered, then they should disillusion themselves at once. Surely they have not forgotten that the grand dragon, the Cyclops and others sought to capture the public schools of the City of Dallas.[81]

The very next day, another letter went out from M. M. Crane in another effort to turn people against Robertson's candidacy. He warned F. W. Hill of Austin, "Their first plan will be to get control of the educational institutions of the state. The University will be the first to suffer. Klansmen regents will be appointed and Klansmen professors will be chosen."[82]

Another sample of anti-Klan argumentation framed by white opponents of Felix Robertson's candidacy is found in a letter to the editor of the *Austin Statesman* published on August 16, 1924. Written by S. W. Fisher, it excoriates then extols, "an invisible government and the dictatorship of secret political organizations are unknown to Anglo-Saxon institutions. In times of war, we fight shoulder to shoulder, regardless of race, religions, creed or political faith." The anti-Klan forces managed to avoid any reference to the status of African Americans. Instead, an effort was made to characterize the Klan itself as un-American. James C. Wright of Fort Worth summarized the case against them in a promotional flier for a book titled *The Unveiling of the Ku Klux Klan*, by W. C. Witcher, also of Fort Worth. Wright described the Klan as

> the most dangerous enemy of modern times. . . . It is AN EMPIRE, a MONARCHY. . . . The very spirit of their obligations and their oath is an INSULT to every AMERICAN CITIZEN; it would, if not restrained by law, ostracize, excommunicate, whip, tar and feather every man who has nerve enough to challenge it.[83]

Ma Ferguson beat Felix Robertson in the August runoff election, tantamount to victory against the weak Republicans. Sam and Rebekah Johnson were Ferguson supporters going back to the 1914 gubernatorial campaign, likely to be one of the first young Lyndon would observe with a watchful eye of someone five going on six years of age. Emmette Redford spoke of another Ferguson supporter during an interview on October 2, 1968.

> I think as early as the Ball-Ferguson election, which must have been in 1914 when Lyndon was six years old, I recall he was handing out folders for Ferguson, and that he was present at a Ferguson rally. He took some active part in other campaigns when he was a teenager, though I do not recall just what they were. This was not merely an interest just in political campaigns; it was also an interest in political issues.[84]

John F. Koeniger's recollections about politics in the Hill Country located the Johnsons in the Ferguson camp. "The Johnsons were Ferguson supporters, very strong. Politics in Texas at that time was sharply divided between prohibitionists and anti-prohibitionists."[85] The Klan stood for prohibition, yet another divisive issue within Texas communities for decades. For a brief interval after 1932, the questions of party identity and loyalty were simple; one was either for the New Deal or not. For more than a decade prior to that, however, deep divisions ran through the Texas Democratic Party. By 1937 the New Deal coalition among Texas Democrats broke apart, but with the worst of the lynching era fading and the KKK less overt in its vigilantism, white elected officials stood solidly for segregation.

African Americans, in the face of the psychological and physical trauma of segregation as administered in these Texas cities, also demonstrated strength in unity in their communities. Despite the shadow oppression had cast since the Reconstruction era, the African American residents of Austin developed a vibrant business district. A middle class of African Americans in Waco grew, too. Individuals, from physicians and dentists to barbers and auto mechanics, provided a wide range of professional and support services. Entrepreneurs and well-educated men and women found a way to prosper, relatively speaking, in a Jim Crow environment. For reasons addressed earlier, the post–Jesse Washington decade garnered little scholarly attention from those interested in documenting the history of Waco, but it is possible to get a glimpse of life in a segregated city by focusing on Austin, where Lyndon Johnson and Bob Poage spent a great deal of time.

Historian Tera Hunter's description of the importance of the church in African American society in Atlanta near the turn of the century applies directly to the circumstances one finds in Austin and Waco in the post–World War I era. In her words, "churches provided outlets of collective self-help, fostered leadership development, sanctioned group morals, and promoted public and private education."[86] The small middle class of the African American community in Austin in the 1920s might be what Du Bois had in mind when he referred to the Talented Tenth. A combination of practical economics, entrepreneurship, and a strong sense of community interdependence made the repressive Twenties a period of growth in the African American and Mexican American business communities. From the ranks of these prominent and successful leaders came a generation of men and women who struggled for social, economic, and political justice far into the 1960s. Within the establishment, there were disagreements within these communities about how to respond to changes in the political climate, notably during the overt expressions of racism associated with the post–World War I era and the KKK.

As opportunities for African Americans expanded in the wartime economy, Texan employers faced the reality of losing labor they had grown dependent upon. Issues of mobility and segregation were intertwined for many African Americans, and the complexities of these issues point to the questions Booker T. Washington and W. E. B. Du Bois raised. The issue of African Americans seeking opportunities outside of Austin illustrates differing viewpoints. In Austin, the leading voice of conservative accommodationism for many years was the Reverend L. L. Campbell. He urged African Americans to stay in Austin, despite the tensions of the summer of 1919: "We have our churches, our schools, our social functions, our fraternal relations, our property and every conceivable advantage and comfort for our physical, moral, and intellectual development."[87] Local African American journalist Mansfield M. Haynes, editor of the *Herald*, offered a different view during the summer of 1917, when the Great Migration was touching Austin: "The Negro has the same rights to go North or to any other section of the country, singly or collectively, just as other people and races do, whenever he chooses."[88]

A report from the Colored Welfare Board to the Austin City Council in July 1918 zeroed in on a major factor in the equation. W. H. Crawford said, "Right here in our city, many of the best colored citizens are leaving daily . . . and unless some inducements are offered in the future for their betterment, more of them will permanently take up abode in other parts of this country." Crawford's voice was important within the African American community, to the extent that when the physician sent a letter to city officials expressing concerns about problems facing the races, the result was the creation of the Welfare Board.[89]

The council called for this new group to "keep in intimate touch with the varied interests of the colored people of Austin." Board members included several leading citizens from East Austin. In addition to Dr. Crawford, the board included William Tears, an undertaker, and a dentist named Everett Givens. The council asked for monthly reports. Unfortunately, minutes form the City Council meetings included none of these reports until 1927. A report was filed on June 6, 1918, one month after the creation of the Colored Welfare Board. A general wage increase went into effect for African Americans in the summer of 1918 as a result of discussion of the Colored Welfare Board's report.

In troubled times, as discussed earlier in this chapter in terms of the summer of 1919, the press and the white political establishment would use the influence of African American ministers to forestall violence in Austin. The state of terror established in Waco effectively precluded violence.

(Near) Triumph of the Separatists

The Reverend L. L. Campbell, pastor of the Ebenezer Baptist Church from 1892 until his death in 1927, often played the role of spokesperson for the African American establishment in Austin. His skills would soon be put to the test. The white executive secretary of the NAACP, John Shillady, was beat up in front of the Driskill Hotel on Sixth Street after a meeting with the adjutant general about the handling of the Longview detainees. Ever since the Longview riots, local NAACP leaders were under increasing pressure from whites. Shillady's assistants included two local officials, County Judge Dave J. Pickle and Constable Charles Hamby. As reported in the August 30, 1919, edition of the *Austin Statesman*, Campbell spoke out as a voice of reason to both sides: "There is no disposition to crush anybody down here, our white friends who know us are not afraid of us and they know there is no danger of our annihilating them."[90] Reverend Campbell was also the publisher of a newspaper for local African Americans called the *Herald*, giving him an even broader audience for his moderate views.

At a meeting of the St. John's Baptist Association on August 30, representatives of church members across eleven counties, led by Campbell, called again for levelheadedness about the aftermath of the riot and the beating. "Speakers are urging the negroes of the South to work and make friends with the white man of the South instead of listening to agitators," read the story in the morning paper.[91]

Since the first state branch organized in El Paso in 1915, interest and participation in the NAACP grew rapidly in Texas, increasing to thirty-one branches and 7,046 members around the state by the end of 1918.[92] By then Texas had the largest number of NAACP chapters of any state. The Austin chapter, organized in 1918, had between seventy-five and three hundred members (sources vary).[93] One of the consequences of the events of July and August, however, was an order from state officials to disband the Austin chapter. Mayor Alexander Woolridge, shortly after stepping down from ten years of service, warned members of an African American audience that whites "will tolerate no idea of social equality" and that the white man "knows his power and knows how to use it."[94]

Woolridge intended to leave no doubt about the status of the impending crisis and conveyed his level of concern. If the audience referred to in the quote above consisted of leaders like Reverend L. L. Campbell, the message received may have come across both as Texas realpolitik and as a blunt, no-nonsense warning. Campbell, like many long-established African American leaders in civic life, had a reputation to uphold and status to maintain within his community and his congregation. As Tera Hunter noted in her study of post-Reconstruction Atlanta, church leaders in the African American community could view the status quo of racism as in their interest.[95]

After the tensions of the summer of 1919 and the remarkable ascension of the Ku Klux Klan in the years following, the forces of separatism institutionalized Jim Crow in Austin. A distinctive enforcement capability in the form of hooded Klansmen sent a credible message to nonwhites that social equality would never be permitted by the white majority, even after the grand jury report issued in 1921. Just a few months later, on February 3, 1922, the *Austin American* reported a story under the headline "Capital Klan Receives 700 New Members." The reporter referred to two hundred Klansmen guarding the rural site seven miles outside of Austin, a description conveying the paramilitary image they cultivated.[96]

In their first appearance in Austin, reported in the *Austin American* on July 3, 1921, a Klan spokesman said, "Our creed is opposed to violence, lynchings, etc., but we are even more strongly opposed to the things that cause lynchings and mob rule."[97]

Based on the estimated membership and the prominence of the Klan's support for Felix Robertson in the runoff election against Ma Ferguson in the summer of 1924, July and August represent a pivotal period. This was a time when Klan influence peaked, then rapidly declined and was rejected. Forces of segregation would continue to gather, reaching their pinnacle in the symbolic and practical effects of the City Plan adopted in 1929. Formal dialogue between the white city leaders and the African American spokespersons would take on a different tone in the years 1925–29. The sound of less accommodationist voices was heard in the chambers of City Council meetings as African Americans pressed for a proportionate share of the resources, especially in terms of schools, parks, and community services.

In a city the size of Austin in the 1920s, long-term personal relationships would be essential in determining how community leaders on their respective sides of the color line would respond to crisis. White community leaders and nonwhite leaders certainly felt the pressure from increased tensions and fears of violence, especially between 1919 and 1924. History does not record for us a name, place, or date of the first white Austinite to speak out against segregation. The mores and strictures of the Twenties would not permit that kind of talk. A southern white heretic might oppose segregation for a variety of reasons, among these could be religious beliefs, or perhaps even the absence of such beliefs. Another significant factor would be the direct or indirect contact of whites with African Americans who played key roles in their community as business owners, physicians, teachers, and dentists. As the grip of de jure and de facto systems of segregation tightened, social contacts between the lower classes of white and black laborers decreased. This served to increase the importance of the contacts still permitted, those that were required for the city of Austin to conduct its public business.

In this environment, African American community organizations flourished. The Ministerial Alliance and the King's Daughters pursued the social and spiritual agendas of several churches. The Colored Knights of Pythias, the National Woodmen, and the Masonic Lodge actively promoted fellowship and community-mindedness. In 1927 the Community Welfare Association (CWA) was organized under the leadership of Mrs. Dean Mohr. The CWA drew its membership from several smaller federated clubs, including the Silver Leaf Art Club, the Dramatic Social Club, the Dunbar Art Club, the Ladies' Unity Social Club, and the Elite Club. The group quickly identified its top priority and mission:

> To purchase a lot and to erect thereon to be used for a baby clinic and health center and to be interested in any activity that pertains to the civic welfare of the community, to engage in other benevolent and charitable work that the organization may see fit to do.[98]

On August 19, 1929, the CWA signed a contract to construct a one-story building at 1192 Angelina Street in East Austin. By the time the building was finished, the total cost of the project was $7,050.[99] When New Deal programs needed a community center in Austin for various functions aimed at African Americans, including National Youth Administration programs Lyndon Johnson administered, this facility would be used extensively.

After the last half-century of public policy aimed at racial integration, it may be provocative to reflect on how the excluded people successfully built parallel, yet culturally distinctive, communities. In 1940 the Negro History class at Samuel Huston College produced a *Historical Outline of the Negro in Travis County*. Referring to the period from 1905 to 1940 as "The Era of Progress," the students' work conveys a mixture of pride and regret in the separation that had been created. "During this period they experienced prosperity, success, failure, need, and occasionally a break in the fine race relationships that existed. They had more to feel proud of, however, than they did to feel sorry about." It is evident from the debates among African American intellectuals from this period that some gave up on ever seeing an integrated society. Some were concerned about the dissolution of African culture. Historic discoveries on the African continent revived interest in the accomplishments of Africans before the cumulative trauma of the slave trade obscured the achievements of major empires, so it is not surprising that students writing a local history would inject a strong sense of independence in their work. In reference to the period from 1905 to 1929, they wrote: "At no time in the history of the city was the business man as prosperous as he was at that time."[100]

Among the most respected people in the African American community in Austin were the men and women who served as teachers in the segregated K–12 system and in the two private colleges. The 1920s was a decade of growth for Austin's schools, but the public school district struggled to provide up-to-date facilities for the nonwhite population. Between 1920 and 1930, enrollment in public and private schools rose from 7,836 to 11,501 students, directly proportionate to the overall growth of the city. The number of teachers increased from 205 to 364 during this time. In addition to six elementary schools for African American children, two elementary schools served Mexican American children only through third grade. The children from these two schools were then eligible to attend "white" elementary schools to continue their education. In the 1924–25 school year, however, fewer than forty Mexican American children were attending elementary schools in grades four or above, and only ten Mexican American students were at the junior high.[101]

Superintendent A. N. McCallum presided over the Austin school system with pride. In 1928, appealing to the city's electorate to support increased taxation for school construction, he declared, "Negro schools of Austin have a higher standard than those of any city in the state. Every negro teacher holds at least a first grade [state] teacher's certificate." Informed parents knew something needed to be done about the crowding in the nonwhite schools. Over a five-year period, from 1924 to 1929, the average teacher-to-pupil ratio in Mexican American elementary classrooms decreased from 1:41 to 1:54. African American schools at all levels stayed about the same during the same five-year period, ranging from 1:42 to 1:40. The ratio for white teachers and students stayed at a noticeably lower ratio of 1:28 for both years sampled. The distribution of funds for education reflected the inequality of the separate-but-equal framework rather dramatically. In 1925, Austin allocated $183.49 for each white pupil, $84.07 for each African American pupil, and only $65.31 for each Mexican American student. Teachers' salaries reflect these disparities. The average salary for a white male teacher in Austin in the 1928–29 school year was $1,872. His white female colleagues averaged $1,207 for similar work. In the schools for African Americans, men earned an average annual salary of $1,027 and women, on average, earned $742.[102]

Chrystine Shackles came to Austin in 1928 to teach history at Tillotson College, a school founded by the American Missionary Association in 1881 (two years before the founding of the University of Texas). She got off the train at the Katy station (Kansas & Topeka rail line, hence K-T, or Katy) for "colored" and took a "colored" cab on unpaved East Austin roads to Bluebonnet Hill, the location of Allen Hall. She remembered her reaction to seeing the fifty-year-old structure in bad repair, a reaction she shared with her new colleagues. She felt somewhat isolated from her new community at first, but the fringe benefits were good: transportation to the college from her home, room and board, and all linens provided. Churchwomen in the North had donated the towels and sheets and had shipped them to Austin.[103]

Shackles developed close friendships with several of her colleagues and considered herself part of a family. "Many of us who came here did find a friendliness not realized in many of the Southern towns which we had visited when there were a large number of Negroes—sometimes equal to the Whites or larger."[104] Enrollment at Tillotson and its fellow AMA school for men, Samuel Huston College, varied during the decade after World War I. School leaders tried various curricular emphases, from skilled trades to teacher training. At Huston, degree completion was a problem, with only four students completing bachelor's degrees in 1923, even though 412 students were enrolled in the 1918–19 academic year. The number of graduates increased to twenty-two in 1927.[105]

People who needed a little orientation when they came to Austin during the 1920s might pick up a city directory. R. L. Polk and Company, compilers of the annual publication, made it very easy for nonwhite customers to choose appropriately from the list of merchants, because those serving "colored" were marked with a (c) after the directory listing. For example, the listing for the barbershop at 103 1/2 West Seventh Street was given as R. S. Harrison (c). Local whites knew, though, that ol' Bob still had some white customers who knew the former slave was not uppity like some of the others.[106]

There were eight other barbers to choose from within seven blocks along East Sixth Street in 1920, and five more shops would be open when the 1930–31 *Directory* would be printed ten years later. Four physicians and three dentists had offices in East Austin. Eight grocery stores and fourteen restaurants gave customers a wide range of choices, whether the customers were planning to cook at home or get out of the kitchen for a meal. There had only been three places to get one's nicer clothes cleaned and pressed in East Austin in 1920, but by the end of the decade, eight shops vied for those customers.

Eunice Lyons Prescott reminisced in 1974 about the days when her family owned a landmark among African American businesses, E. H. Carrington Grocery, Feed, and Produce at Sixth Street and Red River.

> It was all one big room then. I remember going out to the back door to the ice house and the blacksmith shop. We had sorghum right out of the press, and people brought eggs and butter to sell in the store. We had chickens out back, and people could select a chicken to take home—or we'd kill it here.[107]

Upstairs, known as Lyons Hall (named for Louis D. Lyons, son-in-law of the former slave who started the store), served as a reception room for weddings, dances, and birthday parties. Ms. Prescott had fond memories of her twelfth birthday because, "It was my first boy-girl party. And I wore a white dress with a blue bow in my hair. The orchestra was toward the back, and we danced."[108] When funeral services were held for Eunice Lyons Prescott, the program provided to those who came to celebrate her life included this message:

> Her paternal grandfather was the Governor of Texas, with whom she had limited contact because of the racial climate of that era. However, she and her brothers and sisters were often taken to the capitol building through a back door to visit him, and he would hug and kiss his grandchildren, put money in their pockets, and send them on their way.[109]

Relationships between influential whites and prominent African American and Mexican American citizens were worked for mutual advantage. When the Klan's influence ebbed after the election of 1924, it became more common for white politicians to cultivate the image of being interested in the well-being of African Americans and Mexican Americans. Not only did this perpetuate the viability of segregation, but for those seeking votes of nonwhites who had paid the poll tax it was a safe political tactic as well.

Leaders recognize that there is strength to be found in unity that transcends the power achieved through divisiveness. Observing the tactics of Reverend L. L. Campbell offered a telling glimpse into what happened between the leaders of the white and black communities behind closed doors. The heir apparent to the unofficial title of most influential African American in Austin after the passing of Reverend L. L. Campbell in 1927 was undoubtedly Dr. Everett H. Givens, whose dental office on East Sixth Street adjoined that of physician Dr. W. H. Crawford. By the 1930s, whites and African Americans in town would refer to Dr. Givens as the "bronze mayor of Austin."[110]

In their history of Travis County, the students at Huston College characterized the political situation in the latter part of the 1920s: "the Negro began to approach the place where he obtained better consideration from the city. This gave the Negro a chance to improve his status and acquire greater influence than he had previously possessed."[111] Givens has been described as a "soft-spoken but tireless advocate of improvements for East Austin" and is credited with persuading white politicians to build a new junior high, a "Negro Branch Library," and to provide improved health care and waste disposal.[112] After many years of listening to accommodationists like Campbell, the African American community appeared to coalesce around Givens. Praise from the immediate beneficiaries of improvements in East Austin, students at Huston College, came in this fashion: "The Negro's progress in Austin may also be attributed in large manner to the absence of church fights in the latter part of this era, and to the lack of littleness on the part of the civic and denominational leaders of the city."[113]

Shortly after Sam Rayburn's funeral in 1961, the *Austin American-Statesman* ran a story alongside a photograph of a "sad-faced Negro man dressed all in black sitting on a tombstone by a lonely road in Bonham." The subject of the photo was Everett Givens. By this time the distinguished dentist's office was on Chicon Street, and its walls were decorated with photos of Joe Louis, a sailor named Doris Miller, and three white politicians: Harry Truman, Franklin Roosevelt, and Lyndon Johnson. The reporter asked Givens why he went to Rayburn's funeral. "I never thought about not going. I wanted to see Mr. Sam in the hospital, but I was afraid people would think I was seeking publicity."[114] Givens met Rayburn, the legendary Texas legislator who became Speaker of the House of Representatives in Washington, DC, back in the 1920s. "I remember being at a speaking in J. Frank Norris's church. Sam Rayburn was taking his seat. He spotted me and he came over and shook hands. He didn't have to do that. There was no reason. Negroes couldn't vote in the Democratic primaries in those days. That's how I know Sam Rayburn was my real friend." Another visitor to the funeral at Bonham that November was the vice president of the United States, who as a young congressman from Austin used to say Sam Rayburn was "like a father."[115]

A Formal Separation

It was somewhat ironic that the City Plan the Austin City Council adopted in February 1929 came at a time when African Americans could see some progress made in the form of investments by the city in East Austin. Perhaps there had been more to the improved relations than matters of style or quality of presentation. In July 1927, almost two years before the adoption of the plan, the *Austin American* reported about the progress city planners had made. Among those strategizing about Austin's future, some "felt that the unrestricted presence of nonwhite groups had a destabilizing effect upon property values."[116]

Just a year before, in 1926, Dr. Charles Yerwood, a local physician, purchased a house located at 1115 East Twelfth Street from a white man named Michael Connelly (sometimes Connolly). The house was constructed in 1904 when the neighborhood was in a predominantly white, largely German, working-class area. This property, now known as the Connelly-Yerwood home, has been nominated by the Texas State Historical Commission to be registered as a National Historic Place by the United States Department of the Interior. In the section of the application calling for a "Statement of Significance," one finds the following:

> The Yerwoods, an African American family, purchased the home in 1926 from the Connelly's, a typical white, working-class family who had occupied the house since its construction in 1904. This seemingly benign household transition is significant in that it speaks to larger demographic changes which took place in Austin during the early part of the last century.[117]

Evidently city planners did not see this type of transition as benign.

The trend toward ethnic clusters of Mexican Americans and African

Americans was nothing new. As historian David C. Humphrey noted in his book *Austin: A History of the Capital City*, "Black residents and newcomers alike gravitated to East Austin as it developed its own business, social, and religious life and became a haven from white oppression."[118] At the same time as Dr. Givens and the CWA lobbied the city for investments in East Austin, the city was developing a strategy to justify its endorsement of several of the ideas Givens brought forward. Was this a simple quid pro quo deal? Yes, sewer lines will be extended. Yes, a junior high will be built to ease crowding. Yes, more streets will be paved. Yes, there will be a new park. These improvements will benefit 80 percent of the African American population in Austin, because that is how concentrated they have become. In return, the city's new plan will effectively serve as formal recognition of a long-developing reality: Austin is, indeed, a segregated city.

Koch and Fowler, civil engineers hired in part because of the work they had done in Dallas, presented the plan on January 14, 1928. Near the end of the proposed plan, pages 66 and 67, are found these plainly worded suggestions:

> There has been considerable talk in Austin, as well as other cities, in regard to the race segregation problem. This problem cannot be solved legally under any zoning law known to us at present. Practically all attempts of such have proven unconstitutional.
>
> In our studies in Austin, we have found that the negroes are present in small numbers, in practically all sections of the city, excepting the area just east of East Avenue and south of the City Cemetery. This area seems to be all negro population. It is our recommendation that the nearest approach to the solution of the race segregation problem will be the recommendation of this district as a negro district; and that all the facilities and conveniences be provided the negroes in this district, as an incentive to draw the negro population to this area. This will eliminate the necessity of duplication of white and black schools, white and black parks, and other duplicate facilities for this area. We are recommending that sufficient area be acquired adjoining the negro high school to provide adequate space for a complete negro play-field in connection with the negro high school. We further recommend that the negro schools in this area be provided with ample and adequate playground space and facilities similar to the white schools of the city.[119]

Considering the praise given to city leaders in the local history project by the students from Huston College in 1940, it may tempt some readers to view this plan as a coup de grâce by white officials who outmaneuvered the non-white citizens. This seems a rather condescending conclusion to draw. If African American leaders had chosen to make the plan a source of confrontation, what would have been accomplished? Had not the power relationships already been well established by the events between 1919 and 1924?

Part of the value of revisiting the Austin experience with race relations during the 1920s is the strong sense one gets of an ongoing set of negotiations.[120] Integration was not an inevitable outcome, nor was segregation an inevitable future. Lives were at stake, but often the living were treated as extras, not actors. Mexican Americans were relative newcomers in 1919, but by the 1930s and 1940s, their economic interests and political clout would give the Mexican American establishment a voice. The overt racist ideology and genocidal tactics Americans were exposed to in World War II would finally set the stage for white southern liberals to begin to speak about integration as being in the self-interest of whites. Two of these politicians, Lyndon B. Johnson and Bob Poage, learned about the politics of race under home rule in the turbulent Twenties in central Texas. Eventually, one would seek the resources of the federal government to end segregation.

A man from the Hill Country became a race radical among his peers; a man of the Brazos Valley eventually lost favor in his party because of his opposition to its civil rights agenda. LBJ and Bob Poage, whatever their views on race, loved Austin. But under the capitol dome, visible from virtually every neighborhood, the business of bigots cast a dark shadow of racial discrimination. Although the killing of Jesse Washington took place one hundred miles to the north, the lingering stench of the "Waco Horror" hung over Texas (and the nation), in stark contrast to the scent of the bleached white sheets of the Ku Klux Klan. During this time many white Texans responded to the increasing diversity by exercising their majority power to isolate, to control, and to deny others liberty and equality under the law. Postwar dislocation affected the entire nation, and disruptions in the farm economy hit central Texas especially hard, complicating the racial terrain with the trials of deprivation. The "veil" of racism, as Du Bois so aptly described it, served to hide the agency of African Americans and Mexican Americans—combined with traces of tolerant Anglos, all key actors in the growth of Central Texas—from the view of history.[121]

Before the proliferation of federal sources of assistance during the New Deal era, Austinites had established extensive networks of support and advocacy in their respective communities. Service organizations played multiple roles, from fellowship for members to assistance to the needy. Mexican Americans called mutual aid societies *mutualistas*. The formation of these kinds of groups accelerated in the 1920s. For women, there was the Cruz Azul (Blue Cross) and the men, the Comisión Honorífica. These groups played vital roles in acclimating migrants to their new surroundings, taking the place of or supplementing what kinship groups and churches could provide. Sometimes quasi-patriotic groups formed, such as La Orden de Hijos de América (Order of the Sons of America), established in 1921, to emphasize loyalty and commitment to democratic values. These tended to be driven by middle-class Mexican American men and women whose work and good fortune enabled them to devote time to others. By 1929 common interest and oppressive circumstances led men of these groups to unite under the banner of the League of United Latin American Citizens (LULAC). Modeled in many respects along the lines of the NAACP, LULAC became the chief political platform for Mexican Americans in Austin. Successful businessmen like Cresenciano Segovia and Ben Gonzales, owners of the Austin Tortilla Manufacturing Company, and Ben Garza, whose family operated several groceries, served as role models and magnets to newcomers to Austin. Even the barely literate could breathe a sigh of relief when entering a store with a sign reading "Se habla español."

An easily discernible trend in housing patterns over the last five decades of the nineteenth century and continuing into the twentieth century reflected a localized version of a "push-pull" effect. Simply put, the more African Americans moved into East Austin neighborhoods, the more successful businesses serving this population would be in an increasingly segregated economy. Anthony Orum described East Austin in *Power, Money, and the People: The Making of Modern Austin*: "If you should visit here on a Saturday, you will observe small congregations of families along the walks, visiting and shopping in the various stores. This is the heart of Austin for its black and brown residents, the place that will remain etched in their memories forever."[122]

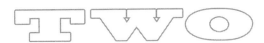

The National Youth Administration,
the State Director, and the State Senator

LESSONS LEARNED AT THE GRASS ROOTS

THE NEW DEAL GREATLY INCREASED the frequency of interaction between federal employees and citizens across the United States in the 1930s as "alphabet agencies" cascaded from Washington, DC. Indeed, the New Deal brought LBJ and Bob Poage together in the autumn of 1935, when their respective career paths intersected because of the creation of the National Youth Administration (NYA). The program aimed at preserving and extending educational opportunities for sixteen- to twenty-five-year-olds by keeping them in school for additional training rather than letting them join the unemployment roll. Like in the Civilian Conservation Corps, eligibility criteria focused primarily on assisting people with minimal income. The expansion of federal agencies also included the creation of public sector employment at managerial levels, with opportunities for those with the right talents and the right connections.

These new political networks often took well-connected, ambitious individuals from local positions to federal assignments. In the case of Lyndon Johnson, the opportunity to serve as Texas NYA director set the stage for success in a special election to Congress in 1937. Meanwhile, state senator Bob Poage's support for New Deal programs like the NYA moved him to the top among Democratic candidates for the Eleventh District seat in 1936; he had lost his previous run in 1934 to the Democrat incumbent Otto Cross. By the time Poage and LBJ were assigned offices across the hall from each other in the old House Office Building, these Texans from adjoining congressional districts in Central Texas already had much in common.

With diplomas in hand—Poage's from Baylor University Law School ('24) and LBJ's from San Marcos State Teachers College ('30)—these two joined perhaps 5 percent of the adult population in Texas who finished college in that era. Poage's parents, as well as Johnson's, placed a premium on the education of their children, to the extent that schooling would shape decisions about where to raise them. Arguably, their real education involved majoring in politics at their fathers' sides. Through the NYA, along with many other New Deal programs, Lyndon Johnson and Bob Poage expanded their political networks in Central Texas. Why select the NYA, rather than one of the more prominent public works programs like the Civilian Conservation Corps? Public schools, more than any other institution in the United States, represent the bedrock of self-government at the local (even neighborhood) level. If one wanted to gain insights into how citizens viewed potential encroachment, federal programs that interfaced with students and the adults responsible for their success could prove instructive.

Locally elected trustees resent any perceived usurpation of their authority from even the state level, so the notion of a federal program would understandably raise suspicions among reasonable people. Concerns about the extent of federal authority extend across the spectrum in American political culture, and across generations.[1] This is why the situation in Central Texas from the mid-1930s into the Johnson presidency is so compelling. An increasingly representative slice of the citizenry had the opportunity to make the federal system function as well as one could expect of a constitutional engine design well over a century old.

Johnson, as well as Poage, saw the New Deal transform the American political landscape in large part by bringing citizens into contact with agents of their government at the community level. For those individuals whose socioeconomic status in the community enabled them to engage in civic affairs in some manner, but had fallen on hard times, the New Deal spawned employment opportunities in federal offices established in cities and rural county seats across the country. For the first time since the mobilization of the nation by the Committee for Public Information in World War I, the federal government had a neighborhood presence reflecting major changes in the political landscape. In so doing, it also

Poage campaign flyer, 1936.
Courtesy W. R. Poage Legis-
lative Library.

. transformed those present at the creation, especially Lyndon Johnson and Bob Poage.

Over LBJ's twenty months as Franklin Roosevelt's appointee as director of the Texas NYA, he can be seen scaling the steep learning curve that accompanied redefining the American citizen's relationship with the federal government. Poage also scaled this curve during this time. A new kind of constituent service, and new expectations as well, grew in proportion to the number of agencies FDR created. The New Deal also created new job descriptions for the public's representatives at the state level. Through analysis of their correspondence with each other, with constituents, and with other public officials, we can see these legislators serve more than ever as headhunters, placement coordinators, and interventionists for individuals seeking aid from newly created institutions of government.

Constituent service matters, and the loyalty of a satisfied citizen, built political capital, as indicated by a letter Johnson received from an African

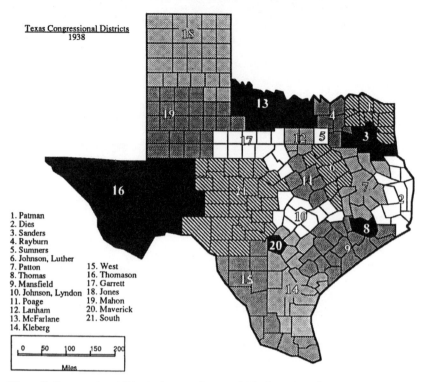

Texas Congressional Districts
1938

1. Patman
2. Dies
3. Sanders
4. Rayburn
5. Sumners
6. Johnson, Luther
7. Patton
8. Thomas
9. Mansfield
10. Johnson, Lyndon
11. Poage
12. Lanham
13. McFarlane
14. Kleberg
15. West
16. Thomason
17. Garrett
18. Jones
19. Mahon
20. Maverick
21. South

0   50   100   150   200
Miles

Eleventh Congressional District in 1937. *Courtesy W. R. Poage Legislative Library.*

American student from Mexia, forty miles from Waco. Lamar Kirven could follow through with plans to attend Huston College in Austin because of the NYA. "Always know that progressive minded negroes the state over take off their hats to you." Kirven wrote that letter to Congressman Johnson more than two years after the director left the NYA to represent the Tenth District.[2] Oral histories support the portrayal of the charismatic Johnson as a hands-on visionary determined to direct federal resources to meet the needs of the poor.

Historian Christie Bourgeois explored the positive perception of Johnson that spread among the African American community, especially when considering that so much of what he did happened quietly, deliberately kept away from the realm of newspapers or radio. Word of mouth favored LBJ, judging from comments by Robert C. Weaver, who eventually got Johnson's nomination to serve as the first secretary of the Housing and Urban Development Department. Weaver recalled hearing about a guy down in Texas who was running the National Youth Administration up on the Hill because he thought that the National Youth Administration benefits ought to go to poor folks . . . to make matters worse, he was giving a hell of a lot of this money to Mexican-Americans and Negroes.[3]

Johnson saw no advantage in the prevailing racial climate to advertise the unprecedented steps he took to expand opportunities for African American and Mexican American adolescents and young adults—the segment of the population white racists feared and loathed most. The environment he operated in seemed hypersensitive to matters of race, and requests for federal assistance from constituents typically included some reference to either the writer's skin color or to someone else's.

Letters from citizens struggling to navigate the new system, as well as the "voices" of those charged with administering a new program in a very fluid environment, add an important dimension to the understanding of how these major figures in Texas political history viewed their roles as public servants throughout their careers. Furthermore, they underline that in the formulation and implementation of economic recovery policies, New Dealers, as did their Progressive predecessors, envisioned public and private schools from K–12 through postsecondary as agents of federal relief, recovery, and reform programs.

Schools served as incubators for the enormous task of reconditioning students, and community members sent their children to school to help them learn to accept all members of the human family as equals. Political scientist John Kincaid identified the 1954 US Supreme Court ruling on *Brown v. Board of Education of Topeka* as the turning point in federal-state relations, but he also pointed to the new Democratic majorities in Congress and new waves of federal aid to state and local governments as marking a new era. Kincaid concluded, "cooperative federalism [was] the reigning conception of American federalism from about 1954 to 1978," attributing this more seamless approach to layered governance as a "political response to the policy challenges of market failure, postwar affluence, racism, urban poverty, environmentalism, and individual rights."[4]

Using Kincaid's periodization, LBJ acts almost as a harbinger of an era yet to come in the United States. A practical political philosophy took form in Johnson's mind as he reconciled his faith in FDR with the suspicions about the federal government he encountered while spreading the NYA gospel across the state. The insistence on well-paved avenues for citizen engagement with public affairs in their communities that comes into full flower during the Great Society initiatives of his presidency, most notably in the controversial Community Action Program, should be known as Johnsonian Democracy.

Lyndon Johnson did not invent the advisory council, but through the crucible of inventing a model NYA program, Johnson fabricated a prototype for a federalism that achieved elusive harmony among local, state, and national authorities when resolving discord on matters of public policy.[5] Kincaid sees the relationships between levels of government clearly stacked in favor of federal authority, which means cooperative models become coercive either in practice or form. Kincaid states that by 1968, the Johnson administration's "creative federalism" had implemented new federal-local attempts at cooperation, as well as partnerships that brought public and private institutions together. He pointed out, "because of its comparatively vast fiscal capacity, the federal government could endeavor, for about twenty years, to purchase state and local cooperation."[6]

This brilliant, blunt formulation works well, but it is based on the policy initiative being generated from Washington. Johnson, through Poage and dozens of other actors across the state, pushed the political tide in the other direction, channeling the agency of citizens so local players could drive the process. The "tradition of intergovernmental sharing" Kincaid referred to informed cooperative federalism as it evolved, and it served the political interests of reformers to keep the role of local and state institutions front and center as a shield against charges of centralization at a time when that would smack of socialism. Nonetheless, when one considers the prominent role Johnson attached to the use of advisory councils, task forces, and other models of stakeholder engagement, one sees this usage as a political buffer or lubricant to serve as a future electoral aid. Working with these citizen-based bodies of the NYA from 1935 to 1937 convinced LBJ that there is potential strength to be found in the unity among local, state, and national actors, but advisory councils need true empowerment to function meaningfully.

Every Johnson biographer agrees on at least one thing: the work shy did not survive around LBJ. He undoubtedly earned the reputation in college that led to the nickname of "Bull" (for Bullshit) Johnson, but his track record exhibits thoroughness, and the official reports for the Washington NYA office submitted by the former teacher showed solid preparation. They also reflected seventeen-hour days for the director and for his staff.[7] According

From the beginning, LBJ nurtured relationships with key Texas politicians. Johnson's note to Poage reads: "To a real friend and a real man—in any league." *Courtesy W. R. Poage Legislative Library.*

to Johnson's credo, individuals who dedicate time and effort to make their contribution to the process need something to show for their work. Give citizens voices in the choir, and they will be members for life. Strong local connections help to minimize resentment of federal engagement when those issues of sovereignty and jurisdiction arise.

Federal officials, notably presidents, use the power of the purse and of eminent domain to leverage state and local policy makers. *LBJ and Grassroots Federalism* emphasizes the agency of the elite and of the once disenfranchised, and at the same time it shows the philosophy, which Poage and LBJ shared, that people at the local level must have a meaningful role to play in the formulation of public policy. When Poage's duties as state senator called upon him to name constituents from Waco to a serve as members of an advisory council to determine projects to be undertaken by the National Youth Administration, he became a stakeholder and made others into stakeholders, too.

Throughout its eight-year existence, this New Deal agency targeted a distinctive population: adolescents and young adults still in school seeking diplomas. The Roosevelt administration's initiatives in arresting the economic free fall in the kinetic first hundred days in the spring of 1933, notably the Civilian Conservation Corps (CCC), provided employment for hundreds of thousands of unemployed teens and young adults. Analysis of the records of participants revealed a high percentage of dropouts and illiterates. CCC enlistees could attend evening classes covering a wide range of subject matter at many camps.[8] The residential nature of the program, of course, made attendance at a conventional high school or college impossible.

Depending on cultural traditions and household circumstances, young women and men could be under considerable pressure to set aside educational goals during times of hardship. To some degree, the CCC may have increased dropout rates by providing a viable alternative for these young adults with no incentive to stay in school. The NYA existed, in large part, to keep them out of the labor force and to avoid competition with older workers that could only drive wages down further for all. In addition to school-based opportunities for part-time employment, local NYA advisory boards planned community-based projects offering applied learning through general labor and in apprenticeships in various skilled trades.

New Deal agencies gained notoriety for duplication of effort, so by the late 1930s, discussions of reorganization and repurposing departments, agencies, and bureaus occupied the critics and pundits. A bill Representative Lyndon B. Johnson of Texas (D-Tenth District) introduced on December 9, 1941, HR 6194, calling for the consolidation of the CCC and NYA, failed to gain sufficient support to get through the House. Carol Weisenberger attributed Johnson's motivation for sponsoring the legislation to a request from FDR. His experiences as director a few years earlier, however, gave Johnson ample exposure to the nuisances of dueling agencies, so while there can be no doubt that LBJ would carry the Boss's water for him up the Hill, prior administrative experience predisposed him to that kind of consolidation.[9]

During that time one sees Johnson's synthesis of lessons learned about the nuances of survival in the political culture of Texas from the boyhood apprenticeship served at his father's side with the insights he gained about poverty and human dignity from teaching in Cotulla. Following that transformative experience working with Mexican American children and completion of his degree at San Marcos State Teachers College, Johnson taught for another year. His charismatic approach to his role as debate coach and his cultivation of a mentor-mentee relationship with the superintendent brought him to the attention of the well connected.

Southern congressmen, including Texans Johnson and Poage, posed at the White House after President Roosevelt's signing of cotton legislation in August 1937. This photo opportunity came early in the first terms of Congressmen Poage and Johnson. *Courtesy Lyndon Baines Johnson Library and Museum.*

In a familiar tale of a northeastern liberal Democrat courting votes from a conservative Democrat from the South or Southwest, Roosevelt's political network among Texans, including Aubrey Williams and congressman Dick Kleberg, led to the promotion of LBJ from Kleberg's peripatetic aide to the position of state director of the NYA in Texas.[10] A prominent Texas Democrat, US senator Tom Connally of McLennan County, supported Johnson's candidacy for the position, perhaps as a favor to Sam Rayburn, an acquaintance of Sam Johnson's who took the "boy" under his eagle wing.[11] No program of its kind heretofore existed. Assessing LBJ's readiness relied on his performance as a highly visible aide to a member willing to delegate authority and responsibility in bites nearly substantial enough to satisfy the hollow-legged political appetite of Johnson.

Connally, like many fellow members of the Texas delegation to Congress, distanced himself from FDR. His distaste for New Deal programs grew as alphabet agencies seemed to multiply like jackrabbits on the recently terraced ranchland in Central Texas. Farmers who owned their land liked the new federal program that increased the productivity of their acreage by reducing erosion and increasing retention of precious rain. This productivity was achieved by grading steep terrain into steps, or terraces, not unlike what Peruvian farmers do on the steep slopes of the Andes. The farmers especially liked getting 50 percent or more of the cost paid by Uncle Sam. They liked FDR, too. Rayburn, Johnson, and his Waco colleague, Bob Poage, did what they could to hold the Roosevelt coalition together, even as Connally and some other loose horses bolted as a third Roosevelt term approached. In Texas, essentially a one-party state since Reconstruction ended in 1877, Democrats never lacked for reasons to feud and factionalize. In the 1936 election, the central issue would be the New Deal.[12]

Despite the real (and exaggerated) tales of unwieldy New Deal bureaucracies that annoyed Democrats like Connally and plagued subsequent federal initiatives for decades, FDR's program administrators in the public works agencies consistently extended considerable latitude to local officials when it came to program design and implementation. These sincere bows to the tradition of local control coincided, however, with a distinctive leftward direction in terms of federal labor policies under the Wagner Act. A generation earlier, a budding socialist movement sewed prolabor seeds into the potentially fertile blackland prairie where the nascent Southern Tenant Farmers Union now hoped to establish itself.[13] Poage and Johnson both steered right of labor unions for fear of being linked to Reds, tending to favor landowners over tenants and sharecroppers. Both viewed agricultural policies with strong federal price supports as the best means to elevate the living standards of all farmers.[14]

When conservatives on both sides of the aisle in Congress became stronger forces of resistance in the late 1930s and ideological lines hardened both rhetorically and in actual votes cast, the political benefits of securing federal projects for one's district, nevertheless, seldom went untapped. Patronage New Deal–style resembled what occurred in the established political culture of the county or municipality, with beneficiaries shifting as leadership in those bodies moved from one faction to another within the Democratic Party in Texas over the eight-year life span of the NYA.

The federal resources came with new expectations for accounting as the agency tried to serve the public as rapidly as possible by running before it crawled. Procedures changed constantly. Certain administrative chores, such as reimbursement for expenditures, called for standardized annoyances for those assigned to accounting at the local level. Long-standing local practices had to adapt to a centralized model, creating a source of friction.

In addition, federal requirements for local or state matching funds could vary from year to year or from program to program, complicating an already difficult planning process. One of the most difficult challenges facing local, state, and federal players arose when federal projects engaged formerly unemployed citizens with residents of a community with individuals from different backgrounds.

Similar to the experiences of the CCC with placement of people of color across the state, ugly grievances developed around issues of race, particularly the use of non-Anglo workers on NYA job sites. Later in this chapter, this point will be addressed in a brief case study that climaxes with a blunt letter from Congressman Johnson to a former NYA associate back in Johnson City. The letter framed the issue in its starkest political reality to those who would find fault with the particulars of working with federal funds. To paraphrase, he asked, "Do you want the money or don't you? Can you meet the needs of your community with your resources alone?"[15]

Upon assuming the NYA post, LBJ operated out of the offices on the sixth floor of the Littlefield Building on the corner of Sixth and Congress in the heart of Austin. There he nurtured a relationship with attorney Arthur J. Wirtz, named by national NYA director Aubrey Williams to chair the nine-member Texas NYA advisory council. Wirtz, the consummate well-connected insider close to the moneyed pooh-bahs of the Democratic Party, helped the ambitious state director to establish key contacts across the vast state. Many of these became part of the system of "approximately 200" advisory groups operating at the county and community level.[16] Several of the 254 counties in Texas remained sparsely populated by the 1930s, so while every county was eligible for NYA projects, no mandate required an advisory board for each. Tapping into these grassroots networks of movers and shakers mobilized public engagement and resulted in federally supported projects aimed at locally identified needs.

The NYA resulted from the equivalent of a triage-style response by New Deal planners to the epic scale of economic dislocation facing what FDR came to describe as a population "one-third ill-clothed, ill-housed, and ill-fed."[17] Although public schools at the beginning of the Depression did not provide federally funded breakfast or lunch programs, they did offer safe shelter for nearly one-third of the day to a population in need of such simple comfort. The colorful state director delineated options for helping 125,000 sixteen- to twenty-five-year-old Texans on relief while speaking to a group of Texas educators in September 1935, listing the choices as he saw them:

We could starve them to death; we could send them to school; we could kill them through war. Obviously the answer lies in sending some of them to school; giving some of them vocational training; finding work projects for others.[18]

Barely twenty-seven years old at the time, Johnson's stunning assessment underlined a deep faith in the power of education. It conveyed the prevailing views of supporters of more federally supported programming for youth that, in Weisenberger's stark phrasing, alleviated "fear that idleness of youth" could lead to a "demoralized, unproductive generation of Americans."[19] Society faced a grave problem. At the time, 14 percent of the sixteen- to twenty-five-year-olds in the nation received relief of some kind. Uncounted thousands bobbed and sank out of reach of the ship of state's life preservers. Believers in the mystical power of the classroom to transform lives, including LBJ, held that schools must accomplish their mission, but only because knowledge equals power. Slowing the entry of young adults into a labor market not producing sufficient jobs to absorb their influx became the NYA's priority.

The NYA strategy of providing direct aid to schools (or other appropriate fiscal agents) for reimbursement for paychecks received for work performed had no precedent in 1935. By the time Johnson launched the War on Poverty and Great Society programs as president three decades later, a generation of school officials, many of whom attended college because of the GI Bill, shared the institutional memory of working with federal programs from subsidized school lunches to a flurry of efforts to boost math and science instruction in the post-Sputnik era. These federal programs involved indirect aid, however, in the form of grants and reimbursements, often linked to obligations for matching funds.

Without question, LBJ and Bob Poage believed productive American citizenship called for all young people to consider their future in terms of becoming educated to his or her potential, whether the path led to vocational skills or toward other academic pursuits. The program Johnson administered affirmed that the nation gained from investments in education at all levels of government. At the local level, carrying out this new mission infused new federal dollars into the system, thereby changing the expectations of teachers, parents, and students affected by the programs and injecting new factors into a school's political culture. The evidence suggests that school districts embraced the opportunities the NYA extended to their communities. This

CHAPTER TWO

kind of mutually supportive interaction between federal and local educational agencies exemplified the model the Johnson administration intended.

In the months leading up to FDR's issuance on June 26, 1935, of Executive Order #7086 establishing the NYA, multiple proposals for addressing youth unemployment circulated in Washington. John Studebaker, then commissioner of the US Office of Education, discussed a "Community Youth Program" in a radio broadcast just two months earlier that would distribute $288 million in federal aid to local school districts for the purpose of establishing "guidance and adjustment centers" for unemployed teenagers.[20] In Waco, these funds could support students attending Waco High School, Paul Quinn College, and Baylor University in their efforts to stay in school long enough to earn a diploma. The federal government declared that society, along with local communities and the family itself, of course, held a stake in young adults' success.

The model Studebaker described called for the creation of community councils across the nation that would play an advisory role in collaboration with locally elected school trustees who would serve as many as two million students. Typical of the hothouse environment for ideas cultivated by FDR, the Department of Labor drafted its own, less expansive plan calling for similar services for half as many students at one-third the cost. Roosevelt looked to a pair of his trusted insiders, Harry Hopkins and Aubrey Williams, to weed through these proposals.

By early June 1935, this process led them to recommend a $60 million program under the auspices of the Works Progress Administration (WPA). The size of the budget belies the perception critics of the New Deal pushed of undisciplined spending, since it represented barely one-fifth of the expenditures of the rejected Studebaker design, while retaining many of its key elements. Indeed, the scaled-back version likely reflects political calculations of what level of spending would arouse opposition by conservative Democrats. To the degree it succeeded, NYA would prove to be a boon to school enrollment. Keeping teenagers out of the general labor force meant giving them incentives, as well as the means, to stay in high school or college by employing them. Anticipated results such as reduced dropout rates and increased graduation rates found receptive audiences.

Then, as now, funding for education invariably involved head count in determining how much each school received; school districts consequently realized benefits in terms of increasing their general operating funds. Given FDR's total mastery of Congress at this stage of the New Deal, the expansion of the federal role into the realm of education provoked no significant opposition in the House or Senate. The White House decision to establish the NYA through use of an executive order, therefore, did not represent avoidance of a fight. On the contrary, it showed the administration at peak confidence.

This is not to say the NYA lacked for critics. In fact, Commissioner Studebaker believed vehemently that placing it under the WPA made no sense, especially given its conceptual origin (in his plan, at least) under the domain of the Office of Education. Denied what he deemed appropriate control over this new federal effort to prevent dropouts and to provide more vocational training opportunities for this key segment of the populace, the commissioner found a powerful ally in his ongoing effort to find leverage. He joined with the influential National Education Association in taking issue with the organizational structure of the NYA, as well as its function, which NEA viewed as a violation of long-established constitutional principles holding education as a responsibility of states. Ironically, attaining cabinet-level status, that is, a Department of Education, ranked as one of the top agenda items for the NEA, as it would until Jimmy Carter sided with the NEA over the AFT on this matter and signed the legislation in 1979.

The NEA shared Studebaker's conviction that skirting the Office of Education meant the NYA would inevitably overstep appropriate boundaries for federal involvement in state and local affairs. Two decades earlier, the NEA endorsed federal funding for vocational education under the Smith-Hughes Act, but it now considered NYA job-training projects as an encroachment on the powers of local boards of education.[21] This conflict smacked of a classic internecine turf battle among interested parties, and it gave the rival NEA and the left-leaning American Federation of Teachers (AFT) another cause for disagreement.[22]

The White House answered the critics. Interior secretary Harold Ickes viewed the risk of the collapse of the capitalist system as so severe that he felt the federal government must live up to its constitutional obligations (presumably under the "promote the general welfare" clause of the Preamble) to ensure that a student in US public schools had "every possible opportunity . . . to unfold to his utmost intellectual and spiritual capacity, regardless of where along the road of education this means that any particular child should stop."[23]

Undeniably, norms of the time left policy making related to assigning students to buildings and classrooms, budgeting, personnel, and curriculum (including graduation requirements) to a board of trustees elected to terms set by the state constitution. In this model, essentially all matters governing day-to-day operations of schools fell under the purview of a county superintendent responsible for hiring and overseeing administrators for the various elementary and secondary buildings who carried out board policies. Nothing about the NYA threatened to usurp any aspect of these standard operating procedures.

Roosevelt directly countered accusations by NEA president Agnes Samuelson that federal intrusiveness in local school affairs somehow threatened the nation. FDR dismissed the criticism in language the union likely saw as condescending, asserting that the relief function of the program involved challenges "with which educational people are not generally well acquainted."[24] Considering that women outnumbered men in the teaching profession by a five-to-one ratio in the 1930s, Roosevelt's paternalistic tone might suggest gender played a significant role in denying teacher organizations greater status in the policy-making process. This analysis may prove problematic, though, given that the rival AFT also had a woman as the designated leader, and because AFT vice president Selma Borchardt accepted the invitation to serve on the national advisory council for the NYA from its newly appointed executive director, Aubrey Williams.[25] Founded by female classroom teachers in Chicago thirty years earlier, the AFT opposed the NEA on many issues, including creation of a cabinet-level Department of Education, another wedge in the relationship between FDR and the NEA.[26]

Organizational dynamics and the profile of the overall membership led the NEA and AFT, as well as their state affiliates, to elevate prominent women educators to largely ceremonial roles in which they would be nothing more than token players.[27] In a profession where men overwhelmingly dominated administrative positions (to the extent that twenty-year-old Lyndon Johnson supervised women who were his seniors in age and experience while at Cotulla's Welhausen School), the importance of a maternal facade in maintaining the desired public image led to opportunities for a handful of talented women to participate to varying degrees.

Still, these steps toward inclusion laid essential groundwork by affording the opportunity for individuals once excluded to have places at the table. This serves as evidence of a shift in the political culture that influenced behavior of public and private bodies because the advisory council model meets the need of public officials to be seen as receptive to input at the same time it offers them the opportunity to strengthen (perhaps expand) their own network through exercising the power to nominate. The nominee gained status among his or her own constituency. Small wonder the advisory council, a remarkably self-reinforcing model of participatory governance, endures. Who would nominate individuals with contrary views?

In her study of the NYA in Texas, historian Carol Whiteside Weisenberger analyzed Williams's strategic decision to embrace the use of an advisory council at the national level; it would serve as a public relations vehicle for the new program. He seized upon every opportunity for speaking engagements, for example, making high-profile addresses at conventions of the National Congress of Parents and to the NEA's Department of Secondary School Principals to build support and to disseminate information to key constituencies. Opposition by the NEA at the national level did not eliminate the need for school administrators to know how the program would work, after all. Furthermore, Williams shared the prevailing view that a decentralized model, operating through state and local NYA bodies, would allow communities to tailor projects to their distinctive circumstances (and politics, of course). Given the inevitable scramble for places at the table, Aubrey Williams's insistence on inclusion of a student representative for each advisory council, along with a seat for an educator, amplified the voice of the teacher in the process, ultimately.

As designed, the NYA allocated federal funds to support the hiring of students for part-time employment at school or in carrying out projects identified by local advisory boards made up of individuals selected by state officials. In Texas, state senators played a role in this process. Consequently, they could bestow rewards to key allies for loyalty, financial support, or favors. Offering a prospective political friend a status-bearing position on an advisory body could be just the right perk. In Waco, the NYA advisory board consisted of figures handpicked by state senator Bob Poage. He received a letter dated October 5, 1935, inviting him to nominate prospective appointees to the advisory board for McLennan County; they were to be "selected from industry, agriculture, labor, education, and youth."[28]

In Texas, committees worked with the state NYA office or its four regional staffs to develop, implement, and oversee projects. McLennan County resided within District #1, assigned to Joe K. Skiles, who sent the request for assistance in getting an advisory council established. On the surface, the letters of nomination Poage prepared, with the exception of the letter to Poage's nominee from the field of education, principal Ben S. Peek of South Waco Junior High School, are identical, yet each has a story behind it.

The letter that deviates from the normal invitation to participate reveals something of the relationship between Poage and Peek. Poage decided to address a question Peek wrote to him about involving a proposed "Chain Store Tax," which Poage supported, as did Peek, evidently. Among the things common to all letters, one sees the senator had no clear picture of the logistics of the program. "I do not know what action will be taken," he straightforwardly admits, "but if you receive inquiries along this line, you will know that it is with a view of placing you on this board. I hope that the State administration will see fit to name you and that you will see fit to serve."[29] In addition to Principal Peek, Poage selected R. E. McCleary, a typesetter at the *Waco Tribune-Herald* with ties to the Texas State Federation of Labor, to represent labor interests. For the agriculture slot, he selected Joe Chapin of Waco. George Jones, another Wacoan, answered similar calls to community.[30]

The reply from George Jones, owner of Jones Fine Bread Company, located in Waco at Seventeenth Street and Mary Avenue, indicated the prospective representative of industry viewed accepting the invitation as an expression of trust in Poage.

> Was glad to have your letter stating that you had recommended me. . . . I am not fully informed as to the aims and objects or purposes of this movement and I am not quite clear on how it is to be financed, however I will be glad to do whatever I can in the situation and appreciate your remembering me.[31]

Poage subsequently received a one-page "Outline of 4-Point Program of National Youth Administration" with the letter instructing him on how to establish a local advisory board, but Jones's comments suggest it may not have been shared. According to the information provided to Poage:

> Employers in all types of industries . . . shall be asked to accept youths as apprentices under arrangements to be worked out with the State Committee on Apprentice Training at Austin, Texas. Also, wherever possible, state, county and municipal offices shall be asked to accept youths as apprentices to train for public service.[32]

This sheds some light on Roosevelt's seemingly dismissive comments about the NEA's concerns about what they perceived as a diminished role for educational expertise in the NYA's organizational structure under the WPA, instead of an enhanced role for the Office of Education they favored. The mission of the NYA called for more than school-based projects. Poage's selection of R. E. McCleary as the voice for labor interests on the advisory board illustrates Poage's approach to the political process. McCleary served as secretary for the Allied Printing Trades Council in Waco, where he became a prominent figure in the labor effort there, as well as through his involvement with the Texas State Federation of Labor (TSFL). McCleary's support for Poage in the quest for a seat in Congress could help to generate hundreds if not thousands of votes in the all-important Democratic primary election in the spring of 1936. Several months before Poage named him for membership on the NYA body, and nearly a year before the primary, the labor leader solicited input from TSFL regarding potential support for prospective candidates for the Eleventh District seat in a letter dated April 30, 1935. McCleary's request received an immediate answer from W. B. Arnold, TSFL president:

In your letter of April 30th requesting information whether or not Senator Bob Poage is a friend of labor, you ask me to use plain terms in my reply, here it is: Bob Poage is the most outstanding member in the Senate *for labor*. He has fought for labor's bills on every occasion. He has never failed to cooperate with Wallace Reilly, our executive secretary. In my estimation, Bob Poage is the best friend labor has in the Senate. Hoping that the above is "plain enough."[33]

For Democrats in Texas in the mid-1930s, being described as a friend of labor came with some risk; reactionaries could paint respect for working people as indicative of socialist tendencies. Paralleling their concerns about centralized governmental authority, many Texas Democrats could simultaneously support protection of the rights of labor while challenging the wisdom of the collective bargaining rights outlined by the newly established National Labor Relations Board. According to this logic, big unions could overwhelm the rights of the individual worker and reward the slovenly at the level paid to hard-working Texans. Yet populist indignation against powerful elites ran as high as ever in a state with a political culture full of Texas versions of David and Goliath. Skill at negotiating such terrain determined one's success in Democratic primaries.

The left-leaning *Waco Farm and Labor Journal*, published weekly for a few years in the depths of the Depression as the self-proclaimed "Journal of

Progress and Champion of a Square Deal for All the People—Standing for Better Relations Between Capital and Labor," had little use for Poage. Instead, editorial support again went to Poage's chief rival for the nomination, incumbent congressman Otto H. Cross, who defeated him in 1934. Well before the 1936 rematch, and three months before R. E. McCleary asked TSFL leaders for their impressions, *Journal* editor J. M. Pittillo directed highly critical language toward Poage. "Cross Replies to Poage's Political Propaganda" reads a lead story on the front page of the January 25, 1935, issue.[34] It quoted extensively from a letter by Cross to Pittillo, wherein Poage's "feverish" desire to "get himself in Congress" sharply contrasted with Cross's account of his own dedication to his constituents.[35] Then, as now, securing the support of working-class voters loomed large in the thinking of ambitious politicians. The circumstances suggest Poage clearly saw the political advantages of naming McCleary to the NYA advisory board for McLennan County.

In the gendered terms characteristic of both time and place, the letter expressed confidence that Poage will "select men who will secure for your county the broadest possible program," even though Aubrey Williams, Arthur Wirtz, and Lyndon Johnson all invited women into the process.[36] Poage did not. Ever the traditionalist, Poage believed women contributed best to society in a role supportive of the men in their lives, especially in the area of child rearing. Despite the irreplaceable role Rebekah Johnson played in her son's life, at no time in his career did Johnson interact with women as peers on the playing field of politics. Census records do not list an occupation for Helen Conger Poage, and the word "homemaker," commonly used by the census takers, does not appear either. The family grew accustomed to having the services of an African American cook and a "nurse." Ironically, some of the NYA programs designed for African American women aimed to prepare them for careers in homes like the Poage's and the Johnson's.

Eleanor Roosevelt rightfully complained that the CCC's virtually all-male programming fell short of expectations for relief opportunities for women. This commitment led to some of the most cross-cultural training in the eight-year program. For example, at the San Antonio Camp for Unemployed Women, one of three such sites Johnson established, Anglos and Latinas met together for songs and games for the purposes of breaking down language barriers and other obstacles to understanding.[37] Some scholars attribute low rates of participation in NYA programs by Latinas to the need to work to sustain the family. Ruthe Winegarten and Teresa Palomo Acosta found "most Tejana NYA participants were sent to poorly equipped and segregated training sites." They also point to a deal between unnamed "government officials and farm agents" that prohibited operation of NYA programs during harvest season, which created major obstacles for many Tejanos and Mexican Americans.[38] In *LBJ and Mexican Americans,* Julie Leininger Pycior mentions a more positive episode involving Manuela Gonzalez, whose NYA placement at the library in Cotulla, where Johnson taught, proved deeply satisfying. Gonzalez became a lifelong friend of Johnson's, according to Pycior.[39]

Another initiative aimed at rural women targeted homemaking skills, such as the one offered at the Prairie View State Normal and Industrial College, a historically black institution, where women trained for careers in domestic service.[40] A less favorable report by an NYA inspector in 1937, however, cited "the projects are not on a par with those for boys, most of them being of the sewing-room variety."[41] Johnson departed to begin his term in Congress, but within the year his replacement, Jesse Kellam, itemized several new projects, specifically in cafeteria and hospital situations.

The issue of diversity was challenging for Johnson. In the area of race, he documented it at considerable length in a letter to John Corson, assistant NYA director under Williams, expressing opposition to integrating the state advisory board. In a statement both revealing of Johnson's perceptions of race relations as a young adult and of his presumptuous application of these views to "negro leaders," the new director framed the situation:

> To one unacquainted with conditions in Texas this may seem paradoxical, but I sincerely believe that an investigation will reveal that negro leaders would have no confidence in any of their number who permits his name to be proposed as a member of the Board, because of the friction they know would certainly ensue. Their leaders are interested in the progress of their race and its development, not by such manifestations of force against the will of white leaders, but by harmony and cooperation. They know there are limits upon this cooperation and that their intrusion upon white boards is beyond the limits.[42]

The letter displays all of Johnson's trademark persuasive tactics, including a fatalistic declaration of doom ("I would, in all probability, be 'run out of Texas'") if he did not prevail.[43] By 1966, Lyndon Johnson's perceptions of race relations evolved into the undeniably radical posture announced in his landmark address at Howard University outlining the need for affirmative action.

In 1935, however, he worked within the highly localized Jim Crow system, and around its fringes, believing no viable alternative existed. The resulting strategy for advisory boards for African Americans, established by Johnson "with the fullest cooperation of negro leaders," in his words, would have the Texas NYA director meet with such bodies. As LBJ schooled Corson about the inner workings of segregation—the white Easterner might only know subtler variations of American apartheid—LBJ noted a key limitation. African American citizens could assist in planning, provided the meetings took place where "they are permitted to concentrate."[44]

Overlooking the contributions of women who contributed to the planning and implementation of programs for African American youth in Texas under the NYA, Johnson gave Corson the profile of the typical individual he had appointed to the advisory board he organized for African Americans. This language from an Anglo Texan who risked being considered too liberal on race by his contemporaries for much of his life came three decades after W. E. B. Du Bois wrote about the "Talented Tenth":

> It includes a number of the finest men of the race—men who have spent many years in their various professions to uplift and better their people. They are men who enjoy the confidence of white people and who are respected by white leaders for their work and ideas.[45]

Comprising the six-member Negro advisory board appointed by Johnson were three college presidents: W. R. Banks of Prairie View College, Mary Branch of Tillotson College in Austin, and Joseph J. Rhoads of the newly established Bishop College. W. L. Davis, principal of Harper Junior High School in Houston, and L. Virgil Williams, principal of Booker T. Washington High School in Dallas, represented secondary education.[46] Johnson did not claim that African Americans would choose the same people, but despite the paternalism, his emphasis on importance of credibility transcends race. Johnson explained that the board he assembled for the purpose of representing African Americans in the state already met in Houston and had another public forum scheduled in Waco. Furthermore, when the NYA conference for college presidents took place in Austin, Johnson arranged for sessions with presidents of "negro colleges" where "negro school problems were brought up and gone over with great thoroughness."[47]

Members of the Negro advisory board proved indispensable in promoting the work of the NYA within the African American communities across

Texas. Johnson selected members from population centers across the state that actively engaged in outreach efforts to serve more students in their region. Some outreach efforts had the added benefit of identifying problems within the system. LBJ received a letter from board member Mary Branch on the lack of cooperation she received from Travis County officials. The issue prompting her complaint—refusal to certify eligibility for relief, and therefore for NYA program participation—led the director to send repeated memos to NYA headquarters: the eligibility formula kept out needy students.[48]

Noteworthy in the communications between Johnson and his superiors in Washington were expressions of frustration with a requirement, for example, that 90 percent of students on an NYA project must come from families certified by the Works Progress Administration. That arbitrary mandate caused unnecessary delays, which inevitably hurt the people to be helped. Within the first several weeks of his appointment, Johnson responded with interest to an inquiry from President Banks of Prairie View College about coordinating an NYA project with a proposed CCC camp near his campus. Aubrey Williams insisted that NYA programs be independent of other federal agencies, however, so LBJ and Banks developed another concept that proved highly successful. These early experiences with federal bureaucracy, itself in its infancy, left indelible impressions on Johnson's sense of how cooperation between layers of government ultimately proved to be the essential ingredient to making the system work.[49]

Always concerned that his efforts to steer federal resources to African Americans could ruin his career, Johnson quickly learned enough about budgetary practices and record keeping to identify his strategy:

We had to use most of our money for wages, the rest for equipment, shovels, etc., and nothing for fancy things like dormitories. What I did was go around and get people to donate money for the equipment in the white areas and then apply that saving to Prairie View and use it to build dorms which they so badly needed.[50]

Johnson and Banks worked well together, but the director devoted attention to Waco as well. Johnson mentioned in his letter to Corson a meeting in Waco at Paul Quinn College, the historically black college that was part of the city's proud claim to be the "Athens of the South." The other schools nurturing the proud claim were Baylor University and its sister school for women, Mary Hardin Baylor, then located midway between Waco and Austin at the old stagecoach stop near Belton. The absence of letters involving African Americans and the National Youth Administration in the late congressman's papers at the W. R. Poage Legislative Library at Baylor University in Waco, Texas, does not provide conclusive evidence of Poage's stance on engaging non-whites in the political process, but the record leaves no question that some African American youth in his senatorial and House districts did participate.

On March 16, 1936, the Texas director's Projects Division issued a "Special Report of Negro Activities of NYA in Texas," with data presented on a county-by-county basis. The range of projects deemed within the scope of the NYA raises the possibility for a variety of scenarios in terms of the prioritizing process in each county. Johnson's letter to Corson emphasizes the role of his "Negro" advisory board, but the impact of locals remains less clear.

For example, one might envision sitting in on a meeting in Waco of local African American community leaders conferring with Johnson about a project sponsored by the Waco Working Boys' Club that employed two individuals for a two-month period beginning February 4, 1936. The report did not indicate whether these part-time employees were male or female. How did they decide that the average monthly wage should be set at $15 per month, even though that set the pay rate at least $1 higher than any other NYA job for "negro youth" in Central Texas?[51]

After all, another project, started just the week before under the sponsorship of the Waco Recreation Department, offered two months of employment to seven African American youth. The report data showed no indication of limitation by gender. These $12 per month jobs paid at the same rate as the three positions that were available for African Americans when the third NYA program started within a week in Waco in early 1936 under the direction of the State Highway Department. Two of the three projects commencing between January 31 and February 4 that year likely involved young adults in work within the African American community. The sponsorship was by the Waco Working Boys' Club and the Waco Recreation Department, both of which organized activities for children on a segregated basis in segregated facilities. The jobs associated with the State Highway Department likely presented more opportunities for a multicultural experience for the young men; they were often assigned to assist with the construction of roadside picnic areas for the increasing numbers of motorists in the state.

The county superintendent in neighboring Falls County, also within Poage's state senate and congressional districts, received approval of his request for funds for a project lasting one month that called for fifteen positions for "negro youth" on an $8 per month basis beginning the last week of February. Dozens of such projects commenced across Central Texas in the first three months of 1936, so this must have been an incredibly busy time for Johnson and his staff. For people like Bob Poage, staying on top of these agencies and of the opportunities they presented for constituents proved a constant challenge under the Roosevelt administration, when a stream of new programs created a flood of requests. When one considers the scope of the problem of youth unemployment combined with the temptation for teens to drop out of school to assist the family, a budget of less than $500,000 for its first year of operation in Texas seems miniscule. Rules for eligibility for funds were standardized, but the strong emphasis on local control left issues of fairness to local sensibilities.

It appears that Mexican Americans' access to sources of federal relief depended on the local political culture. For example, the state of Texas reported "90% of the NYA program operating in San Antonio and south of San Antonio to the border of Texas was composed of Mexican youth."[52] A project in Austin found the school district converting a school formerly used only for Mexican American students into a community center for the city's fluctuating numbers of Spanish-speaking residents.[53] By the time the NYA program came to Texas in the autumn of 1935, however, tens of thousands of adults and children of Mexican heritage left Texas by force or less coercive means in the deportation movement spurred by hard times and bigotry. For those who remained, "local discriminatory practices" limited access for Mexican American youth.[54]

There is some reason to conclude that as late as October 1935 Poage had not yet encountered the man who would be a vital link for Waco to federal resources, as well as an indispensable ally. Poage's letters to prospective members of the NYA advisory board for McLennan County mentioned that their nomination would be directed to the attention of the "Honorable *Linden* Johnson" (italics added for emphasis), the "National Youth Administrator of Texas."[55] Poage would not have to wait long to know Johnson and his pathbreaking program better.

Johnson's approach to the job showed evidence of his ambition and keen sense of the future value of establishing contacts around the state with people like Poage. Some of these amounted, no doubt, to little more than token acquaintances to be tapped later for support in campaigns for the US Senate, but the evidence of Johnson's hands-on approach to administering the Texas NYA points to more than glad-handing good ol' boys. Undoubtedly, trips to

Waco, just one hundred miles north of Austin and half-way to Dallas, meant he and Poage met early in Johnson's stint as director, if these strong party men did not know each other from previous campaigns. And the possibility remains that the two knew each other from their fathers' careers in the Texas legislature.

The director assigned two of his college friends, H. A. Ziegler and Jesse Kellam, to handle the details of the school aid portion of the program, but Johnson apparently struggled to delegate key aspects of the job. Weisenberger's study offered evidence of Johnson working with Ziegler in order to teach high school principals about working effectively with federal paperwork to avoid delays in payments. Johnson, according to NYA staffer Sherman Birdwell, "had to make many trips to Washington" during his twenty months as head of the Texas NYA for "training seminars and program developments . . . because this was strictly a Federal program, this was not a Federal-State program . . . so instructions came from the source."[56]

Serving eligible students in high schools and colleges, NYA established a two-tiered system of payments. Family eligibility for WPA benefits automatically qualified students for assistance. Instead of making payments directly to the students, however, the WPA paid high schools six dollars per student, "depending on the size school and the number of students they had," reported Birdwell. School administrators operated within distinctive political cultures, of course, so Birdwell's description of how funds would be handled in practice is telling:

> The superintendent, at that time, would take the six dollars for one person—it was not designated for an individual, but it was designated for, we'll say, ten students, so he'd get sixty dollars a month—and divide it maybe three ways and have thirty people working where each of them got two dollars a month, because this would buy them a better pair of tennis shoes, in those days, and some pencils and paper that people badly needed to go to school.[57]

Rugged individualists proclaimed the use of direct federal aid to students and to the citizenry in general as counterproductive in the long term, predicting a problem with dependency. For K–12 districts and higher education, however, resources of the kind the NYA provided quickly became indispensable, despite the frustrating accompanying bureaucratic features. Even with restrictions on use of federal funds, school districts looked to underwrite general operating expenditures in any legitimate manner, perhaps in the form of charging a fee for rental of facilities or for indirect costs associated with operating federal programs.[58]

Changes emanating from Aubrey Williams's headquarters in Washington reflected ongoing debates about eligibility requirements. Effective October 1935, scarcely four months into the NYA's eight-year existence, policy changes relaxed eligibility requirements by making students from families not on relief eligible for NYA jobs. This change required local school leaders to "exercise every precaution to make certain that funds were not made available to any student who did not produce satisfactory evidence that NYA employment was essential to the proper continuance of his education."[59] Meetings with those officials emphasized significant local control of the project design process. Out of this decentralized model came partnerships between Waco's educational institutions and community organizations. Baylor University and Waco public school officials, for example, conceived a plan to use sociology students to reduce dropouts and improve school attendance for "underprivileged students of school age . . . who were maladjusted both in the home and in the school."[60] The project employed ten Baylor sociology majors to conduct home visits to the truant students and their families.

Using the clout attendant to holding the purse strings for NYA programming in Texas, Johnson assembled a group of college presidents in September 1935 to pool ideas and to share their concerns about their early experiences with the agency. Out of these interactions came the establishment of twenty "Freshman Centers" (officially known as Emergency Education Freshman Colleges) across the state aimed at assisting high school graduates with the transition to college. This was the first initiative of its kind in the nation. Black colleges, including Paul Quinn College in Waco, hosted fifteen of the twenty centers.[61] This ratio reflects the lack of resources available for elementary and secondary preparation of African American students in the segregated system Texas operated. The "Special Report of Negro Activities of the National Youth Administration in Texas" confirmed greater participation by African American youth in NYA programs overall, citing a margin of 24.2 percent to a 12–14 percent rate for white students.[62] All programming decisions were local. Curiously, the waiver of eligibility requirements for other NYA projects announced a few weeks later did not apply to these centers.

A meeting with one hundred African American educators and civic leaders on October 12, 1935, conducted by the Negro advisory board signaled strong interest, but planning for implementation of the centers taught Johnson another lesson about federalism, because only 471 students of the 2,000 interested could be served because of insufficient funds to pay the four hundred teachers necessary to deliver the program.[63] By tapping into the innovations local school districts, colleges, universities, and community-based organizations conceived, Johnson's NYA efforts resulted in high praise from the national office: "Texas is so prolific in projects that every new batch of project applications is greeted with 'Oh's and Ah's'"[64]

In a report Johnson submitted in February 1936, the state director provided evidence of a growing sense of the limits of both local control and centralization; these limits stand out in his analysis by revealing the challenge of meeting rural needs with the current delivery system. Speaking of communities with fewer than ten eligible students, Johnson informed NYA officials in Washington of his assessment:

> Experience has demonstrated the inadvisability of operating a project without frequent inspection by persons paid from federal funds. It therefore appears that the excessive overhead of Federal cost will prevent operation of small projects for the employment of many youths scattered in small communities.[65]

That month, February 1936, the Texas NYA opened junior placement offices at four Texas state employment service centers around the state, including Waco (but not Austin). "Junior counselors" screened applicants, whether they qualified for relief or not, resulting in the placement of over five thousand young people in the private sector in the first eighteen months of its operation.

By November 1936, Poage's constituent services, already acclimated to the role of interface between needy citizen and potential employment, extended to those seeking placement through NYA. That month, Roy Malcik, formerly a student at Sam Houston State Teachers College, from rural Rosebud, Texas, contacted Poage with a request for assistance in finding a job that would enable him to "reenter school at midterm," as Poage described the situation in his letter to Professor H. R. Brentzel at the college in Huntsville in East Texas. Advocating on behalf of Malcik for any kind of employment, "if nothing more than one of Federal Government places," Poage told Brentzel "this is the kind of student, who is the most deserving of help, having exhibited his own willingness to help himself just as far as possible."[66]

For the young men and women employed in NYA programs as part-time clerical staff in school offices across Texas, or as full-time laborers on a roadside picnic area project for the Texas Road Commission, these programs represented a lifeline. File after file in the papers of Bob Poage and Lyndon Johnson contain letters from citizens who put self-preservation ahead of pride, until, often at moments of obvious desperation, they break down and write for help from the federal government.

Letters from students reveal the extent of the need for programs like the NYA; at the same time the letters demonstrate the distinctive circumstances facing individuals like John Griswell of Marlin, Texas. He could not continue at Baylor because, as he explained to Poage, "I cannot get the course I want there, therefore I wish to transfer to State. I plan to get a Chemical Engineering Degree." Griswell was referring to the University of Texas in Austin, where he stated he had "been down there all last week trying to secure work for room or board . . . tried to get on the N.Y.A. jobs, with no success." [67]

At some point early in his quest for a job through the NYA, Griswell likely received a copy of form A-155, issued by the Texas NYA office, located in room 605 of the Littlefield Building in Austin. Reflecting fewer layers of bureaucracy than students encounter today at any institution, instructions told students to "Write direct to the president of the institution you wish to attend, and apply for one of the part-time jobs available through the National Youth Administration."[68]

The very concise, one-page document informed students that the part-time jobs averaged $15 per month for "students of good character, between the ages of 16 and 25, who cannot otherwise attend college and who are able to do high grade academic work."[69] Such assistance would be welcomed by anyone, even a steadily employed educator, based on a letter Poage received from Raleigh Moses in early April 1936. Moses taught in Orange, Texas, near the Mexican border, but had acquaintance with Poage, apparently, from previous residence in Hewitt, a rural community southwest of Waco.

He commended the senator for "helping the school [in Hewitt] out of a jam" and predicted Poage's campaign for the House seat in the upcoming primary: "from what I hear you do not need any help." Moses then moved to the heart of the matter—a plea for assistance in finding "any possible part-time work I can get in Austin this summer." He described the circumstances behind his request:

Unfortunately, we teachers in Orange will not get paid in cash the last month this year. Furthermore, we have not been paid yet for the last month of last year. This leaves me short of cash for summer school.[70]

The letter Poage composed the next day upon receipt of Moses's call for help displays open frustration with the inability of even the New Deal programs to address the scope of the needs among his constituents.

I have just received your letter of the 6th, and certainly wish that I knew of some kind of place that I could advise you to apply for, but I just don't know of a thing in the world that you could get. There is never a week that passes but what there are dozens of people come to me, and ask me to write letters from [sic] them to various State Departments, trying to get some place, but I know that most of these are utterly hopeless efforts.[71]

Part of Poage's transparent feeling of powerlessness derived from the aforementioned uncertainty regarding the continuation of programs like the NYA. Within a single academic year (1935–36), students and school officials across the nation became reliant upon these supplemental sources of funding. The University of Texas quickly established a Committee on Federal Aid for Students to monitor developments. As summer approached, all stakeholders would wonder about the status of NYA funds for the 1936–37 school year. Chaired by V. I. Moore, dean of student life, the committee responded swiftly when good news arrived early in July. Citing confirmation from Lyndon Johnson, state NYA director, Dean Moore informed UT students, "we are therefore accepting tentatively applications for part-time jobs for the coming session." Moore cautioned students about the limited resources of the NYA and how those supplemental payments fit into the larger picture of college expenses:

Attention is called to the fact that the income from these jobs will not by any means meet all expenses at The University of Texas. Last long session the maximum allowed each undergraduate student through NYA funds was $15 per month for nine months. This amount will probably be less than one-third of the actual expense.[72]

Students at the University of Texas received a two-page application form enclosed with this letter from the dean. After entering basic identification information, students were given two lines to "Explain fully the conditions that make it impossible for your parents to provide full support." Another set of questions, "Do you keep a car? For what purpose?" sought to sort and select worthy applicants by gleaning individual spending profiles before leading up to a simple yes-or-no question that provided a full line for the applicant's response: "Is your entrance into this institution or your continuance here absolutely dependent upon your obtaining some employment?" The second page of the application amounts to a template for a résumé, requesting information ranging from words per minute from those with typing skills to foreign languages individuals might be capable of translating.[73]

A letter from Poage to Dean Moore written a month after the mailing to UT students suggests the communications loop among public officials needed attention. Citing inquiries from "a number of young men and a few young ladies . . . relative to the possibility of securing some kind of work to assist them through the University," Poage wrote: "However, I am not advised as to just what they should do in order to secure one of the Federal positions for college students. I would appreciate your advice in this connection."[74]

Poage took the opportunity to include a reference on behalf of a constituent from a Falls County resident from the village of Lott, located twenty miles south of Waco on Highway 77. Jack Ruble "heretofore attended Sam Houston Teacher's College, but hopes to take his degree from the University of Texas." Referring to Ruble as a "very fine young man," Poage closed with an expression of appreciation to Dean Moore for "any suggestions that you can offer."[75] In this instance, it appears that the senator's efforts received prompt attention, because a follow-up letter from Poage to Moore dated August 14, 1936, reported, "since that time Mr. Ruble has received and filled out N.Y.A. application blanks." There are no indications in the files of the nature of Poage's familiarity with Jack Ruble, but the wording of his second letter to Moore about Ruble conveys such a strong endorsement that it does not read like a standard referral. Poage informed Moore that his purpose in writing again after just nine days was that Moore "may not overlook his application." Poage continued, "There is no question, but what he needs the help, and that he is striving to get an education. If you can be of assistance to him, I will greatly appreciate it."[76]

As members of Congress, Poage and Johnson required that their office staff consistently replied to constituent letters within one day, regardless of the topic. In the case of LBJ, less admirable traits of his management style included a reputation for blistering criticism of his staff alternating with gifts and expressions of gratitude for endless office hours. An inviolable rule required written responses to constituents within twenty-four hours.[77] In the early congressional years, especially in the case of Johnson, one finds many replies quite expansive, as in the case of a series of communications related to an NYA project underway in Johnson City.

In LBJ's first coup for the Tenth District, he famously persuaded FDR to approve funding for a hydroelectric dam to provide Austin and the Hill Country with power. Ancillary needs associated with this vast undertaking included buildings such as one to house the Pedernales Electric Cooperative in Johnson City, the seat of Blanco County. In his capacity as a member of Congress, the former state director applied the lessons he learned running the Texas NYA. His familiarity with the personalities involved and the intricacies of budgeting meant LBJ undoubtedly played a central role in securing NYA funds for this project to supplement the Rural Electrification Administration (REA) budget. Delighted with the approval of the project, Congressman Johnson undoubtedly recalled Aubrey Williams's refusal to allow for CCC-NYA collaboration on the Prairie View College venture. Nevertheless, there may have been moments when he regretted it by late May 1939. Complaints from old friends about the NYA project back home could not escape Johnson's attention.

Charlie Stevenson and Dan Rose of Johnson City, where LBJ spent a portion of his youth, contacted him regarding some concerns about recent labor issues on the building project. When Johnson read Stevenson's letter and came upon the statement, "Everything has been going on fine up until today," he surely knew the pleasantries were over. Sherman Birdwell, then an NYA director himself in the area, instituted ten-hour days, effective immediately. Stevenson reported:

it don't set at all with the Mexicans. They claim he tricked them. I am afraid they are all going to quit. He certainly has made it hard on the white men and I'll say Claude Kidder is the best foreman they could have gotten . . . they all have confidence in his ability & every man on the job honors & respects him. If they will leave it to him he will get the job done. It looks like every time we get things to working smooth there is a monkey wrench tossed in from somewhere.[78]

Stevenson's relationship with LBJ went back at least to their teen years, when they worked on a road construction crew together. In recalling those days, he insinuated to Johnson that some of the worksite issues derived from unwelcome diversity, stating, "Lyndon we white boys get along fine. Just like your Dad old Shock, Bob Paterson and the rest of us on the Hiway in 1926." From Stevenson's description, peaceful coexistence and productivity relied in part on separating Anglos and Mexicans into work crews focused on different parts of the building. "These Mexicans are not doing any of the outside wall work. There is 6 white boys doing the work & believe me they are doing a neat job."[79]

Collaboration between NYA and REA in planning the construction of the building anticipated a labor force consisting of Anglos and Mexicans. A two-page listing of job descriptions for fourteen supervisory positions for various skilled trades, from general superintendent of construction to plasterer, assigned nine of these to REA and the remaining five to NYA. These positions paid well, demonstrating the impact of New Deal programs on more than the indigent and poorly educated members of society. The general superintendent earned $175 per month, or $2,200 annually, compared to $100 earned by the REA plasterer, whose job included some supervisory duties. NYA pay for minority laborers on construction projects ranged between $8 and $15 per month, dependent on skills and responsibilities. Pay for whites, as evidenced by rates listed on the "Suggested Labor Supervisory Requirements" document, could vary widely for the same reasons, but would generally be in the $30 per month range.[80]

Johnson characteristically replied immediately, expressing appreciation to his friend Charlie for "writing me the picture as you see it—frankly and honestly." He did not address issues of ethnicity. Instead, the letter served as a pep talk, attributing the work schedule changes to "Birdwell's doing what he has to do in order to get it done," before, as LBJ put it, "It isn't at all impossible that funds will run out by July first." In typical Johnson fashion, he then elevated the project's importance to maximize pressure on Stevenson, stating, "I don't know of any project that means more to me than that building and I feel that knowing this you'll try to help Birdwell every way you can and will spread the Gospel to the boys."[81]

The "boys" he refers to may be just the white personnel on the NYA-REA project, or perhaps LBJ intended a broader audience. Letters crisscrossed in the mail between Johnson City and Washington, DC, in late May and early June, including the complaint from Dan Rose, a local service station owner, about the use of Mexican labor on the NYA-REA project. Despite its two pages, Johnson's explanation comes across as terse—the kind of corrective tone one might sense in the words of a teacher disappointed that a student did not "get it," again.

And Dan Rose received a reminder from Lyndon that he did not forget previous negativity. Johnson said he recalled that "you wrote me when it did not look as if we could whip the power companies."[82] No need to remind Rose any further, apparently, of the essential role Johnson played in bringing electricity to the Hill Country, or that without that dam, there would be no need for a new building in Johnson City for use by the new electric co-op. As Senate Majority Leader and as president, Johnson would employ a similar line of argument when dealing with racists. Highlighting areas where self-interest could serve as a counterweight to prejudice, he wrote to Rose:

> Dan, here is the situation briefly: Except for outside money, we could have no REA project. . . . We could not have had a building project except as an excuse to employ needy youth labor on a worthwhile job.
> . . . It seems to me very obvious that we are getting a headquarters and a building and a few jobs without spending a cent.[83]

One can almost detect the changing inflection in his voice as Johnson explained to Rose that NYA had been instructed to direct eligible white men in the area to the project. "Yes, Dan, we could have had all white boys on the project to do all the work on the building. But who was to put up the money?" Using his knowledge of NYA and taking advantage of ongoing relationships with his NYA colleagues, Congressman Johnson saw the opportunity to infuse some of those funds into the Pedernales Electric Cooperative Building project planned for Johnson City, only partially funded by the REA. Along with other ailments afflicting politicians, LBJ showed symptoms of an edifice complex, so in addition to bringing jobs to the community, the project would serve as a continuing reminder of his civic-mindedness.

Briefly reviewing Keynesian economics, Johnson explained the pump-priming effects of the project: "Thousands of dollars will be spent in our little town as a result of this development. A few local men will get jobs that they would not have otherwise. All you fellows in business will benefit a little bit." Were these words uttered face-to-face, one can picture LBJ adjusting his still lanky six foot three inch frame for maximum effect just before driving his point home. Rose knew Johnson well enough to picture that, and by this time in reading the reply the service station owner wished he had not mailed his letter in the first place. Johnson bluntly informed Rose that if the benefits derived from the project

> are not sufficiently attractive . . . then we can get the NYA to move their camp and work out a local plan whereby the county puts up some money and some of the local citizens contribute, and we can then finish the job with our own labor. I just didn't feel like the business men and the county were able to do that and no one suggested it, and I did the only thing that could be done to get the building built.[84]

The school year Johnson spent in Cotulla seared impressions of the lives of children in stark poverty into his memory. Throughout his political career as a program administrator, legislator, and as chief executive, LBJ harkened back to that experience. Touting education policy initiatives, but most famously promoting voting rights legislation as president, he drew upon those memories. Those who never had their own classroom could understandably scoff at this as melodramatic. The subtle exercise of power by Johnson as state director and as representative of the Tenth District directed resources to Mexican Americans and to African Americans by artfully playing the system.

Dan Rose barely finished reading the verbal spanking from the former teacher in the form of Johnson's letter before Sherman Birdwell stopped by to see him and "explained a few things was not clear to me, which puts me in a better position to explain or answer any one who has some criticism to make. You know I regretted sending my first letter." By this stage of Lyndon Johnson's career, well into the first year of his second term in the House, constituents of the Tenth District had tangible evidence that the big-talking son of Sam Johnson could get results. Perhaps Johnson's effort to get Rose to focus on the color of money instead of on the NYA-REA workers' sweating faces paid quick dividends, because he literally rewrote his concerns about Mexicans. At the risk that Johnson might have perceived some anti-Mexican bigotry, Rose explained:

> One reason I wrote to you was that I was afraid that 4 or 5 of the boys who have been griping might get to talking to some of the boys who come from Sandy and Round mountain or out of town and they would make some kind of move against the Mexicans. . . . So what I really wish to say Lyndon is that I think all of the business men in town and others

around here that are directly concerned will not be making any sympa-
thetic remarks when some one who is prejudiced against the Mexicans
are making wisecracks and every thing will work out fine.[85]

The famous "Johnson treatment," the no-holds-barred forays into the art of
persuasion that would eventually live forever through White House recordings, earned a place in political folklore as a face-to-face experience. Johnson's
telephone performances, captured on tape during the White House years,
convey some of his seductive craftsmanship. The letter to Charlie Stevenson,
like the aforementioned letter from LBJ to assistant NYA director Corson
about African American representation on the state advisory council, stands
among the most revealing documents of this stage of his career. It conveyed
the passion of an individual focused on delivering services to a grateful citizenry who grated at second-guessing by those he viewed as spectators, not
doers.

To examine the work of the NYA in Central Texas, notably in the Waco
area, under Johnson's leadership, is to witness the emergence of the political partnership between Johnson and Poage that spanned more than three
decades. Director Johnson's and state Senator (soon-to-be Congressman)
Poage's entry-level, hands-on experience would forever influence their sense
that federal programs should operate in conjunction with elected state and
local officials and other stakeholders.

These new relationships between community leaders and a federal agency
with resources for teenagers and young adults suggest a mixture of pragmatic
thinking modeled after Progressive Era initiatives like the County Extension
Act that brought federal resources close to home, where state and local officials played key roles in determining how to use their requisite contributions
to greatest effect. Evidence of the enduring impact of the NYA model can be
found in work-study programs for students in every state in the twenty-first
century.

Flood Control, Federalism, and a Ford Dealer

HOW THE GREAT SOCIETY CAME TO WACO, TEXAS

THE PREAMBLE TO THE US CONSTITUTION sidesteps the issue of natural disasters. Yet in the third century of these United States, even libertarians interpret "provide for the common defense" and "promote the general welfare" as a federal mission statement allowing for direct intervention in local affairs when catastrophe strikes. Indeed, public expectations for presidential leadership during such crises seem at an all-time high. Questions arose about the very competency of federal officials and their agencies, hardly a new concern among conservatives, when Hurricane Katrina slammed the Gulf Coast in 2005, and the woefully inadequate federal response to the flooding of New Orleans shocked the nation. Those images of families stranded on rooftops evoked commentaries on the nature of modern poverty on one hand while on the other levee breaches highlighted infrastructure deficits awaiting federal resources. Clearly, the "system" did not work, providing fodder for table-top simulation exercises by emergency management personnel around the globe.

Since that debacle, devastating outbreaks of extreme weather provided far too many opportunities for implementation, evaluation, and adjustment of emergency plans developed by virtually every community. Failures like the response to Hurricane Katrina potentially instruct, as do those times when local, state, and federal officials manage to work together to successfully implement solutions to environmental problems. The choice seems clear—we can have weakness from dysfunction or strength in unity.

One example demonstrates how persistence and political know-how overcame the long-running problem of flooding in Waco, Texas; this persistence culminated in the dedication of a new dam at Lake Waco in 1965. This case study examines the alliance of Senator Lyndon Johnson, Congressman Bob Poage, and the local Ford dealer, J. H. "Jack" Kultgen, whose combined efforts to address water management issues in the Brazos River basin finally gained federal support for the Lake Waco project. LBJ used his mastery of the Senate to give longtime ally Bob Poage and his Central Texas constituency an apparent victory over nature. By this time in his career, LBJ had developed circles of advisers all across Texas capable of relaying changing political conditions like Doppler radar spots potential heavy weather. In Waco, Poage's network became LBJ's network.

In the summer of 1965, arguably the peak of Johnson's mercurial presidency, the dedication of the new dam at Lake Waco symbolized a federal, state, and local partnership that connected Johnson's New Deal roots with the Great Society, even though the political spadework by Kultgen, Poage, and Johnson had begun decades before. All three came of age in the New Deal era, when managing the landscape for the twin goals of conservation and economic development came into full flower. The convergence of their efforts makes a good dam story.

Like the rest of the uniformly Democratic Texas congressional delegation in the Sam Rayburn era, Bob Poage knew one had to "go along to get along," in accordance with Mr. Sam's dictum.[1] Poage navigated the cross currents of the Democratic Party in Texas well enough to be elected to Congress twenty-one consecutive terms from 1936 to 1976. A fixture in Waco, Poage started serving in the Texas legislature in 1925, and his father before that. Over all that time, Poage's relationship with the business community, notably with automobile dealer Jack Kultgen, newspaper publisher Harlan Fentress, his editor in Waco, Harry Provence, and Waco Chamber of Commerce president Sidney Dobbins proved essential in creating a highly effective lobbying strategy for directing federal resources to Central Texas. LBJ's indispensable help in the Senate, especially during his years as Senate Majority Leader (1955–61), enabled Poage to play a pivotal role in decision making that would shape life in Waco for generations. In Kultgen's words, "the building of the Waco Dam was the biggest single factor in the progress of Waco in the last hundred years."[2]

The ravages of 1957 spring rains in Texas captured the attention of the nation. The *Kalamazoo Gazette* story on Vietnamese visitors just below the headline eerily points to issues that would take down Lyndon Johnson eleven years later. *Photograph in author's collection.*

The circumstances facing Waco in the 1950s present an opportunity to bring together elements of environmental history, policy analysis, and biography to remind ourselves of what the American political system looked like when it worked, with the stark exception of near-paralysis on civil rights. The stains of Jim Crow and cultural constraints upon women so evident during this era receive minimal exposure in the telling of this project, although one finds some foreshadowing of greater inclusiveness. We see a cross section of the political system of that era at work, "with the bark off," but not without an admirable public-mindedness.[3] Consider Jack Kultgen's reflections on his service on the Brazos River Authority. It captures the essence of the transformative power of an inclusive approach to governance, because Kultgen addresses personal growth through civic engagement.

> Well, I don't think that you work for any agency of this type without learning a lot about yourself . . . it broadens you and teaches you a lot about things that you wouldn't otherwise know. I think that people who don't . . . take an interest in the affairs of their community are missing

a whole lot in their own education. You learn to get along with people. You learn to compromise things that you think there's only one side to . . . you learn you can't have everything just the way you want to have it but that there is a way that can be arrived at that gives both parties what they're entitled to. You learn to get things done.[4]

No wonder Kultgen and LBJ worked well together. Wheeler and dealer that he was, LBJ could have been an outstanding car salesman. Jack Kultgen, a transplanted midwesterner, hardly fit the mold of the back-slapping good ol' boy car dealer, but he got enough things done in Waco that a stretch of Interstate 35 there bears his name. The success of Bob Poage and Lyndon Johnson in bringing federal resources to Central Texas for flood prevention and control depended upon ambitious, civic-minded individuals like him.

Out of the Woods and into the Arms of God

Before air conditioning, the slowly turning rotisserie of a Central Texas summer seared into its people a dread of the flames of eternal damnation. Water represented salvation there, as generations of god-fearing residents could attest. Despite its cleansing properties, fire has been associated with Waco in two nationally notorious episodes. The burning and lynching of Jesse Washington by a mob in May 1916, discussed in a previous chapter, was among the starkest examples of race-based terrorism. More recently, the communal funeral pyre of David Koresh and his followers, members of a sect called the Branch Davidians, transfixed the nation's attention when it ignited April 19, 1993, during a dispute over federal authority. Given the notoriety of these episodes, perhaps few today would consider Waco a remarkable success story of federal-state-local relations, consummated not by flames but by water in the 1950s.

The combined effects of perennial floods in the Brazos River Valley with a deadly tornado through the city center in 1953 changed both the physical and political landscape, leading to a decade of intense interactions between Waco and Washington, DC, which would transform the city. Natural catastrophes led the century-old city along the historic Brazos River to reengineer its relationship with the river, as well. Since the story at hand involves the enormous endeavor of dam building in Central Texas, let us first consider the landscape and the issues it presented. The North, Middle, and South Bosque Rivers originate in limestone formations some 125 miles west of

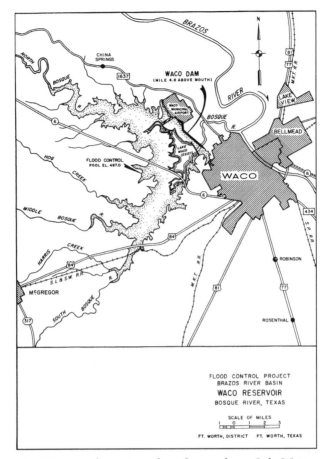

Constituents with questions about the new dam at Lake Waco
received copies of this Army Corps of Engineers map from Congressman Poage's office. *Courtesy W. R. Poage Legislative Library.*

Waco. The longest of these tributaries, the North Bosque, carries precious
spring water from Erath County before spilling into the Brazos River.[5] The
headwaters of the Middle and South Bosque form in Coryell County and
merge just a few river miles upstream from the modern dam site.[6] The three
main forks of the Bosque (Spanish for "woods" or "forest") provided potable water in sufficient quantities to sustain the city's residents for several
decades after the founding of Waco in 1849, but rapid growth and occasional
droughts brought recurring crises to the city. Characteristic of many riverside communities, the role of the artery in human affairs changed over time,

with the nature of each transition shaped by a love-hate relationship with a vital force that can destroy as surely as it can nurture.

Established at the same water-rich location chosen long before by a succession of Native American cultures, including the Waco (or Huaco) band of the Wichita nation, the city owed its early livelihood to cotton production and, by the 1870s, to rail transport.[7] The land use patterns established in this portion of the blackland prairie, which included the Brazos River system, reflected the influence of the river and its tributaries on soil conditions.[8] Cotton plantations on the rich bottomlands downstream from Waco prospered, in part because of heavy erosion upstream from the flash floods that scoured the feeder creeks gushing into the forks of larger tributaries like the Bosque and the Leon Rivers. The juncture of the Bosque and the Brazos at the city's north end became the site of Cameron Park, a gathering place for many generations to come—and come they did.[9]

Census tallies in 1870 enumerated 3,000 residents of Waco. The population tripled by 1900 and reached 35,000 by the time the Great War erupted in Europe in 1914.[10] As Waco's population swelled, city boosters pursued a wide range of economic development strategies in the late nineteenth and early twentieth centuries. Proposals to make the Brazos navigable from Waco to the Gulf took form, only to dissipate like the smoke rings of cigar-chomping dreamers. Such dreams led to the Panama Canal, reasoned Robert Lee Henry, a ten-term US representative (D-Waco, 1897–1917), who unsuccessfully promoted a system of locks on the Brazos, hoping to connect Waco businesses with the Gulf of Mexico just 420 river miles downstream.[11]

Among those who knew the Brazos Valley best, perhaps none captured the cycles of abuse and dependency between the river and those who lived in its sway better than chronicler John Graves, whose eulogy *Goodbye to a River* described the give and take between raw landscape and development from the late nineteenth century to the 1950s.

After the eighties the Brazos country needed rest. It pulled up its blanket of scrub oak and cedar and had itself a doze, a long one that is only now ending as the city money pulls away the blanket. The frontier had moved on and petered out, with most of its violence. The Brazos country ranched and farmed, or its people did—without knowing, most of them, any more about soft treatment of the land than their fathers and grandfathers had, so that they went on to compound the old error. They money-cropped when they could make the money crops grow, ... and where nothing else would grow they ran cattle, too many of them always, so that the grass went from the slopes and then the dirt, and the white lime rock showed through and the brush spread, and we've gone into that before. . . . In the end the country's sleep was one of exhaustion.[12]

These land-use patterns promoted erosion and siltation of the river, exacerbating an inevitable problem with water conservation. The Anglo machismo of the political culture of Central Texas in the 1920s did not promote regional cooperation and intergovernmental collaboration, as would be the case following the introduction of the New Deal. City officials in Waco determined the immediate challenge was increasing the drinking water supply, rather than flood control or a hydroelectric project.[13] Proponents of the project fended off critics who predicted the lake would "result in sickness and typhoid and would attract crap shooters, ukulele players and venereal bathers," all cavorting in the newly pooled Lake Waco. A petition drive organized by concerned mothers opposed to the dam called upon city leaders to use taxpayer money "for the construction of new schools." Opponents of the project even paid $7,500 to General George Washington Goethals, chief engineer for the Panama Canal, to review the plans for the proposed dam.[14]

Despite the spirited campaign against the dam, the dire circumstances facing Waco voters led them to approve $3.5 million for a project located at the convergence of the South and North forks of the Bosque, about four river miles above where the mainstream of the Bosque enters the Brazos.[15] No federal or state funds went into construction of this dam, owned and operated by the city of Waco. Engineers from W. E. Callahan Construction Company of Waco, Dallas, and Saint Louis determined that upwards of twenty billion gallons of "high grade water" coursed through the Bosque Hills on the way to the Brazos and the Gulf of Mexico. Throughout 1928 and 1929, heavy equipment reshaped the rugged countryside. When the work was done and the machinery fell silent, an earthen dam 4,700 feet long and 65 feet high symbolized a bright future for Wacoans. Capturing that water represented the "crowning achievement of Waco's 80 Years of Romantic History," or so nearly 54,000 city residents were told in May 1930 in the *Waco Tribune-Herald*, courtesy of a somewhat self-congratulatory advertisement W. E. Callahan placed.[16]

Despite the absence of data on incidents involving gambling, stringed instruments, or diseased bathers, critics of the dam eventually claimed vindication. Within fifteen years of its construction, erosion and siltation reduced the storage capacity of the newly formed Lake Waco from 39,378 acre-feet by nearly 50 percent, with only 22,030 acre-feet available for water storage in the mid-1940s. In short, the first dam at Lake Waco, conceived, funded, and constructed locally, served rather poorly. Even the heralded rugged individual, an iconic image in Central Texas, calls upon neighbors for a barn raising. The city of Waco took a different approach the next time.

Many Texas communities faced similar questions about how to deal with the cyclical problems associated with too little water, or too much, leading the Texas legislature to establish the Brazos River Authority (BRA) in 1929, a pioneering agency of its kind in the United States. The unprecedented state action indicated the seriousness of the water rights issues facing Texas. Charged at the outset with maintaining and distributing water supplies to communities along the river system, the self-supporting BRA later assumed responsibility for wastewater treatment and for monitoring water quality, using revenues from water sales to carry out its charges.[17] Evidence of the political significance of water management shows in the *Waco Farm and Labor Journal*, wherein editors termed Poage's assertion that incumbent Democratic congressman O. H. Cross had an "unsympathetic" record in terms of the Brazos River project to be "political propaganda in no uncertain language." Cross described Poage as "feverish to get himself in Congress at the expense of the Brazos River project."[18] As discussed in a previous chapter, Poage reversed the defeat from 1934 by beating Cross in the Democratic primary race two years later.

As the monumental Tennessee Valley Authority undertook its work in the East, the BRA completed a "Master Plan" calling for construction of dams at thirteen sites along the Brazos system. The first began in 1938 with a three-year project that would create Possum Kingdom Lake (later named Morris Shepherd Lake) in Palo Pinto County. Congressional action in 1939 to empower the Army Corps of Engineers to pursue flood control and water supply projects pointed toward a future wherein these water management issues would involve local, state, and federal stakeholders.[19]

By the time of the dedication of the dam at Possum Kingdom Lake in 1941, after the New Deal and escalating spending related to preparation for entry into World War II, one could see Uncle Sam's indelible footprints across the Central Texas landscape. With the help of the Civilian Conservation Corps, for example, Texas established several new state parks, including the Mother Neff State Park along the Leon River, another tributary of the Brazos downstream from Waco. Unfortunately, one of the BRA projects called for a dam to be constructed on the Leon near the town of Belton, meaning a portion of the CCC's work would be submerged when lake levels were high after the Belton dam was completed in April 1954.[20] Proximity to Camp Hood (as it was known prior to the Korean War) meant the newly filled Lake Belton would serve as the primary source of drinking water for the military base, which expanded quickly during the Cold War when powerful Texas legislators like Lyndon Johnson and Bob Poage directed defense appropriations back home. In 1957 the two collaborated on getting Waco's James Connally Air Force Base designated as the home of the Twelfth Air Force. As biographer Robert A. Caro detailed in *The Path to Power*, Johnson learned very early the value such massive projects could have for firms like Brown and Root, and their political allies.[21] These lessons were not lost on Bob Poage.

Johnson and Poage understood the political advantages of leaving communities considerable latitude with federal monies when tailoring projects to meet their needs. Backs could be scratched. Logs could roll. Local contractors could be rewarded or recruited for support in an election down the newly paved road. Local customs did not always promote efficient use of funds. Working on an NYA project in Waco, for example, meant setting up one Freshman College Center for white students at Baylor and another at Paul Quinn College for African American students.[22]

Johnson used a statewide advisory board for "Negro" projects, which would interface with local leaders, such as representatives of the Board of Trustees of Paul Quinn College. New connections among stakeholders led in some cases to lifelong alliances. Such is the case of Lyndon Johnson and Jack Kultgen. One of the first white men to be appointed to the Board of Trustees of Paul Quinn College, Kultgen saw Waco for the first time in 1936, when "East Waco was under two feet of water . . . this happened frequently. When you've got a segment of your city that's subject to floods of that kind, it means the people are just not going to build anything there that amounts to anything."[23] As co-owner of a Ford dealership in Waco, Kultgen played a pivotal role in the transformation of this storied Texas city. A devout Roman Catholic from the comparatively integrated Midwest, Kultgen left Chicago during the Great Depression to sell cars in the flood-prone Baptist stronghold of Jim Crow–era Waco. There, he teamed with Harry Bird, a successful grocer, to establish Bird-Kultgen Ford at Thirteenth Street and Franklin Avenue.

When World War II called citizens to service of all kinds, Kultgen followed Bird, now a "$1 a year man," to Washington, DC, to assist with home front logistics.[24] Bird's connections in the food business helped Kultgen land a job in the sugar rationing division of the Office of Price Administration (OPA), where he worked his way up to a regional directorship covering six states and thirteen district offices. "I had the whole office there," he recalled of his time spent at the Dallas OPA headquarters, "rent control, price control, shoe rationing, stove rationing, sugar rationing and meat rationing—everything."

In the corporate version of selective service, the Ford Motor Company had no vehicles to sell once production shifted to military necessities, so Kultgen seized the opportunity, thereby gaining experience that would make him an invaluable player in securing federal resources for Waco.

> I learned the workings of bureaucracy from the federal to the state level all the way down. You're a lot more patient with the United States government if you work for it a little while because you realize the huge size of it and the terrible problems about running it due to size and complexity.[25]

Like countless Americans of his generation, Jack Kultgen's eyes were opened by the war to a world unimaginably vast yet potentially responsive to properly channeled political skills. When he returned to Waco in 1946, Kultgen found that his experiences in the OPA gave him the skills to fully engage himself in civic affairs. For the next three decades, as Waco grew to 100,000 residents, Kultgen played a pivotal role in building the city's future.

James McEnteer's aforementioned study of the degree of influence Texans held in the United States determined that "thanks to the powerful Texas politicians in Washington, an inordinate share of the federal military budget was expended in Texas during and after World War II." These men "expanded the alliance with the national defense establishment . . . that transformed the Texas plains into a burgeoning national armory."[26] The US government proved to be hero and villain to Wacoans, who experienced that same curious patriotic cynicism found across the nation, as reported by Agnes Myers in her wartime travelogue, *America's Home Front*.[27] With victory in hand, the public vented its collective frustration in the 1946 elections, which in two-party states broomed out Democrats and swept in Republicans at all levels of government.

Jack Kultgen remembered his tour of duty as regional director of the OPA as a lesson in human nature. When it came to sugar rationing, for example, everybody hoarded it, but there wasn't too much to hoard. People on the whole were very patriotic. Of course, there were a lot of people that cheated. There were a lot of manufacturers, there were a lot of business people that cheated—ice cream people, soda water people and so on and so forth. But there was a lot of them that didn't cheat.[28]

Kultgen's assessment of the realities of wartime patriotism amid consumer resentment of federal intrusions into the marketplace underlined the nobility of sacrifice for the greater good, side by side with simple self-interest. Throughout many years working with the Brazos River Authority, he would exercise every means within his grasp to use the muscle and resources of the federal system so that the needs of the many would outweigh the needs of the few.[29]

All of this economic expansion and the movement of people greatly increased the need for a solution to the unresolved issues of flood control and water supply. Despite the presence of the Waco Army Air Field (renamed Connally Air Force Base upon reactivation in 1948 after closing in the brief postwar demobilization), meeting the needs of the Waco base did not approach the demands of Fort Hood and other major installations, so the community had to wait. The historic cycle of drought and flooding continued, however, and so did persistent lobbying for a new dam at the silt-filled Lake Waco. Determined to keep the project on the minds of members of Congress, between 1945 and 1956 these civic leaders "made 35 trips to Washington to push for the project," according to one local historian. At the center, along with Bob Poage, stood Harlan M. Fentress (owner of newspapers serving Austin, Port Arthur, Lufkin, and Waco), his Waco editor in chief Harry Provence, and Kultgen. Among a rotating roster of other Waco civic leaders, as evidenced by inclusion on a list of VIPs receiving telegram updates from LBJ, these three were omnipresent.[30]

In 1946, flood control issues on the Brazos upstream from Waco, near Hillsboro, led to federal approval for construction of the dam that created Lake Whitney, as anticipated in legislation enacted seven years earlier. Meanwhile, yet another deluge caused Waco to "nearly wash out during a flood."[31] Despite the construction of the dams creating the Belton and Whitney reservoirs, the postwar trend toward a reduced federal role slowed the pace of such massive projects, leaving disappointed Wacoans to strategize how to move to a higher rung on the priority ladder.

Bob Poage and Lyndon Johnson continued to win their respective House races as the Roosevelt coalition broke apart in the conservative resurgence after World War II, but it took Johnson's subsequent victory in a special election of the US Senate seat in Texas in 1949 to change the political calculus in Austin and Washington, and therefore, in Waco. Indeed, Poage's loyalty to Johnson paid off over the years, at least in terms of Waco receiving a stream of federal funds. As LBJ gained power in the Senate, Poage's clout increased proportionately. Consequently, civic-minded business leaders in Waco, like Jack Kultgen, gained significant influence on a broad swath of issues central to Waco's development. From Kultgen's oral memoirs, it appears that in these postwar years a shadow government emerged in Waco, consisting of a combination of elected officials and influential whites interested in circumventing problems:

we always had a loosely knit group around here. I think they call them the Committee of Fifty, although it included about forty or seventy or whatever. It was generally the idea that when some local emergency came along . . . you'd get together and probably get the combined ideas of people to find the answer to the problem.[32]

Out of this informal model arose the Waco Community Relations Committee. Consisting of "maybe a dozen people, maybe seven whites and five blacks—maybe that ratio—could be six and six, depending on who showed up. An equal number were invited."[33] Consisting of Kultgen, Mayor Joe Ward, and a rotating cast of businessmen, newspaper editors, clergy, and other opinion leaders, the group often dealt behind the scenes with tense race relations. Kultgen recollected an example of what might be termed pragmatic progressive accommodation:

For instance, we got in touch with the bottlers who hired drivers and hauled and delivered Coca Colas and things like this and stopped in the black areas. They demanded that they have black drivers in those areas—the dairies that delivered milk at that time and people like that. So, whenever there was a demand of this sort, why, we'd try to get people in that business together and talk it over with them and generally come up with a concession of some kind on both sides.[34]

This "come, let us reason together" style epitomized consensus politics and an emerging factor in the political culture of Anglo males in Central Texas in the Johnson era favored: tolerance. Although his own political skills were quite evident, Jack Kultgen never sought elective office, explaining that he "didn't want to ever want to have to express an opinion to get somebody to vote for me that I don't feel." While Johnson and Poage anticipated voter support in their respective Democratic primary races in the summer of 1946, Jack Kultgen returned to the automobile business in Waco with his partner Harry Bird. "I . . . have always been interested in civic affairs," he reflected years later.[35] In 1948 Kultgen's business colleagues in Waco elected him president of the Chamber of Commerce, but his range of interests and commitments continually expanded. Kultgen "just had to take over" the effort to build a new football stadium for Baylor University in 1949, because, as he acknowledged, "Baylor is a big element in this city and a very valuable element."[36]

By 1951 Kultgen's leadership role in the city and region seemed to grow exponentially, perhaps an indication that his OPA and business experience bridged the major factions within Waco. He led the Texas Good Roads Association ("simply lobbyists, if you want to call them that") from 1951 to 1955. Kultgen also served as chair of the Waco Community Chest in 1951. Given his midwestern roots, Kultgen clearly did not coast into these positions through the kind of familial entitlement that comes to the descendants of city founders. When Governor Alan Shivers named him to the board of the Brazos River Authority in 1951, he set the stage for Kultgen's greatest contribution to the future of Waco. Kultgen reflected:

I frankly don't remember how I got interested in water, except that Governor Shivers appointed me to the Brazos River Authority board, which then had its main office in Mineral Wells and had under its control the Possum Kingdom dam. That was the only dam they had. There was a measure that had been passed by Congress in the late thirties, I believe it was for twelve new dams all along the Brazos River by the Corps of Engineers . . . but the money had never been appropriated. So we decided that we'd go to work on that, which we did.[37]

Correspondence between Johnson and Kultgen throughout LBJ's years, but especially when he was Majority Leader, clearly demonstrated a close working relationship with the Ford dealer on issues grand and trivial. They exchanged letters regarding Kultgen's concerns about insufficient appropriations for cadets at the Merchant Marine Academy and the auto dealer's predictable endorsement of what would become the interstate highway system.

Kultgen tried to use Johnson's clout to get a parachutist to drop in on the Heart o' Texas Fair. He hosted a visit to Waco by Senator Johnson in late September of 1953, for which he received a typically effusive note to "thank you most sincerely for the many courtesies" and "excellent" lodging.[38]

The collaborative efforts of Jack Kultgen, Bob Poage, and Lyndon Johnson produced the results thousands of Wacoans prayed about for nearly a century: relief from the killer floods of the Brazos Valley. The system worked so well that the construction of the new dam at Lake Waco may represent the high-water mark for truly collaborative federalism in Central Texas.

The Heart of the Deal

In the dawn of the age of television in the 1950s, fans of Gene Autry, the famed singing cowboy of radio, film, and Saturday morning TV, represented a huge new market for souvenir items promoting the future owner of a major league baseball franchise. As the company stationery proudly proclaimed, "jeans, jackets and shirts," for Autry fans around the world came from J. Carroll Wood's shop in Waco. Like many successful Central Texans in the

House Agriculture Committee chairman Poage with gavel. *Courtesy W. R. Poage Legislative Library.*

post–World War II era, using his wealth to acquire lakefront property in a thirsty state appealed to him. He chose frontage on the original Lake Waco, never imagining that a new dam might one day raise lake levels and submerge his dream home. Writing to his friend Bob Poage on March 15, 1954, Wood stated, "if this dam is built as originally proposed, it would put me under water."[39]

Poage replied a few days later, attempting to distance himself from the intense lobbying effort underway on behalf of the dam project, while acknowledging he "had been discussing the possibilities both with our folks from Waco, who have been up here, and with the Army Engineers, and with the Chairman of the Committee in Congress." Poage assured Wood that "you are in a better position to decide what the local people are going to do than I am," but he also expressed his opinion that either Waco would have to do something on its own again or he expected that "we will ultimately get the federal government to build a large dam which will provide Waco with both water and flood protection."[40]

Acknowledging that the dam project anticipated by the Corps of Engineers would raise the water level twenty feet, "which would seriously affect all the surrounding property except that on the hills on the southeast side," Poage told Wood that he did not "really think there is any prospect of getting any action on this in the near future," and that Wood "will surely have several years in which you can use your property without any effect from this program, no matter if it were approved this year."[41] As it turned out, the groundbreaking ceremony for the new dam would take place little more than four years after this exchange. Poage's dim assessment of the prospects of ultimate success appears disingenuous in retrospect. For example, LBJ wrote to Kultgen on April 14, 1954, about the status of the dam in the House. "I have just talked to Bob Poage . . . regarding the possibility of setting a definite hearing on the Bosque Dam Project," referring to a meeting Poage had with Congressman Peter Mack (D-IL), chair of the House Subcommittee on Commerce and Finance. Election year politics arose as a topic of conversation between Kultgen and LBJ. On the same day LBJ wrote about Poage, Kultgen sent a letter to the senator that Johnson said gave him "strength and courage." Asking Kultgen to "please help to keep me informed of any significant developments in the Waco area," Johnson thanked him for offering to provide a campaign headquarters at the Roosevelt Hotel. Among his many other roles in the city, Kultgen served as hotel president. Both men understood how to attach themselves to those with power.

In terms of formal opposition to the project, Robert Brown, an attorney from nearby Gatesville, presented a three-page brief to the Flood Control Sub-Committee of the House Public Works Committee in anticipation of a hearing scheduled for May 13, 1954. Sidney Dobbins, president of the Waco Chamber of Commerce; Jack Kultgen; and newspaper publisher Harlan Fentress testified on behalf of the proposed dam at the same round of hearings. An upset Poage sent a letter to the Gatesville Chamber of Commerce and to the Gatesville Lions Club. Not mentioning names, Poage made it clear that he did not appreciate being undermined, stating "it had not occurred to me that any civic group in the valley of the Brazos or its tributaries—as Gatesville is—would for a moment protest this project which seems to me to be essential to the area."[42]

Taking the constituent to task, Poage wrote a letter to Attorney Brown that quoted none other than Abraham Lincoln, the personification of federal intrusiveness for many in the old Confederacy ninety years after their Lost Cause. "Let not him who has no house pull down the house of his neighbor."[43] A struggle between proponents of a new dam engineered and located upstream of the Brazos for flood control and those who advocated instead for a hydroelectric project on the Brazos itself threatened the whole endeavor. Poage never wavered from his emphasis on flood control. Complicating the legislative agenda further was the St. Lawrence Seaway bill, a priority of congressman George Dondero of Michigan, who chaired the Public Works committee. Writing to Sidney Dobbins on May 1 about the upcoming hearing, Poage shared his somewhat awkward political position. "I wish we could have been heard before the debate on the St. Lawrence Seaway Project on the floor. I still expect to vote against that project, but I will, of course, try to keep from giving any more offense than necessary to Mr. Dondero."[44] Although Poage, like Jack Kultgen, would consistently downplay his role in getting federal funding for the new dam at Lake Waco, the congressman's performance belies assertions that he did "nothing except lobbying with the members."[45]

On June 30, 1954, fifteen years after Congress first recognized the significance of water management issues in the Brazos Valley, Bob Poage sent a telegram to the usual VIPs in Waco announcing that the "full Public Works Committee approved Brazos Report this afternoon with $40 million authorized as the subcommittee had recommended."[46] This represented a breakthrough in the funding process in the House of Representatives, but it also seemed to reenergize opponents of the new project. An article appeared in the Waco Tribune-Herald hinting at the possibility of malfeasance with public

CHAPTER THREE

projects, specifically warning readers of "a possible reoccurrence of the famous 'Circle Development Company,'" referring to a scheme hatched in the
1930s by individuals hoping to reap ill-gotten gains from the construction of
the traffic circle on the south end of the city.[47] Nevertheless, the momentum
continued in the Senate. Within a month of action by the House Commerce
Committee, Johnson sent Kultgen a copy of the "Report of the Senate Committee on Public Works" that gave its blessing for inclusion of the Waco project with others on the Brazos River system.[48]

The ultimate determination of the water level of the lake proved the single
most important piece of insider information for property owners or speculators. Poage's critics accused him of deliberately hiding that information. With
the publisher and editor of the local paper as close friends, Poage tended to get
more positive coverage, such as the editorial that ran on November 16, 1954:

> There are two major hopes for advancing the Brazos (and Waco) dams
> in the next session. One of them is Bob Poage's energetic, tireless work
> in persuading his colleagues from Texas to support the plan and in win-
> ning friends for it among congressmen from other states. Coupled with
> this, of course, is the backing of Senator Lyndon B. Johnson and Senator
> Price Daniel, especially Johnson's.[49]

The principals held meetings in Waco during the postelection congressional recess. As prospects for a new dam improved, some members of the Chamber of Commerce evidently looked ahead to the day when the larger lake might
spark new opportunities.[50] For example, Poage wrote to Sidney Dobbins, in
April 1955, regarding an inquiry received from some chamber member considering "skeeter" or "paddle boats" on the new lake. Apparently the watercraft
available at the Tidal Basin in Washington inspired the entrepreneur. Poage
contacted Benjamin Hall, the boat concessionaire who informed the congressman that the widow of the man who built the boats intended to retain the
rights "for her teen-age son as she expects him to re-open the business after
he becomes older." Having advised Poage that these boats were not manufac-
tured at the present time, Mr. Hall allowed that he would give consideration
of reasonable offers for some used boats. Poage passed this all along to Harlan
Fentress, whom he told that Hall said, "the larger boats cost him a little over
$600 and the small boats about $450 each when they were new."[51]

If, as Reagan-era Republicans argued, a rising tide lifts all boats, then
it follows that a rising lake lifts investors. This entrepreneurial example, a

Harlan Fentress and LBJ at Waco Dam groundbreaking (mislabeled in the photo as "dedication"). *Courtesy Lyndon Baines Johnson Library and Museum and by special permission of the Fentress family.*

discussion of buying paddleboats to rent to carefree recreationists out for a day at the new, improved Lake Waco, exemplified the kind of stimulus Kultgen, Fentress, and Poage sought for Waco above and beyond the long-desired promise of flood control. Since decisions about lake levels could determine whether one owned prime lakefront property for speculators or a sunken parcel with an outbuilding housing catfish fifteen feet below the surface, the final determination could mean sink or swim, literally.

Another indication of the range of interests the project piqued came in the form of a petition signed by some five hundred people, directed to the US Army Corps of Engineers:

> We, the undersigned, do respectfully request that you discontinue your plans for acquiring in fee title any of the land above the 470' above sea level owned by K. H. Easley out of the site on which he has planned to relocate the Lake Waco Golf Course which will be inundated by the new Waco Reservoir, thereby releasing Mr. Easley to proceed with the

development of the new golf course without any further delay. As the Lake Waco Golf Course is the only public golf course in the Waco area and as Mr. Easley's new course is the only other such course completely planned and under construction, we, the undersigned citizens and participants in the game of golf will be without a golf course to play on unless Mr. Easley is permitted to complete his new course as planned.[52]

Winners and losers would emerge from the project, especially those losers with property on or near the banks of "old" Lake Waco, and those winners whose properties gained instant value from the expansion of the lake. Inevitably, grumbling losers gave way to what most people saw as progress. In the 1950s the local newspaper publisher and editor carried significant clout, and in the medium-sized city of Waco, the political culture found them deeply engaged with efforts of friendly persuasion. Winning federal funding for a new dam represented a top agenda item for these community boosters. Appearances at congressional hearings were carefully coordinated with Bob Poage.

For example, Harlan Fentress received this background letter from Poage concerning final arrangements for their visit to Washington in May 1955, when they would testify before a House committee:

> I know Joe Evins, John Fogarty and Ben Jensen personally, and I do not expect any trouble from them. I do not know Mr. Murray and although I know Mr. Hand, I do not know him as well as I do the first three. I will try to find an opportunity to discuss the project with each of these men and will, of course, keep you advised of any difficulties that might arise.
> I presume that you boys will be here a day or two in advance of the hearing anyway, and that you will have an opportunity to meet some, if not all, of the members of the Sub-Committee before the hearing. Yesterday afternoon, Arthur Perry [Johnson aide] called. He stated that inasmuch as your group will be here around the 11th of May, that he has been trying to get the Senate Committee to grant you a hearing on the morning of May 11, but up to the present time he has been unsuccessful.[53]

Previous correspondence between Kultgen and Johnson addressed maritime issues, so perhaps the "trip situation" Johnson aide Walter Jenkins referred to in late March 1955 referred to something other than a reward for a loyal Democrat in Waco.

In any case, Jenkins referred to the logistics of a cruise to Hawaii (a "Navy orientation program") Lyndon Johnson arranged for Jack Kultgen that June. The trading of political favors cementing alliances intensified in that buoyant spring after Johnson's ascension to the newly powerful role of Senate Majority Leader after the November 1954 elections gave Democrats the smallest of majorities. Unprecedented national news media coverage of LBJ followed, accompanied by extensive profiles in the Texas press. Just two days before a near-fatal heart attack felled Johnson, Kultgen and newspaper publisher Harlan Fentress received grateful praise from him for their efforts to highlight LBJ's contributions to the quality of life in the Waco press.[54]

Ironically, the political momentum to minimize the risk of natural disaster by providing resources for a new flood control dam in the summer of 1954 can be traced to the plight of the city in the aftermath of the horrific damage wrought by the tornado of May 11, 1953, that put Waco in the national spotlight. As discussed in the next chapter, the twister opened the funnel for federal disaster relief. Whatever reservations other cities may have had about embracing new ventures in partnership with the federal government, Kultgen praised the aggressiveness shown by Waco in obtaining federal funding for "six or seven" urban renewal projects.[55]

The second factor involves Lyndon Johnson securing the position of Majority Leader within a few days after the 1954 elections.[56] Bob Poage's loyalty to Lyndon Johnson over the previous eighteen years paid off, and Waco would see increased federal support that effectively previewed the urban development strategies of the Great Society. Virtually all LBJ biographers describe Johnson's ability to maneuver the Senate agenda for action, but Poage leveraged his experience and the power of the Texas delegation artfully during that window of opportunity as well. Their combined ability to secure federal funds for the new dam at Lake Waco increased incalculably when an entry titled "Loss of Water Projects Points Up Need for Dam at Waco, Tex." appeared in the Congressional Record Appendix on May 24, 1955. Senator Johnson remarked, "some two weeks ago I appeared with several citizens from Waco, Tex., before a Senate subcommittee to urge an appropriation to complete final plans for the building of the Waco Dam and Reservoir, an authorized project on the Bosque River, in Texas."

In the extension, Johnson cited an article from *Waco Tribune-Herald* of May 20, 1955, describing the city's plight. "Waco lost a 6-month supply of water Thursday because Lake Waco couldn't hold a drop of the new rainfall on the Bosque watersheds, and the loss was called a perfect illustration of why a new and larger dam on the Bosque is needed." Referring to the recent lobbying effort by Waco representatives, LBJ reminded his colleagues that Bennet Watson of the Waco Chamber of Commerce was in Washington "a week ago, asking for $100,000 this year to complete final plans." Clearly, Johnson intended to finally commit the Senate to enabling Waco to do something about "its reservoir being filled with silt."[57]

Given Lyndon Johnson's legendary cloakroom tactics in the art of persuasion, these official remarks likely extended even further, with Texas downpours described as "toad chokers" and far earthier colorful metaphors that enliven the aural landscape of Central Texas and the Hill Country. Bob Poage's letters to constituents and colleagues characteristically contain phrasing reflecting the speech pattern of a "good ol' boy." His efforts to line up votes to support the planning funds generated a favorable response from several House members.

After the skies opened up with some particularly fearsome storms that spring, Poage sent a letter to Representative John E. Fogarty (D-Rhode Island) of the Public Works Sub-Committee of the House Appropriations Committee:

> You may be interested in seeing just what has happened in Central Texas recently. You will note that while last year we received less than 15 inches of rain in Waco during the entire twelve months, some of the areas in Central Texas got a full 15 inches last week. As we tried to explain to your Committee, we need a dam on the Bosque to protect against the 15 inches of rain in one week. We also need a dam to protect against the years when we don't get 15 inches a year. You will recall that we are asking your Committee to retain the $100,000 recommended by the Engineers for planning work for the Waco Reservoir. While you were unable to be present at the hearing when our group discussed this matter, we do appreciate the interest you have taken and the help you have extended in this matter.[58]

Poage mailed at least three more letters on May 24, 1955: one to Chair of Public Works Sub-Committee Joe L. Evins (D-Tennessee) and another to members Ben J. Jensen (Iowa) and James C. Murray (D-Illinois) of the Public Works Sub-Committee. On May 27, 1955, Representative T. Millet Hand (R-New Jersey) thanked Poage for "giving me your views on the need for a dam on the Bosque to protect Waco and other areas in Central Texas against too little or too much rainfall. Your thoughts are helpful, and will have my attention."[59] Eighteen years of cultivating relationships in the House paid off.

Poage's mailbox also contained several letters from constituents, some who wrote on multiple occasions, sometimes prompting a characteristically folksy, familiar reply from the congressman. Sam McCracken, for example, wrote often enough that he began one message by noting that "me and this old typewriter are about worn out" before launching into his questions and opinions about the proposed new dam and the effect it would have on property owners.[60] Sidestepping McCracken's pointed commentary, Poage sought safer ground, explaining, "Mama told me that you had called when I was in Texas, but I was not at the house. I am sorry I did not get to see you."

In the weeks following Johnson's heart attack, aides Walter Jenkins, Booth Mooney, and, of course, Lady Bird handled waves of correspondence urging a speedy recovery to the senator, who skirted death when stricken on July 2, 1955. At forty-six years of age, Johnson's appetite for whiskey, tobacco, and barbecue proved a bad combination with his work habits, temperament, and genes. Poage did not partake of the bourbon and branch water sessions that lubricated the legislative process, but the friendship that developed over time between Mrs. Poage and Mrs. Johnson added an important dimension to the relationship between the two men. This appeared to be the case especially in the aftermath of the health scare. Kultgen kept in close contact with the Johnsons, too, though the formality of Lady Bird's letter to him on August 4, 1955—she does not refer to him as Jack, but as Mr. Kultgen—suggests that he had not been to the LBJ ranch, unlike the Poages. Grateful for Kultgen's expression of concerns to Johnson assistants Walter Jenkins and Jesse Kellam, Lady Bird expressed confidence about the prognosis for recovery and closed by stating, "Lyndon appreciates your interest so much and I just want to drop you this note of thanks."[61]

Correspondence points to a growing appreciation of Kultgen's role in the civic life of Waco; it shows Poage's admiration for the businessman. Thanks to the strong ties nurtured with Kultgen, the Johnsons could stay at the Roosevelt Hotel in Waco as Jack Kultgen's guests, as they did in late November after the senator spoke in nearby Whitney. On Thanksgiving Day, LBJ dictated a letter to Walter Jenkins, thanking Kultgen for "fine accommodations . . . and for the beautiful flowers."[62] Three days later, Kultgen received an even more effusive letter from Johnson, stating, "You really proved what I have known all the time—when you need a job done in Waco, call on Jack Kultgen."[63] As Christmas approached, they exchanged letters yet again, leading Johnson to comment, "It has been wonderful to see and hear from you often this fall. I am so grateful for your friendship, and I look forward to a continuation in the coming years."[64]

The Johnson "treatment" occupies a special place among students of the art of politics. These examples of his ability to cement relationships with opinion leaders outside of the Senate cloakroom with a well-crafted letter indicate that he had not lost the touch so evident early in his NYA and House career. His aides learned well under his infamous tutelage.

Progress in Washington, DC, in both the House and Senate, spurred rumors to circulate throughout the summer among property owners around the proposed dam site. Rumors also circulated about the negative impacts of the project. Poage sent a letter to Mrs. Edith Scott of Route 1, Box 110, Waco, Texas, on September 10, 1955, in response to the plain folded notecard she sent him the day before: "Please let us know where they will start the lake as we are having trouble finding us a place to live do we have very much time." Poage's reply revealed something of his "bedside manner," as he helped a woman sort out what would soon happen to her because of the project he championed. Choosing his words carefully, but revealing his own uncertainty about timelines, he wrote:

> It would be some time before you would have to move, unless you live directly where the dam will be built. If work starts on the dam, it will probably take 4 or 5 years to complete it. I think therefore that you can safely count on several years in your present location . . . my office has a map of the proposed construction, which they will be glad to show you if you care to come by.[65]

The actual time to completion was twice as long as Poage had advised Mrs. Scott and other constituents. When confronted about the proposed expansion of Lake Waco, Bob Poage depended heavily upon information he received from the Army Corps of Engineers. Poage relayed updates from Colonel Harry Fisher, the district engineer who oversaw much of the project, back to interested citizens. Many of the letters from Fisher show the ongoing uncertainties about funding. Fisher reported on November 30, 1955, "engineering planning work, being accomplished with the $100,000 appropriated during the last session of Congress, is on schedule." He reminded Poage that this amount represented only 25 percent of the funds needed for the engineering studies that precede actual construction, stating, "in view of the progress now being made, I am confident that these planning funds will be expended by the end of this fiscal year."[66]

Shortly after Congress reconvened in January 1956, Poage heard again from Sam McCracken, whose questions suggest an element of suspicion about federal spending habits:

> We would like to know why, we should spend 12 to 18, million dollars, more by, trying to build a dam, below our present dam, and Utilities when we could go up the North Bosque, above the Dehay bridge, and build one almost as big as The Whitney Dam. I have made three copies of this letter, and wonder, if you would permit me to send, one, to, EISENHOWER, NIXON, and BENSON?"[67]

This citizen's obvious disappointment in the spending habits of Congress and the Army Corps of Engineers did not appear to carry over to expenses incurred by the Department of Agriculture, for in a handwritten postscript, he implores, "Please have the department to send me the *Free* Booklets or Pamphlets on the propagation of Pecans."[68]

The issue of where to locate the dam generated several constituent remedies early in 1956. Some enclosed a sketch of the proposed alternative, as did a citizen named W. P. Lester Jr., who illustrated placement of the dam one mile farther downstream, to which Poage pointed out, "The engineers are supposed to have considered all of these possible sites and to have determined that the general area they are now planning is the one most feasible." This nonjudgmental response represented Poage's stock answer to this kind of citizen input.[69]

Constituent service could engage citizens directly with the Corps of Engineers, but even this attempt to relieve uncertainty ultimately depended on the political process in Washington. When the owner of the Fulton Gin in the riverside town of South Bosque wrote to Poage in February 1956 regarding his desire to move his gin before the land was flooded from the new dam, he got attention, but little satisfaction. Colonel Harry Fisher of the Corps of Engineers and Poage's office responded to his inquiries right away, but told him no action could be taken unless Congress had approved the funding. Poage sent him copies of the Corps of Engineers' pamphlet published by their Fort Worth District office titled "LAND for Flood Control." The concluding statement of the fourteen-page guide to the finer points of eminent domain property seizures reads, "The Corps of Engineers will be pleased to assist you."[70]

The prospect of rising waters meant something altogether different for E. F. Grimes, a resident of the nearby village of Clifton. He used stationery from the Equitable Life Insurance Society of the United States to promote the importance of the project to fishing opportunities arising through proper management of the

> upper reaches of the Bosque Rivers, prior to or in conjunction with the new dam below the present Lake Waco Dam. Storage of water in these installations will provide normal flow of the streams, which will produce a balanced condition for the best fish life, keep the steams [*sic*] clean of sewage contamination, as well as provide replenishing supplies of water for the needs of the City of Waco, plus the control of flood waters. This matter has been discussed in several Sportsmans and Anglers Clubs in this area, and they feel that such a dam location near China Springs and Iredell on the North Bosque River, near the intersection of Bluff Creek and Middle Bosque River just north of the City of Crawford would be fine.[71]

With varied interests in his district to contend with, Poage still found himself responding to citizen concerns in guarded language. In a letter to Harlan Fentress and Sidney Dobbins dated January 21, 1956, Poage's diagnosis and prescription suggests the House tended to be stingier than the Senate with regard to funding the project. Referring to a newspaper report from a Texas journalist making inroads on the Washington beat, Poage relayed:

> You doubtless have seen the story by Sarah McClendon to the effect that the Bureau of the Budget has recommended to the Congress that $100,000 be appropriated to carry on planning. . . . I hope that you are not disappointed. . . . I had hoped, however, that this year the Bureau of the Budget would recommend the full amount that would be needed for planning, which I recall was $400,000. I am wondering if we should make an attempt to get the additional amount needed (about $300,000) either in the House Appropriations Committee, or better still, to see if we can get Lyndon and Price to use their influence in raising the total appropriation in the Senate.[72] The latter procedure will probably be easier, but I shall, of course, be glad to do what I can on the House side if you think it is advisable. Your thoughts on this matter would be appreciated.[73]

A letter from Walter Jenkins to Jack Kultgen indicated the potential impact from a "negative report" the senator received requiring answers from the Brazos River Authority about "objections raised" by the Army Corps of Engineers in February 1956.[74]

After more discussion, Kultgen, Harry Provence of the Waco Chamber of Commerce, and city officials geared up for another trek to Washington for a round of hearings, fortified by voter approval of a $6 million dollar bond issue aimed at expansion of facilities to handle the anticipated increase in the water supply. A telegram from Poage to Sidney Dobbins at the chamber explained that they had two weeks notice to prepare for the Appropriations Committee; flood control projects were on the docket for the last two weeks of March 1956.[75] Poage's calculation of Johnson's critical role in the pursuit of $300,000 for planning funds proved on target.

The Wacoans contemplated a repeat performance before the Senate Appropriations Public Works Subcommittee in April or May, but after considering ill-fitting schedules, Walter Jenkins suggested to Kultgen that submitting the report by mail would eliminate the necessity for "a personal trip here to be heard."[76] LBJ confirmed inclusion of Kultgen's statement encouraging support for increased funding for the Waco dam in the "Record of the Hearing on the Waco Dam" on May 15, emphasizing the "strong plea" he delivered to the members personally. As if winking by mail, Johnson concluded, "I hope the Committee may see fit to grant it."[77]

In early June, LBJ sent a telegram to Poage as well as to Jack Kultgen, Harlan Fentress, and Sidney Dobbins of the Waco Chamber of Commerce. The brief communiqué spelled out Waco's future in just ten words: "Senate Appropriations Committee has approved $300,000 for planning Waco Reservoir."[78] Almost twenty years later, Kultgen downplayed his role in the lobbying process:

> We began getting money appropriated . . . we wanted Waco Dam built
> because Waco is the heart of the deal, I think, between all of us—
> and when I say all of us I'm talkin' about Harlan Fentress and Harry
> Provence and Sid Dobbins and various mayors of Waco and myself.
> Why, we made—I think we had an actual count of forty-two trips to
> Washington in connection with these various dams, helping appear
> before legislative committees. It was more or less routine because I suppose it would have come anyway.[79]

Others differed with this modest assessment and said so. Kultgen received a letter from attorney John D. McCall of Dallas distributing the credit: "Congratulations . . . I see the Committee has approved $300,000 for planning for the Waco Dam. I am sending this to Bob Poage because he is entitled to a big share of the congratulations."[80]

With publisher Harlan Fentress part of the inner circle on the dam project, the local newspaper alternately played the role of doomsayer, cheerleader, or gadfly, as needed. When the unrelenting heat of the summer of 1956 carried well past Labor Day, the *Tribune-Herald* reported that Lake Waco held but two months of drinking water. Seeing no sense in wallowing in negativity, the paper extended an invitation to the public on behalf of lake superintendent Turner and water superintendent Harlin:

> to come out and get as much of the exposed lake bottom as they can haul away free. It is alluvial soil and fertile. Two years ago the water department issued the same invitation; Wacoans went out there in large numbers and about the time the movement got started it rained cats and dogs and little gunboats.[81]

By this time Jack Kultgen's attention had turned to another federally funded project for Waco: a new building to serve as headquarters of the Flying Training Air Force located there in the latest incarnation of the Waco Air Field from World War II. Following Kultgen's attendance at the 1956 Democratic Convention in Chicago in August, LBJ expressed gratitude, indicating he knew Kultgen "did a great deal to keep things so well in hand." In closing remarks, LBJ reminded his Waco ally to contact him "if there is anything I can do on the Waco Dam, the FLYTAF Building, or any of the other matters affecting Waco."[82] Pursuant to the project, Kultgen and other Waco dignitaries met with General Kelly at the Pentagon on October 2. Someone else must have been minding the car dealership as Ford unveiled its 1957 models that fall, because Jack Kultgen followed up that meeting with another session about the budget for the dam with the Army Corps of Engineers on October 11.

Hopeful news came for parched Waco residents a few weeks later from Colonel Harry Fisher of the Corps of Engineers, when he confirmed the "level of the new reservoir will be 20 feet higher than the present Lake Waco Dam." Speaking in October 1956, Fisher assured anxious listeners that the planning process would keep apace and allowed that the "construction could begin in late 1957 or early 1958, if Congress provides the money." The colonel demonstrated good public relations skills by putting the long-anticipated project in a broader context, while heaping praise on stakeholders:

> As far back as the late '30s, the Corps of Engineers, at the suggestion of local interests and at the specific request of the Congress, has been active in developing the water resources of the Brazos basin. In this effort we have worked in close cooperation with the BRA, which as an agency of the State of Texas, represents the State and, together with local leaders provides a partnership under which our joint plans are developed. In 1954 Congress authorized a plan calling for the development of six additional reservoir projects on tributary streams . . . with the active support of the Honorable Bob Poage and the truly amazing vitality of many civic leaders here.[83]

As the public came to grips with the implications of the project for their own personal circumstances, a predictable increase in constituent contacts came to Poage's district office in Waco. The day after the Waco newspaper accounts of Fisher's remarks appeared, an assistant encountered a citizen digging for information about the future of their burial plots at the Greenwood Cemetery, located near Speegleville, a valley community subject to submersion by the lake waters. Mrs. Bennett, holder of the plots,

> wants to know if this cemetery will be moved because of the Waco Dam and if so, whether the government will bear the cost of moving the bodies to another cemetery in this area. If the cemetery is to be moved, she wants to place the bodies of her relatives in a perpetual cemetery.[84]

Within the next few weeks, Poage followed up with a phone call to Mrs. Bennett advising the family to

> hold off on this for a couple of years and see how the dam was finalized, etc. But that the general policy was to buy another cemetery site and move all the bodies to that site, but that if you wanted to move them to some other site, they would pay the cost of moving the body but not the cost of another lot.[85]

With each step of the planning process, speculators learned of the fate of their ambitious dreams. From time to time it fell to Bob Poage to dash the last hopes of the entrepreneurs, such as he did to those behind the idea of using the increased capacity of the lake to establish an ordnance plant for Cold War munitions. In a letter to Leon Dollens of the Waco Chamber of Commerce, Poage refers to the receipt of "documentary evidence that deep water was a prerequisite . . . I am sorry that we cannot hope to get anywhere with this project, but certainly it is better to try and fail than to pass up some possibility that might have worked out."[86]

One gets the sense that the coalition of supporters for a new dam and a greatly expanded Lake Waco showed signs of unraveling somewhat in the late winter and early spring of 1957. A report from the Soil Conservation District added to the sense of urgency by announcing that twenty-five years of siltation had filled in 60 percent of the lake's storage capacity. According to the study, by 1973 Lake Waco would no longer be a source of water for a projected 100,000 residents. Some city leaders considered the option of foregoing federal support and repeating the strategy of the late 1920s, when the original dam came from entirely local funds. The city of Waco adopted a resolution on February 12, 1957, indicating support for the new dam, a decision echoed in mid-April by the Brazos River Authority, under the leadership of Jack Kultgen.[87] In the interim, Sidney Dobbins met with General Persons of the Army Corps of Engineers and reported to Poage that the planning costs for the early stages of dam construction could amount to $400,000 in fiscal year 1958. Poage's reply suggested the Senate held all of the cards at that stage.

When Poage wrote to Sam Rayburn on April 12, 1957, however, he voiced fear that "if we do not get any construction started that the demand may become irresistible for the city to go out and build a small lake." Poage believed that a small demonstration of good faith by the federal government could help. "We just need enough to stop the agitation for a separate city dam. We think $250,000 for construction purposes will do this."[88] At some point during this period, the strategy emerged of the city of Waco putting forward $250,000 through the Brazos River Authority as a demonstration of commitment, a move approved by voters by an astounding margin of 44–1. It would take time, but the strategy worked in giving advocates of the project in Washington the leverage necessary to win the funding battles looming as the nation slid into recession in 1957.[89]

The dam would serve the dual purpose of flood control and water conservation; it would supply the city's water needs. But perhaps after five years of drought the memories of floods subsided much as water itself recedes. Hydrologists advising Waco civic leaders in 1954 reported that the Brazos near

Waco measures "a bankful capacity of 65,000 cubic feet per second . . . there have been floods in this area of over 350,000 cubic feet per second."[90] Terrifying tales of children and livestock being swept away never lost their morbid appeal. The victims rarely had any warning, as John Graves recounted in *Goodbye to a River*:

> You don't have to be an old-timer in that country to remember when it was common, there being no dams above to take the shock, for a three- or four-foot curl of angry red water to roar around a bend upon a party swimming in quiet pools under a blue sky. A cloudburst far out on the plains could cause that.[91]

Deep into another dry spring, Kultgen made plans for more meetings on April 24 in Washington with General Persons of the Army Corps of Engineers. An abrupt change in the weather put the conversation in a more urgent context.[92] The deluge of April 19, 1957, marked the end of the five-year drought, seeming as it might make up for the lost years of rainfall all at once. Cameron Park, on the north side of the city, attracted many families on spring days like that Friday, so when the raging forks of the Bosque joined a few miles upstream from the park and entered the Brazos, its sudden power left "stranded people in pecan trees in Cameron Park and washed 60 cows away."[93] The churning horror of the waters added a chapter to the local folklore, which was replete with tales of five hundred fatalities along the Brazos system over the previous fifty years, and gave worried parents cautionary tales to tell wide-eyed children. In the preceding half-century, annual losses from flooding in the lower third of the Brazos basin averaged some $9.8 million, with untold human tragedy hidden in those estimates.[94]

Poage's reputation for effectiveness may have suffered in Waco as frustrations grew. A letter from Lou Holze, the local music store impresario, written two weeks after the April flood, echoed some of this feeling. Holze praised Poage, then delivered the real message: "but we really need to start this construction this year and I know everyone who is interested in the future of Waco agrees to the importance of getting more done this year." Holze went on to remind Poage of his service on the local flood control committee, saying, "everyone agreed that no time can be lost in taking immediate steps in that direction."[95] The reply to Holze conveyed an essential political truth that resonates across the decades, as Poage confronted the gap between needs and resources: "Everybody wants to reduce the budget and to reduce taxes, but we all try to maintain our individual projects. I want both a reduction in the budget and some money for the Waco dam."[96]

Twenty years after taking the oath of office for the first time, Bob Poage, and his fellow members, voted on funding one of his major priorities. Between Poage's personal diplomacy among House members, the ongoing pubic relations effort of Kultgen and his allies, and a supporting storm from Mother Nature, the tipping point came on June 19, 1957. Lyndon Johnson did his part in the Senate, and the congressman from Waco did his. A relieved Poage shot off a telegram to Harry Provence at the Waco *Tribune-Herald* that the House finally passed a flood control appropriations bill including $150,000 to complete planning and giving authority to engineers to use the $250,000 appropriated by the city of Waco. The strategy of priming the federal pump with locally committed funds worked beautifully, and the project moved forward, with the Fentress-owned press keeping the story front and center. When Johnson traveled to Waco in early November, Kultgen put him up again at the Roosevelt Hotel. Johnson's thank-you note on November 4 expressed appreciation for the "beautiful flowers," and referred to a party he and Kultgen attended at the home of Waco businessman Woody Callan, founder of the Central Freight Company.[97]

That celebration among some of Waco's new generation of progressive Democratic entrepreneurs, festive as it surely must have been, anticipated the next requisite step: the president's budget. Back in Washington after the Christmas holiday recess, Johnson told Poage that Eisenhower's new budget proposal for fiscal 1959 included the first $1,000,000 for construction.[98] Harlan Fentress's *Waco Tribune-Herald* crowed on January 19, 1958:

> The $40,000,000 project is being developed in close cooperation and partnership with the BRA and the City of Waco. . . . To serve the city of Waco, the Federal government will provide conservation storage space in the new reservoir equal to that in the existing lake, and the city will contract with the BRA for additional conservation storage space. The cost of this additional storage space will be paid by the local people under a contract between the BRA and the federal government. Based on an equitable percentage of the total cost of the undertaking, it is estimated at about $6,000,000.[99]

This model of planning, funding, and constructing a dam morphed as it went along, since all parties found themselves in a new kind of partnership.

Poage recognized his own journey away from ideological posturing to prag-matism. Responding to charges leveled by Baylor law professor Dr. Angus McSwain Jr. that the dam represented "federal encroachment," Poage stated:

there has to be some compromise between the extreme views which lead to complete anarchy on one side and the extremity of socialism on the other side. As a practical matter, we are going to have government and we are going to have more, not less.[100]

The collective lessons of the New Deal and World War II seem well learned in this symbiotic loop of shared responsibility. In this arrangement, the US government built a dam and contracted with a state agency (BRA). The feds sold to the BRA water captured by the dam, which the BRA would then sell to the city of Waco. As Mayor Truett Smith explained it in advance of a referendum on the project, "the cost of the city's participation will be paid off by sale of city-owned land around the lake to the federal government with the balance of the cost paid in 50 annual payments at 2 ½ percent inter-est."[101] The local homeowner or business paid the city of Waco, enabling the city to meet its obligations. As Jack Kultgen explained:

The BRA . . . was the one agency that could and would and did contract with the United States government to buy all of the conservation water that would be created in the Brazos River by all of the conservation and flood control dams that the government proposed to build. Had they not done so, the government would not have built these.[102]

None dared call it socialized water. On the contrary, praise came in heaps to the city, even if at times it looked like a mutual admiration society. For example, on February 17, 1958, Colonel Walter Wells, a colleague of Colo-nel Harry Fisher with the Army Corps of Engineers, spoke to Rotarians at the Roosevelt Hotel (where else?) of the "excellent cooperation between Wacoans, BRA members, congressmen and representatives in Washing-ton," which allowed the project to move ahead faster than anticipated. Wells congratulated Wacoans for "an almost impossible job of getting the lake au-thorized and for offering the advance of the $250,000 of the city's share of the cost of the reservoir to get work started this year."[103] This kind of ritual-ized cheerleading served as a reminder to the many stakeholders that they worked toward a common goal, undoubtedly exaggerating the actual level of cooperation, but required for the occasion.

A *Report of the Comptroller General* issued at the time of the dam's completion in 1965 described the terms of the contract:

> the contract was executed on March 1, 1958, and approved by the Secretary of the Army on April 15, 1958. Costs estimated then at $42,570,000, of which the BRA's share was $5,871,050. Of the Authority's share, $250,000 was to be paid in advance, with a balance to be paid in fifty equal annual installments of $193,353.46 including interest of 2.5%.[104]

A federal commission charged with identifying long-term water issues Eisenhower established in 1958 took Jack Kultgen away from the presidency of the BRA; he would spend the next four years on "the most definitive report that's ever been published on the rivers of Texas."[105] Kultgen's memories of the project convey his idealism about what could be achieved for the common good, if only people had the resources to determine a consensus course of action:

> We had forty-four engineers on our staff ... we got all sorts of reports. We asked each city and each industry along each river to give us its requirements for the next fifty years; we studied those and then came up with a story of how much water was going to be needed in these rivers for the next hundred years ... the Brazos was the only river in Texas that had just about all that it would need.[106]

Reflecting on the difficult politics surrounding water issues in Texas, Kultgen sounded more like a philosophical cowboy than a wheeler-dealer of Fords, saying, "when you start fighting about water, you've got the most violent fight that you can have, because the fight over the water hole has always been that."[107] Without question, Jack Kultgen's leadership in promoting the project positioned Waco to achieve a political and engineering feat that would define life in that city for as far as the eye could see. Because of the strength and unity of the team of Jack Kultgen, Bob Poage, and Lyndon Johnson, the new dam would be built at Bluebonnet Cliff overlooking the merging forks of the Bosque.

The president's 1959 budget proposal calling for $1,000,000 in construction funds for the Waco reservoir offered evidence progress had been made, but the contingent maintained hopes for an increase as the budget worked its way through Congress. Kultgen jumped right on the issue, as evidenced by Walter Jenkins's response on January 15, 1958:

> As far as the money for the Waco dam is concerned, we, of course, had hoped it would be more also. You know we are going to do everything we can on the Senate side. I would, however, suggest—if you have not already done so—work through Bob Poage to see what can be done on the House side. We have no way of knowing whether or not we will be successful in the matter, but we are certainly going to try to get all we can for that project.[108]

Jenkins's guarded tone reflected the realities of the impact of the recession on spending patterns on Capitol Hill. The recession of 1957–58 made restraint the byword of both parties. For the Democrats to lobby for expenditures beyond the $1 million in the Eisenhower budget, the Senate Majority Leader would have to find cuts elsewhere.

Bob Poage wrote to Harlan Fentress after a round of hearings the publisher could not attend in May 1958: "I felt that our group made a very creditable presentation and I am very hopeful that we will get an increase in the money available for the Waco Dam." Evidently frustrated by the fiefdoms in the House that would stall much of JFK's legislative agenda a few years later, Poage then pointed to the pivotal player. "I think, however, if we do it must come, as usual, through the Senate," he acknowledged. "Lyndon made an appearance at the Senate Committee, but as you will realize the real test of the matter is his insistence to the Appropriations Committee that additional money be included for our project. I think he will insist on this."[109]

Insist he did, which resulted in adoption of a budget in early July 1958 calling for $1.8 million for the Waco dam, almost double what the Eisenhower proposal outlined. Characteristically, LBJ announced the breakthrough in the telegram sent to the Waco team on July 3.[110] The timing proved exquisite, with LBJ and Bob Poage scheduled to attend a groundbreaking ceremony for the dam in Waco on July 5. The Johnsonian flare for the dramatic never more evident, the stage was set for a marvelous fireworks display in Waco that Independence Day. A great deal of groundwork, literally, allowed this celebratory moment to occur. The accelerated schedule Colonel Wells referred to during his remarks to the Waco Rotarians back in February meant that the process of awarding contracts would begin in the spring. Despite the concerns expressed a few years earlier about possible insider deals on such a huge project, there appears to have been a clean competitive bidding process from the start. In early May 1958, Wells and Poage received an update from Lieutenant Colonel J. H. Hottenroth of the Corps of Engineers, indicating the extraordinarily detailed work of preparing materials for prospective contractors to review had

> progressed to the point of readiness to advertise for bids on construction of the first segment of the project . . . a 2,750-foot-long segment of earthen embankment north of the Bosque River in the vicinity of the Waco Municipal Airport. We propose to advertise for bids on this embankment on 10 May 1958, and to open bids on 10 June 1958.[111]

This meant the least appealing aspect of this great leap forward in Central Texas, that is, seizure of privately held land, commenced forthwith. In another letter to Poage, later that month, Lieutenant Colonel Hottenroth addressed current condemnation proceedings, which did not get off to a smooth start. Hottenroth reported:

> To date, negotiations with owners of two of the three tracts needed for the initial phase of construction have failed to produce agreement as to a fair price for the land. Therefore, in order that we may get the project under way before 1 July 1958, we have requested that condemnation proceedings be filed in the Federal Court at Waco to obtain possession of the land. . . . It is expected that condemnation actions will be filed within a few days concerning 49 acres of land owned by Mrs. Olive Talbert and 59.8 acres owned by Mrs. Mildred H. Orelup, who are sisters. These tracts are adjacent to a 63.7 acre tract which is being obtained from the City of Waco and on which we have a right of entry to begin construction.[112]

Such is the collateral damage of progress. Chances are that few of those in attendance for the groundbreaking ceremony on the fifth of July gave much thought to those two sisters. It must have been quite a spectacle. The *Waco Tribune-Herald* claimed, "the largest group of state, local and federal water conservationist ever assembled" gathered for the event. As fate would have it, they "ran into a flood they couldn't handle. Heavy rain," reported the *Tribune-Herald*. Faced with a major storm, the affair moved to the nearby Waco airport, where some creative mind located a planter box complete with dirt for the ceremonial silver shovels. Johnson often began remarks with hyperbole akin to what he said at the groundbreaking: "No amount of satisfaction can be greater than this I feel today." Standing by a ticket counter, he told the gathering that he preferred "to be remembered for my brevity rather than for my eloquence here today," which generated some laughter. And even these few words could be interpreted fifty years later as standard patronizing by a master politician, but they rang especially true. "The citizens of this area have found there is strength in unity and the various agencies working together have brought about a much-needed result." As the Senate Majority Leader headed for his limo, Poage explained to the crowd that LBJ wanted to beat the storm to Austin. "I don't blame him. He just got us $800,000 more for this project, so I guess we'd better let him go."[113]

With the bulldozers ready to "change the course of mighty rivers," as the introduction to the popular *Superman* television show of the day would say, construction plans mapped out a four-year timeline. The funding pipeline to support such a schedule looked secure when Poage and Johnson issued a joint telegram to Kultgen, Harry Provence, Sidney Dobbins, and Mayor Joe Ward, stating, "Please be advised President's budget for 1960 recommends $4,000,000 for Waco Reservoir."[114]

The economic impact of this project in terms of stimulating the construction industry could be felt nationwide. Colonel Walter Wells of the Corps of Engineers updated Poage on the response from contractors during the spring and summer, reporting "widespread interest shown with 24 bidders from 15 states" on a major piece of the initial work on the embankment and spillway excavation. For this phase of construction engineers from the Corps of Engineers budgeted $3.6 million, and Wells indicated to Poage that six of the bids came in below that figure. The contract award went to Moorman and Singleton of Wills Point, Texas, for $2,830,339, a full $2 million below the high bid.[115] A few months later, Poage would inform Harry Provence of the *Waco Tribune-Herald* that the company also won a $1,575,034 contract to build a new bridge where Highway 6 would cross the expanded lake.[116] Of the Waco-based firms bidding successfully, the Corps of Engineers awarded the largest contract to Hoffman and Borders Construction Company in the amount of $1,825,743 for construction of outlet works, a 145-foot tower located toward the south end of the dam.[117] The stimulus to the local economy would continue through 1961, with Eisenhower proposing another $11 million for the project.[118]

As Eisenhower began the last year of his presidency, a school superintendent in the Central Texas community of Speegleville composed a letter to Bob Poage. Within its highly professional discussion of the impact of the expanded reservoir on his school district lies Lloyd H. Taylor's acknowledgment of the greater good achieved by the new dam. When it came time for the waters to submerge the homes of students and to wash over the roadbeds the buses used to transport them to school, who would help the district? From a financial standpoint, the loss of property taxes and enrollment

> will dig deeply into our school finances . . . damaging results to our revenue property. It will take time for this revenue property to be re-established . . . these lean years between Government acquisition and re-establishment will seriously damage our financial stability. We do not submit this letter as opposition to the Lake Waco Reservoir Project. However, we do think that our school district, the very foundation of a "Democratic Way of Life," should receive due financial consideration for the very serious financial losses that will result during the interim period between Government acquisition and the re-establishment of the many homes and businesses located within the boundaries of the Speegleville Independent School District.

Taylor would learn that many aspects of the situation he faced were analogous to what happened to school districts affected by the creation or expansion of military bases, as had happened not far from his district when the US Army developed the Waco Air Field during World War II and expanded it as Connally Air Base as the Cold War worsened.

During the build-up to official US entry into World War II, the Lanham Act established categories of impact aid for communities and school districts, but these tended to be aimed at shoring up the lost tax base. A key distinction is that military bases, unlike reservoirs, bring children to a district. Under the Lanham Act, districts could receive impact aid to help them add faculty, in accordance with various "trigger" numbers that would make a district eligible.[119] It is this friction point between governmental entities, where the legitimate needs of both parties cannot be reconciled, that creates the sparks to light the historian's path.

With another budget cycle came another pilgrimage of Wacoans to the Capitol, where soon the winds of change would blow. Unlike previous audiences with LBJ, this time Kultgen, Poage, and their compadres shared a bourbon or two with a prospective nominee for the Democratic Party for the election in November. It would take an unusual turn of events for Kennedy to lose to Johnson, but a favorite son for the region could wield some influence at the convention. Poage's ties to LBJ also gave the entourage access to other Senate VIPs, such as Bob Kerr of Oklahoma. Anticipating the visit scheduled for early April 1960, Poage sent Harlan Fentress a letter with a friendly reminder of Topic A, stating,

> [LBJ's] office has worked with us in making arrangements for this meet-ing [with Senator Kerr]. It will, of course, be helpful for you and other friends at Waco to remind Senator Johnson of our interest in this autho-rization, along with our interest in the appropriation.[120]

They asked for an appropriation of $11 million, explaining to the Senate Public Works Committee that this would allow the new dam to begin impound-ing water by the end of 1962.[121] Various configurations of the delegation from Waco had made dozens of these trips since the early 1950s. Congress com-mitted to the project in 1957, but the budgeting process remained competi-tive, so Kultgen and company kept the pressure on as the new decade prom-ised great progress. Wherever Lyndon Johnson's political ambitions took him, his connections to these progressive members of the Waco business establishment remained strong.

By the time Lyndon Johnson took his oath of office as vice president, the giant Caterpillars sculpted the landscape in a renewed effort to man-age the precious water. Work halted abruptly on October 4, 1961. A slide had occurred in the dam embankment, leading to a two-year delay in proj-ect completion. Engineers estimated construction costs would increase by $7,729,000. Finger pointing commenced immediately, especially when the BRA received notice that the authority must pay $1,174,000, or 20 percent, of the amount.

Poage wrote to a professor at Baylor's Department of Geology, Dr. J. W. Dixon, expressing frustration with "a system which relies too strongly upon the knowledge of the Corps itself and does not go far enough in the way of securing local information." Dixon reminded the congressman that Baylor's own Dr. Lula Pace, who Poage had as botany professor, produced scholarly work as early as 1921 confirming that a portion of the site engineers from the Corps of Engineers selected for the new dam "was built on solid limestone."[122] According to the Corps of Engineers, what "existed far under the surface about

40 or 50 million years ago . . . became stable except in a very narrow area."[123] By this time Kultgen no longer presided over the BRA, which requested to be released from this obligation in December 1961. The Corps of Engineers supported waiving of the contractual language, but Frank H. Weitzel, the acting comptroller general, rejected these appeals. He indicated that exposure to risks of this kind were known to BRA and refused to waive the obligation. He was later overruled. Ever vigilant in its role as booster of the project, Harlan Fentress's *Tribune-Herald* informed citizens that despite the delay, "the dam is still scheduled for completion late in 1964, with closure of the tainter gates and the impounding of the water starting in June, 1963."[124]

Poage tried to get LBJ to speak at the dedication ceremony. In a letter to Johnson's close aide, Bill Moyers, dated February 10, 1965, Poage made his appeal primarily on the basis of loyalty.

> I am sure that I need not call your attention or his to the splendid vote which Waco has always given to Mr. Johnson in every election in which he has participated and in which our people could vote. The point is that he will be in the hands of friends. He will receive favorable news coverage. The Waco papers are owned by Mr. Harlan Fentress and are edited by Harry Provence. The Johnson Foundation is interested in one of the television stations. The other is owned by Frank Mayborn and can be counted on to give wide and favorable publicity. Waco has suffered a serious economic loss by the closing of James Connally Air Force Base but there has been a very minimum of criticism of the President in that connection. It seems, however, that it might be helpful if he could appear in Waco as evidence of his continued interest in this area.[125]

Poage, ever the gentleman, might have just as accurately said, "LBJ stabbed me in the back on the Connally Air Base, but he is the President, so here is an invitation. If he can't make it, it hurts him, not me." From the research conducted for this book, it does not appear that Poage ever took into consideration that his obstinate, though very quiet, opposition to the civil rights agenda of his longtime colleague hurt his chances of keeping that base. Johnson did not pressure Poage to support the landmark legislation he pursued with a tenacity Poage could recognize as well as anyone, but the timing suggests LBJ hurt him as soon as he could.[126]

Many years had passed since those two new House members from Central Texas went to Washington to help FDR look out for farmers and the little guy. With very few exceptions, Lyndon Johnson and Bob Poage supported each other like the friends and true believers they were. But somewhere between that bluebonnet-lined highway from Austin to Waco and what activists would call the road to freedom, Lyndon Johnson and Bob Poage parted company. Perhaps Poage really did believe that the methods Kultgen and other local leaders used to address the expressed concerns of the African American community worked more effectively than federal mandates ever could. He and LBJ agreed on so much, including the vital role citizens play in shaping the destiny of the community they call home, but differed on who could live in that community.

Beyond Sandtown

COLLABORATION BETWEEN Lyndon Baines Johnson and W. R. "Bob" Poage, allied with key members of the Waco business establishment, played a significant role in bringing federal resources to the Central Texas city in the mid-twentieth century. Chapter 2 demonstrated how, during the 1930s, New Deal programs such as the NYA required the political culture of Waco to adapt its historic suspicion of centralized authority by forming partnerships in aspects of civic affairs where none existed before.[1] The previous chapter dove into the quest for a solution to the city's perennial flooding problem. The long prescribed answer, a new dam at Lake Waco constructed under the direction of the Army Corps of Engineers, resulted from commitments and sacrifices by local units of government, the regional Brazos River Authority, and taxpayers. Individuals and businesses whose properties became lake bottom as the larger reservoir filled sacrificed, too, although they received payment when the Corps exercised its option to seize the land. The government giveth, and the government taketh away.

All across the United States, policies the federal government had enacted during the Great Depression and World War II increased the frequency of contact between Washington, DC, and the nation's citizens. During this time, it became increasingly evident that the federal government, despite its reputation in the South among many whites for destroying a way of life, happened to dole out money. Texans with connections learned to work the system and make more connections. Even when fatigue from rationing and other Home Front inconveniences, followed by steep inflation as price controls expired, enabled Republicans to campaign successfully with the slogan "Had enough?" in 1946, ambitious civic leaders who had tasted of the sweet green water of the well in Washington still thirsted. They knew it could irrigate the pet projects of conservatives or liberals, if one knew the right people. The right people were white, as were the ambassadors from Central Texas who entered that world of power heretofore closed to people of color. In pursuit of the federal dollar, however, they committed to the engagement of stakeholders from affected communities and began the process of cracking open those doors. For children, the schoolhouse doors mattered most, but for an emerging generation of African Americans and Mexican Americans with agendas of their own, the advisory boards created to qualify for federal funds enabled them to cross the threshold.

For the elites, frequent trips by delegations of Waco VIPs to Washington (at least forty-two to lobby on behalf of the dam project between 1946 and 1954, according to Jack Kultgen), with doors opened by LBJ and Poage, cemented effective working relationships. Kultgen, the transplanted midwesterner whose skills proved so vital to success with the Lake Waco dam project, praised the city of Waco and the Chamber of Commerce for pursuit of federal money, even though accompanying requirements regarding civil rights issues contributed to tightening the noose on Jim Crow.

> One thing, too, that helped Waco, was Waco accepted Urban Renewal quicker than most places did. Most places fought Urban Renewal pretty hard. Waco accepted renewal right off the reel. Not only accepted them but went all the way. There were five or six projects here. Waco showed itself ready to do those things.[2]

Kultgen moved comfortably in fast company in Central Texas politics and showed similar ease when interacting with his future colleagues on the board at Paul Quinn College or working behind the scenes with fellow business owners to manage a tense situation when the old ways of Texas collided with the new in the sensitive area of race relations. In the case of urban renewal programs, the eager embrace of federal assistance in Waco testified to the groundwork laid by Poage and Johnson since the 1930s. They developed a

In 2013, the Bird-Kultgen Ford website proudly shared its history by displaying these photographs and commentary: "One evening in October of 1936, just before the shop was closing, a muddy Model A pulled into the Ford agency on Fifth Street between Washington and Columbus. Jack Kultgen got out and introduced himself as the new operator of the store that he and Arthur Bird, a San Antonio investor, had just purchased." *Courtesy Bird-Kultgen Inc., used by permission.*

"One other thing Jack Kultgen brought with him back in 1936 . . . a dedication to making his city a better place for everyone living there. Through four generations the Kultgen family has been involved in more civic projects and agencies than we have room to list." *Courtesy Bird-Kultgen Inc., used by permission.*

model of what political scientist John Kincaid referred to as "cooperative federalism" to a level of acceptance and efficiency that featured high levels of citizen engagement.[3] In this chapter, the focus turns to the role, intended and unintended, urban renewal program requirements played as springboards for the newest stakeholders of an increasingly diverse Waco, the fast-growing Mexican American community.

In the final paragraph of her examination of the evolution of Lyndon Johnson's political connection with Mexican Americans over the course of his career, historian Julie Leininger Pycior asserted, "by welcoming Mexican Americans into the political process, Lyndon Johnson accelerated their integration into national life."[4] Like most historians focused on LBJ, she did not mention Bob Poage, who continued to represent Waco for ten years after Johnson's presidency ended in 1969. The political backlash against the perceived excesses of the Great Society gained significant strength throughout that time.

The environmental movement LBJ helped to spur with the Clean Air Act of 1966 continued to gather momentum, however. Indeed, the most significant legislative accomplishment of Poage's career, the Poage-Aiken Act of 1972, provided rural communities with federal funds to modernize (or build their first, in many cases) sewage disposal and waste treatment facilities. The act summed up his career by combining his lifelong interests in improving water security, enhancing the quality of rural life, and ensuring processes for ample local control, through Kincaid's "cooperative federalism."

This chapter deals very little with Johnson and Poage in a direct sense. Rather, it examines the consequences of the work they did collaboratively, and work only Johnson could claim credit for in the area of civil rights. In chapter 1, African Americans in Austin under the leadership of Dr. Everett Givens and the Colored Welfare Board presented their agenda and engaged in negotiations with the city of Austin for the best possible outcomes from the planning process the progressive city had initiated in the late 1920s. Although aspects of that plan bring to mind a quasi–Negro Removal Act akin to what Andrew Jackson used to force Native Americans west, by formally setting aside East Austin for African Americans, Givens secured a new school, a park, and assurance of city utilities to those who could afford them.

The leadership skills of the man known locally as the "Bronze Mayor" tested the limits of acceptability in a city just a few years from Ku Klux Klan parades down Congress Avenue. One looking for glimmers of a more progressive posture among whites could point to this outcome with the Austin

City Plan of 1929, since Givens's requests could have been denied. Certainly, no such accommodations were forthcoming in Waco for African Americans, where a far more violent tradition served as the backdrop for a less interactive version of segregation than the political culture that evolved in Austin.

For Mexican Americans in Waco, as well as in Austin, a generation of experiences in the League of United Latin American Citizens prepared individuals to seize the opportunity to be heard when it arose in the 1950s. In this chapter the experiences of individuals who would soon give voice to the Chicano movement in Waco reveal how the citizen engagement process created opportunities for constructive engagement between the Waco Independent School District and the Waco Alliance of Mexican Americans. It represented a substantial contrast to the experiences of Everett Givens in Austin in 1929.

Tentative steps by the centrist Eisenhower administration toward an economic development strategy known as urban renewal during the economic downturn in the late 1950s in Congress expanded the federal role in stimulating targeted segments of the economy.[5] From their earliest experiences in public service, Bob Poage and Lyndon Johnson understood the significance of strength in unity across the levels of government in this federal system. Such was the creed of these New Deal Democrats who learned firsthand how to bridge the gap between the individual and Uncle Sam. Much had changed since their political alliance reshaped Waco. The smart politics effective New Deal agencies practiced, whereby local VIPs had a voice in selecting projects, contractors, and gained credit, became standard operating procedure. By cracking open doors to allow more citizens in, the city could now capitalize on human capital. This "boilerplate" language from a planning document used by the city of Waco describes the system:

> The Federal government has expressed clearly through Congressional legislation and Administration policy its preference for cooperative policy-making activities at the metropolitan level by locally elected officials. Recent legislation calls for increasing the role of locally elected officials in the comprehensive regional planning process.[6]

According to the *Strategy for Regional Planning and Policy Guidelines Waco–McLennan County Region* prepared in October 1967 by civil engineers W. F. Soule and Associates, Waco first undertook the process in 1956 (excluding Progressive Era and New Deal forays into urban planning). The timing suggests that the community response to the tornadic hell of May 1953, accompanied by legislative breakthroughs with funding for the dam project, created an atmosphere of teamwork among influential Wacoans. The triumvirate of Ford dealer Jack Kultgen, publisher Harlan Fentress, and Chamber of Commerce president Sidney Dobbins spearheaded a remarkably focused mission. The goal was to anticipate city needs in terms of infrastructure and to anticipate levels of service delivery by city agencies for 1980.

Jack Kultgen correctly recalled the enthusiasm for urban planning Waco civic leaders demonstrated. As detailed in the previous chapter, city officials spent the first half of the twentieth century struggling with water resource management and periodic crisis response to flood or drought. Waco grew, and many segments of the community prospered. Serious planning could only take place, however, after confirmation that the flooding would stop. After the federal government finally committed to building a new dam, long-term planning for the city on the Brazos that boosters once heralded as the "Athens of the West" could move forward. As they did with a ballot question of committing the local contribution to the dam project, Waco voters approved the local share of funding for an urban renewal referendum in 1958 by a 7–1 margin.[7]

After two decades of maintaining a very effective relationship with LBJ, Poage's ability at the federal level to deliver for his constituents unquestionably increased when Johnson became Senate Majority Leader. Marveling at the artfulness he witnessed routinely, Poage described Johnson's ability, along with House Speaker Sam Rayburn, to secure federal funding from Eisenhower to support local initiatives like the Waco plan years ahead of the Great Society:

> I don't think he [Eisenhower] understood it at all, and I don't think he understood what those men were doing to him or for him, and they did a great deal for him. I think they kept him afloat. They brought into the administration—the Eisenhower administration—a considerable degree of Democratic doctrines . . . urban renewal . . . obviously was not something dear to a majority of the Republican leadership, but it was something that came in at this instigation of the Democrats that controlled the Congress, to wit, Mr. Johnson and Mr. Rayburn.[8]

Even in the 1960s as federal forces, eventually led by LBJ himself, battered down walls and chipped away at the jagged edges of segregation, the conservative political culture in Waco calculated that benefits outweighed costs, even when federal funds came tied to ongoing challenges to the racial hierarchy. Elected officials managed to compartmentalize views on the demise of the old ways as long as the federal money flowed. At least Poage's interest in securing federal funding for the Eleventh District did not wane demonstrably as requirements for fair employment practices, including nondiscriminatory wages, and calls for increased engagement by community stakeholders opened doors for African Americans and Mexican Americans into overdue positions of opportunity.

In the wake of the tornado and the dam expansion, the combination of Congressman Poage's leverage with Lyndon Johnson and the engagement of community leaders spurred Waco into an early phase of federally assisted urban renewal, anticipating the Model Cities and the Community Action Programs of the Great Society era. Changes in the physical landscape affected the political landscape and vice versa. The documents created by urban planners contracted by the city of Waco from the late 1950s through the 1970s confirm the growing importance of Mexican American civic leaders in planning processes. The bonding referendum in 1958 committing Waco taxpayers to the local share of urban renewal funds led Anglos to bring them into the circle of strategic planning. Wacoan Tomas Arroyo recalled serving on one of the first of these planning committees and conducting on-site inspections. "And we went all over the community around here—First and Third to Fifth Street, I believe, house to house to see the conditions that people was in. It was awful."[9] Arroyo, Robert Aguilar, and Ernest Calderon were among many Mexican Americans in Waco whose activism grew out of not only the political and cultural challenges of their environment but also those of nature itself. The chain of events illustrates how local and federal initiatives intertwine with geography to alter housing patterns, thereby changing school attendance boundaries as well.

Lyndon Johnson's pluralistic vision of a Great Society included virtual passports from poverty for children in the form of dozens of federal initiatives. These education policies, especially involving school lunches, had the strong support of Agricultural Committee member Bob Poage. Johnson's speechwriters used his deeply rooted experience to give voice to those yearning faces as he addressed Congress on the Voting Rights Act in March 1965:

My students were poor and they often came to class without breakfast, hungry. They knew even in their youth the pain of prejudice. They never seemed to know why people disliked them. But they knew that it was so, because I saw it in their eyes . . . somehow you never forget what poverty and hatred can do when you see its scars on the face of a young child.[10]

That searing experience, though it lasted just one school year, informed Johnson's pursuit of the Elementary and Secondary Education Act (ESEA), Head Start, the Higher Education Act, and a host of others, all of which moved Uncle Sam closer to meeting student needs. LBJ believed teachers play an essential role in uplifting the disadvantaged in this nation with staggering gaps between rich and poor, where bigotry still prevailed—even in schools. By expanding the range of federal programs available to students in Waco and other communities, LBJ intended to increase the likelihood that all children could access educational opportunities from preschool through college. Significantly, Johnson did not abandon his long-held belief in the merits of English-only instructional practice in the classroom, nor did the Bilingual Education Act he signed in January 1968 require schools to abandon it. Promoted by Texas senator Ralph Yarborough, with whom Johnson had not enjoyed close relations, the Title VII amendment to the ESEA Act moved quickly through Senate and House versions to conference and enactment without significant attention by LBJ, whose domestic agenda felt the weight of the debacle in Vietnam.

Johnson's mark on the bilingual education legislation, in fact, seemed most discernible philosophically in terms of its recognition of local circumstances. The distinctive political culture of individual school districts would lead school officials to either embrace or reject the opportunity for federal funds to address student needs.[11] In the grassroots democracy of public education, the bedrock of the republic for both Democrats and Republicans in that era, school board elections could best determine such matters. This formula Johnson had learned as NYA director in Texas in the 1930s proved to be all the political calculation necessary: Federal resources + local decision making by stakeholders = Great Society.

And so the decision-making process on bilingual education and other matters related to multicultural curriculum would unfold. Circumstances in Waco, however, led to an outcome few could have foretold. There, the impetus for a successful community campaign for increased attention to the needs of students from Spanish-speaking households came from an organization created by federal Model Cities funds obtained through the efforts of Bob Poage and Lyndon Johnson, the Waco Alliance of Mexican Americans.

From the time Model Cities program funds allowed for the creation of the Waco Alliance of Mexican Americans in 1967, to 1973, the year of LBJ's death, the influence of this growing segment of the Waco community rose substantially. Indeed, in that span of just six years, the Waco Independent School District (Waco ISD) Board of Education came to see a potential adversary as a key ally. The significance of this development is that it demonstrates what might be termed "collateral construction," as opposed to damage, from a Great Society initiative that gave enormous latitude to local officials. The Model Cities program, dismantled under the Nixon administration, claimed too few successes, perhaps. In retrospect, the leverage the program gave to community-based organizations by insisting that all stakeholders be "at the table," clearly had substantial spin-off effects, including opportunities for emergence of dynamic leadership, as happened in Waco.

A native Wacoan, Roberto Aguilar traced his commitment to community-based activism to 1964, when LBJ's declaration of war on poverty stirred his twenty-year-old soul. Aguilar played a key role in mobilizing a new coalition into a force for change that spoke with a distinctively Chicano voice, the Waco Alliance of Mexican Americans (WAMA), into a meaningful force for change. The alliance represented, at first, a largely conservative coalition of elements of LULAC, local *mutualistas* (such as "MoJo," a group for Mexican American journeymen), and church or mission groups. These groups, which undoubtedly looked far more homogeneous to Anglos than they did to the twenty-three-year-old hired to unify them, brought their own agendas. Inspired by readings, rallies, and lectures about the untapped potential of his people, Aguilar moved too quickly for some, as he acknowledged upon reflection forty years later. Referring to the increased consciousness among the younger generation, increasingly identifying as "La Raza," Aguilar recalled, "That's when it got really active and strong. In fact, it got so active and strong that I think a couple of the organizations pulled out."[12]

Federal programming associated with urban renewal and subsequently with Model Cities and other initiatives gave him valuable experience in civic affairs and help to channel other talented Chicano/a leaders into the system. Robert Aguilar completed his studies at Baylor University in time to be considered for a position funded by Model Cities. "Four hours a day for Model Cities and four hours a day as Executive Director for the Alliance of Mexican Americans . . . they took the business end of LULAC and really made it more of an activist type of organization rather than being passive."[13] Aguilar described the generational politics:

Our parents were hard-core Democrats and "don't change" and "you guys are crazy." But it was a young people's movement. We were all in our twenties and thirties, and we said, "We're gonna make change in the political structure." The Democratic Party wanted our vote but used us. The battle was not with the Democratic Party. The battle was with our parents and our neighborhoods that didn't want us to set up a party that was radical in their mind because they were conservative.[14]

In terms of his political maturation, the War on Poverty inspired activism, and his father's involvement in the Viva Kennedy! movement in 1960 also clearly influenced his commitment to social change. "In fact, I joined LULAC in my junior year in high school. . . . I stayed a LULAC member for almost twenty years," but, later, he continued, "they were too conservative for me . . . slow to move." Evidently, Aguilar's view of LULAC reflected a growing generational rift within the politically minded Mexican American community in Waco.[15] Over time, Aguilar's experience around the state gave him a broader perspective on Waco, which he viewed as "kind of limited because we're just a small group of people here. The level of education was high in the Alliance of Mexican Americans . . . every region is different . . . in South Texas, more knowledge of politics, economics, social dynamics . . . over there they had a lot more diversity in terms of things that happened to 'em in their lives."[16] Like their restless Anglo and African American counterparts, the spirit of liberal activism called them to action.

Among those answering the call was Ernest Calderon, a prominent Waco activist who served as the state treasurer for La Raza Unida Party in the early 1970s. Calderon, too, credits the 1960 campaign and the Kennedy Clubs as the "seed" of a more politicized generation. In later 1962, he learned of efforts to establish a Political Association of Spanish Speaking Organizations (PASSO) chapter in Waco. Kennedy's election made a difference, Calderon said, because young Mexican Americans like himself found the "Kennedy Clubs were so successful that they felt there had to be something to take its place as an ongoing thing." By 1965, Calderon rose to chair of the McLennan County PASSO chapter. Working within the Democratic Party structure, because, as Calderon put it, "historically, that's where we were," Mexican Americans in Waco entered into precinct- and county-level politics on an organized basis for the first time. Like many of the Chicano generation, Calderon, too, tasted his first experience of the political process on a personal level. "I'll never forget the first time we went to a precinct convention here," he recalled. "I think it was five of us controlled the precinct. It shows the apathy on these things. Here's a precinct of eighteen hundred voters and five can control the precinct convention."[17]

Calderon became deeply involved in electoral politics, while conversely Aguilar expressed the view that

> we never envisioned the Raza Unida Party as being something perma-
> nent, but a way of playing one party against the other . . . when I say we
> weren't involved in the politics of elections, we were involved in the poli-
> tics of everything else—socially, economically, politically to a great sense
> that we would present platforms to both candidates and said here's what
> the people need in your area . . . we never endorsed one candidate against
> the other, even though we could do that in local elections, but not in the
> state or federal elections because of the law that came with the programs.[18]

Addressing the significance of the generational differences within the Mexican American community, Calderon speculated, "I think probably it was
because of the older people who were involved in PASSO . . . were merely
giving lip service that the young people picked the interest up . . . and I think
it was about this time the MAYO (Mexican American Youth Organization)
started getting pretty active." Calderon pointed to the Del Rio Manifesto of
March 30, 1969, as a pivotal event in the minds of activists who decided the
traditional two-party system did not address their issues. Calderon found it
possible to be "a staunch Democrat but . . . relate to some of the people in the
MAYO group and subsequently the Raza Unida group."[19]

Spurred by idealism, leaders within the "Chicano generation" in Waco
quickly gained experience, albeit not without friction from the establishment. Calderon referred to this period as a time of "growing pains," due in
part to procedural hurdles. A visit to the McLennan County courthouse by
a longhaired or bearded member of the fledgling Raza Unida Party to file
papers could result in a confrontation. "You know what kind of reception
the guy's going to get. He's going to get thrown out of there. They couldn't
approach the officials of the city or county without being harassed because
of their appearance."[20]

Provocative reappraisals of Mexican Americans in the political culture of
Texas in the past decade emphasized changing perceptions of identity when
comparing the LULAC and GI Forum generation with the La Raza Unida
generation. *Claiming Citizenship*, Antonio Quiroz's penetrating analysis of

the accommodationist approach he discerned among Mexican American community leaders in Victoria County, Texas, contrasted Victoria's moderation with the relative radicalism of Crystal City and other Winter Garden communities.[21] When looking back at the role of Henry B. Gonzalez, a member of Congress from San Antonio who helped to break the political barrier against candidates with Hispanic surnames, Aguilar spoke admiringly. "He opened up a lot of doors to the Hispanic . . . but Henry B. was—we were young; we were aggressive; we had all these—we had all this energy. We got these hormones flowing, and we felt the older group was too slow."[22]

The perspectives of prominent activists like Aguilar and Ernest Calderon of Waco actually demonstrate a sense of agency and realpolitik. Calderon served as the first chair of the PASSO in Waco when it convened in 1965. According to him, PASSO "always worked with what's commonly called the coalition. Not only here but on a statewide basis. You know, the black, the labor, organized labor, the independent liberal and the Mexican American who is the coalition."[23]

The spectrum of interests under the Democratic umbrella Calderon described represented some alliances dating back to nineteenth-century populism. Other Mexican Americans found common ground in supporting the New Deal. Mexican Americans joined last, in accordance with the changing demographics in Waco. The Mexican American population in Central Texas rebounded and grew following the deportations of the 1930s. Their influence grew in the party, but it bears reminding that even by the time LBJ signed the Bilingual Education Act, despite their impact on the city's development, only 10 percent of Wacoans were Mexican American.

As one would expect, the political circumstances Aguilar, Calderon, and their contemporaries in Waco faced are inseparable from the distinctive Central Texas climate that froze Bob Poage in a segregationist posture, despite his long attachment to LBJ. By the time of the Johnson presidency, LULAC and the GI Forum members identified strongly with the Democratic mainstream, to the extent that historian Julie Leininger Pycior argued Mexican Americans were effectively taken for granted.[24]

In 1967, frustration with the pace of change affected the direction of WAMA as chief advocate for the social, economic, and civil rights of Mexican Americans in the city. When its status changed under Nixon, WAMA would incorporate in August 1969.[25] One of their chief strategies in the post–Model Cities years, supported by years of experience around soft money in Waco's urban renewal projects, involved aggressive pursuit of grants. The introductory material accompanying grant applications from that period contains phrasing reflecting the ethnocentric rhetoric of La Raza Unida (RUP), prepared by Robert Aguilar. For example, showing deep pride in the resilient heritage, Aguilar credited the cohesiveness of the Mexican American family unit as the factor enabling "La Raza to maintain its cultural identity which has served as a survival mechanism."[26]

To contextualize Aguilar in the broader Mexican American community in Waco, one must reach back to the time of his boyhood in 1953, when the tornado struck, and after. Since the defining event for that generation of Wacoans in the city center was the tornado that wiped much of the housing slate clean for blocks, attention will now shift to a closer examination of the tornado and its role in changing the political landscape of this deeply segregated city in the 1950s.

The Tornado and the Mexican American Community

A massive tornado (considered EF5 today, with winds exceeding 260 mph) leveled the central business district in Waco on May 11, 1953.[27] For Waco's growing Mexican American population of three thousand, concentrated in the Sandtown district along marginal riverfront land, nature's form of renewal often took the form of floods, and survivors returned as waters receded. Located just two miles downstream from the confluence of the three branches of the Bosque River, where they join the mainstream of the Brazos, the Sandtown neighborhood knew the hardships born of natural calamities and human failings.

The havoc the tornado wreaked triggered a small-scale diaspora by Waco's poorest families out of the Sandtown neighborhood, with changes in where hundreds of pupils, many of them from Spanish-speaking households, would attend classes. The decimation of the central business district and nearby neighborhoods by the tornado, combined with the elevation of Lyndon Johnson to the role of Senate Majority Leader after the 1954 midterm election, made longtime slum areas very attractive to Baylor University.

Even so, stunned Waco residents wandered through the wreckage of their homes and businesses in the aftermath of the horrendous twister, and no one could fathom how the storm that killed 114 people would alter race relations in their segregated city. No more than 5 percent of its population counted as "Spanish speaking" in the 1950 census. Prior to the tornado, housing options in Waco found most of these Tejanos and Mexican Americans concentrated in the notorious barrio/ghetto. The broad floodplain of the Brazos rendered properties on the south bank marginal, resulting in lower real estate values and the substandard housing slumlords favored. However, after the tornado, land that once suited the needs of slumlords looked more appealing to developers, and it represented a dream situation for planners, especially with federal support.

Within five months of the tornado, in October, community activists Almarie Bulloch Blaine and Mardell Armstrong, white women deeply involved with their Council of Church Women, established the Latin American Christian Center at 1618 Clay Street in South Waco. Armstrong, the first president of the organization, recalled "the greatest need at that time was a nursery and kindergarten for the Latin American children."[28] Blaine named the nature of the challenge bluntly, noting, "there was no place for the Latin American child to go and get preschool education."[29] By 1956 the successful center received half of its annual budget through the United Fund.

The efforts of Blaine and Armstrong documented the impact of the religious community on children, who would, in many cases, transition to a public school setting. Anglos established the Latin American Christian Center, but Mexican Americans also responded to the increased needs of the community. Margie Lopez Cintron emphasized the importance of the church as a source of solidarity in Waco. Born in 1956, Margie spent her early childhood on the locally infamous "Calle Dos," the red light district on Second Street. At one time, she observed, "St. Francis was the prominent Catholic Church for Hispanics because the masses were done in Spanish. In 1956, when people started locating to South Waco, enough people located there where they started Sacred Heart Church."[30] This church construction project, necessary because of sweeping changes to Waco in the old downtown area near the riverfront, would prove central to the identities of a significant segment of Waco's Mexican American population.

In 1950, five-year-old Robert Gamboa moved to South First Street in Sandtown with his family from Kansas City, Missouri. Years later, Gamboa described Sandtown boundaries as "a long rectangular area of maybe four or five, six blocks. And the community was made up of probably I'm going to say 98% Mexican families. There were a few African American families. No Anglo families I can recall."[31]

In a culturally homogeneous neighborhood, locally owned businesses served as anchors to the community, often as key supporters of the local place of worship. Many parishioners have a personal connection to their church. Carol Duron's family had operated the grocery store El Progreso, at the corner of Second and Jefferson, since arriving in Waco in 1920. The family actively rallied support for the church project. Construction of the church began with five families who decided, Duron recalled, "to ask each family to donate one hundred bricks—each family for starters. And like my aunt said, 'Papa Marcial,' meaning our grandfather, was never going half on anything. He said, 'I'm going to give you one hundred bricks for each member of my family.' And so, he donated one thousand bricks for the starters for the church." After several years of community-based effort, the volunteers saw their church dedicated in October 1931.[32] When neighborhoods fall victim to the forces of nature directly or indirectly, the deep-rooted sense of loss includes memories built around such manifestations of faith. Schools and places of worship serve as hubs. They represent stability and tradition.

Robert Aguilar spent his entire boyhood in South Waco, residing for all but one of those years at the family's home at 1608 Webster. He benefited directly from the work done by Almarie Blaine and Mardell Armstrong by attending preschool at the Latin American Christian Center they established three blocks from his home. Blaine's observation that the "biggest problem the Latin American child had was the language barrier" applied to young Robert.[33] The transition to public school at Bell's Hill Elementary on Cleveland Street proved daunting, as Aguilar recalled:

> There were English speaking teachers and Spanish speaking teachers, but Spanish was still my first language and it hurt me when I got to elementary because they put me in third level reading, which was the lowest reading there was—one level above mental retardation. And they kept me in that level for six years.[34]

Overcoming odds that found 75 percent of his fellow Mexican American classmates dropping out of school before graduation, Aguilar persevered.[35] Aguilar graduated in 1962 from Waco High School, but his memories are largely painful ones of lice checks and insensitive educators. From his earliest days in elementary school, where his teacher characterized Spanish as a "stupid language" and punished him for using it, through high school where "everything was slandered against the Hispanics so we had no roots in this country," he felt teachers resented his very presence. Aguilar considered his sixth grade teacher his favorite, "the only one . . . that really spent time with me."[36]

The recollections of Margie Cintron shed more light on the complexities of the changes occurring within Waco's Mexican American community. Like black or white "radicals" who faced communication issues with their Depression-era parents, differences of style and substance emerged in many Mexican American families. Reflecting on her upbringing, Cintron recalled, "You know, there was a language barrier between the generations." Her parents were "punished severely for speaking Spanish in school. Because my father and mother were punished severely, the generation that I'm in—we lost the Spanish language."[37]

The political fault lines were many, so power resided in the hands of those community leaders with the skills to assemble and maintain coalitions of interest despite their almost amoebic tendency to divide into rival factions. By the time Ernest Calderon, Robert Aguilar, Margie Lopez Cintron, and other key figures in the Waco Alliance of Mexican Americans organized in 1967, legislators like Bob Poage seemed too entrenched and hopelessly out of step with society. From a cultural standpoint, for Chicano/as to challenge elders required disregard for a deep-rooted norm. Aguilar's strategy of school-based action could sustain important alliances by keeping attention focused on the needs of future generations. A little more respect for the elderly would have been appreciated by Bob Poage, who would eventually lose his treasured chairmanship of the House Agriculture Committee to a new wave of Democrats in the post-Watergate purge of New Dealers who had become the old guard.

As Pycior discussed in *LBJ and Mexican Americans*, by the late 1960s, many Mexican Americans believed that the federal antipoverty programs gave disproportionate attention to the problems of African Americans at the expense of Mexican Americans. From Aguilar's perspective, "to the Anglo, poor means being Black," so Great Society programs "were designed of Blacks and staffed by either Blacks or Blacks and Anglos. . . . When I started providing services for Hispanics the black board members and Anglo members got really upset," he recalled. "Consequently," Aguilar concluded, "we had to get into the business of operating programs ourselves if anything was to be done at all to help."[38]

As events progressed in the Waco ISD, the leaders of the Waco Alliance found themselves being courted by the board of trustees as potential allies in the increasingly complex political culture of the district. This takes us to 1973, the year LBJ's sixty-four-year-old heart stopped, but the events show how so many of the issues the community dealt with were rooted somehow in the work Johnson and Poage did to bring federal resources to Waco.

Both men certainly understood that from time to time, circumstances call for the extension of an olive branch, the strategy used by the Waco ISD Board of Trustees in contacting Julian Vasquez, a leader in the WAMA. M. M. McRae, writing for the board, expressed her gratitude to the alliance for its "contributions to the partial restoration of confidence in public education" in the community. Mrs. McRae's letter characterized the school system as the victim of heavy-handedness of an encroaching federal government:

> So, in the wake of a traumatic experience following the school district's efforts to implement a Federal Court Order, requiring massive reorganization of our entire educational plan and program, it seemed natural and proper to ask representative, straight-thinking, and direct-talking people to come to our aid.[39]

Likely no one knew the troubles she had seen as president of the Waco ISD board, but Mrs. McRae's letter masks the avoidance behavior of the district dating back to the US Supreme Court ruling in the *Brown* case in 1954. This was the context for school officials in Waco when they considered the implications of the *Brown* ruling. The language used in *History of the Waco Public Schools*, a district publication, insinuates that the federal government created, in effect, a disturbance of the peace. The longest journey, which in this case lasted almost two decades, began when the Waco board "like [in] so many other communities, started to work with its problem of implementing the 1954 decision, that the separate but equal idea was unconstitutional."[40] The *Brown* decision came six years after the *Delgado v. Bastrop* ruling in 1948, when US District Court judge Ben H. Rice of the Western District of Texas sustained LULAC's argument that separate schools for Mexican American children were unconstitutional.[41]

Wilbur Ball, who would serve as the first president of McLennan Community College when it opened in Waco in 1972, laughed when he remembered how his tiny community of eight hundred people dealt with diversity prior to *Delgado*. He experienced the Great Depression as an elementary school student in the town of Berclair, located about two hundred miles south of Waco in Goliad County. "We had the Mexican school, we had the

Negro school and we had the white school. Three! And, of course . . . when the integration of the Mexican American into the so-called white schools happened, it was a much more serious thing and harder to do than integration of the blacks later."[42]

Perhaps Ball's laughter acknowledged, from his perspective as a school administrator, the inefficiency of such an operation. Or, perhaps verbalizing how much conditions had changed simply amazed him and elicited a laugh. The Tejanos and Mexican Americans of Goliad historically outnumbered the African American population by 7–1, hence Ball's recollection of the relative difficulty of the integration process in that school district. The very history of Goliad, site of a legendary encounter in the formative stages of the Texas Republic, could significantly color relations between local Anglos and residents of Mexican ancestry.[43]

The culture and climate of a school building derive not only from policies and programs but also from the building's location, because the history and geography of the school setting matter. In Waco in the 1950s, Robert Gamboa attended the partially integrated Sul Ross Elementary School, where Anglos and Mexican American children attended together, but no African Americans learned with them. The teachers there touched his life in a manner he fondly recalled fifty years later as "unbelievable." Because of their efforts, Gamboa experienced "warmth, the encouragement, the ability to accelerate," even though none of them shared his heritage. "There was not one African American teacher; there was not one Hispanic or Mexican American teacher. All my teachers were Anglo. And it didn't matter."

But after promotion to the junior high, trouble set in, shocking the young Gamboa. As he recalled, "the racial prejudice that existed I truly . . . didn't realize it existed." Speaking to a friend one day while walking through the hallways of South Junior High, Gamboa found himself on the receiving end of "brutality."

> I felt a hand literally wrap around my throat and another hand to get one of the belt loops in the back of my pants and literally lifted me. It was the assistant principal . . . he said, "Boy, didn't we tell you not to speak that shit here?" And I promptly got several licks with the paddle all because I spoke Spanish. You know, that's the oddity of it. I never once was corrected at South Junior by any of the teachers about my language ability or capability.[44]

These examples illustrate the variance in patterns of discrimination not only within a school district but also within a school building. Policies issued from on high, even when legitimized by the trappings of democratic institutions, stand or fall by the actions taken by individuals (teachers) at the operational level. More importantly, they highlight how a school can become subdivided into zones of relative safety or danger for students. Within a school, students communicate with one another about their teachers. Gamboa's experience, liked Margie Cintron's description earlier in this chapter, reminds one of the power of individual action within an institutional setting.

The importance of decisions involving the hiring and assignment of teachers, then, cannot be overestimated, whether school policies call for segregation or integration. Waco ISD superintendent Avery Downing began the portion of the integration process that garners insufficient scholarly attention—the integration of school faculties. The first court order directing Waco ISD to integrate schools came in 1963, but the order did not address faculty issues. According to the district's official history, by the 1965–66 school year only eleven Waco ISD faculty members taught "on an integrated basis," a phrase left unexplained. By January 1971, the district initiated a more extensive plan to integrate the faculty, but by that time lawsuits, one filed by African American parents and the other by Mexican Americans, charged Waco ISD with operating a "dual school system . . . with schools left racially identifiable."[45]

The mobilization by WAMA of an increasingly politicized Mexican American community to put pressure on the Waco schools began the previous spring. Charles Gonzalez stood before the Waco ISD Board of Education on May 21, 1970, as WAMA president, which he stated "represents the largest segment of organized Mexican Americans." Gonzalez's call for reform echoed LBJ's appeal for reason; Gonzalez maintained that "most of the problems are also those that plague the Negro and the poor White in some manner or another." Several areas of concern followed, including the school lunch program, counseling services, and teacher qualifications. Gonzalez then pointed specifically to issues limiting the success of Mexican American students. He grounded his argument in his role as a parent. "As you know," he told the board, "we are not educators, but we see our children having problems."[46] By first calling attention to the common needs of all the district's children, Gonzalez displayed keen political skills and modeled an approach of constructive confrontation that the alliance would follow in years to come. The aforementioned letter from board president McRae speaks to the long-term effectiveness of the strategy Aguilar and his fellow WAMA members adopted in 1967.

When Charles Gonzalez delivered his remarks to the Waco ISD board, did he know that a representative of the Waco Classroom Teachers Association, Mrs. Ollie Posey, listened as several of his sharpest criticisms struck at the association's membership? After personnel issues such as hiring practices, teacher training, and supervision were discussed, Gonzalez continued, "We are not saying there is discrimination. We are saying there is complacency, apathy, and indifference."[47]

Gonzalez asked, in effect, "where are the Mr. Johnsons?" Did anyone teaching these children actually care about their futures? Gonzalez turned one of the gravest concerns among teachers—that parents are disinterested in the progress children make in school—on its head. Speaking on behalf of WAMA, he urged the board and the administration of the Waco ISD to see indicators such as high dropout rates and low grades among those still in school as evidence of problems with teacher quality. Then Gonzalez offered solutions:

> There should be a method to periodically check on the qualifications of teachers and we do not mean their academic achievements. We want their productiveness checked. Teachers with master degrees who cannot relate or communicate their knowledge to youngsters is like having the blind leading a person with 20–20 vision. The youngsters can learn, but teachers must be able to teach. We want to suggest that teachers should be moved and not stagnate in areas where the people do not have their displeasures heard or they are unable to articulate their problems.[48]

If parents could not rely on the professionalism and basic humanity of the faculty, could they not rely on the school's administrators to monitor, to discipline, or to remove bad teachers? This public rebuke, aimed at the faculty and administration of Waco High School, represented the palpable tension between the many factions of the school community. Closing on a note that many teachers and principals would have agreed with, Gonzalez called upon the board to spend more money. Chiding them for their priorities, he said, "You did not bat an eye for raising our taxes for new buildings, how about raising our taxes for new levels of human achievement?" Gonzalez stressed the importance of hiring bilingual aides "wherever needed" for elementary and junior high classrooms to "supplement the teachers in communicating instructions to the students and we suggest you begin studying and implementing bi-lingual education where needed in the immediate future."[49] In this context, Gonzalez envisions bilingual programming as more than a strategy for teaching. He sees it as a means to break down barriers to mutual understanding among teachers and students.

A few passages in the Gonzalez statement to the Waco ISD board on behalf of WAMA hinted at political action but made no specific demands. From the official minutes of the meeting, it appears all participants remained professional and businesslike. In fact, the minutes specifically stated, "Superintendent Downing expressed appreciation . . . for the fine manner in which their reports were prepared and presented." The vice president of the board, a local Oldsmobile dealer named Gordon Rountree, "assured the visitors that the study of the reports would be discussed at a subsequent meeting."[50]

The end of May brings the close of the school year in Texas. Teachers earning low salaries hustle for ways to make ends meet. The school business office gets ready to conclude one fiscal year while principals approve purchase orders for supplies billed to the next. The pace changes for administrators. During the summer, no Waco ISD administrator or Board of Education member contacted Charles Gonzalez. Instead, Superintendent Avery Downing waited until September 22, 1970, to respond to the issues the WAMA president had raised four months earlier. Even before that spring meeting, Downing had to weather turbulent periods in Waco ISD's history. The worst was yet to come, perhaps, as his response to Gonzalez was not only far too late but far too little as well. Downing's letter extends the barest courtesies in defending the district's performance. He begins by indicating that the idea for writing the letter germinated elsewhere. "I have been asked to give a report on the status of the main topics mentioned in your letter," Downing stated. He detailed efforts to boost reading achievement scores in elementary schools, informing Gonzalez that "an allotment of $7 per pupil is spent to purchase reading materials for slow readers in disadvantaged schools, a sum which is over and above the regular budget allotment for this activity."

Twice in his two-page report, Downing uses the term "Mexican-American." Both instances involve the issue of participation in school activities. The school principals told him of "several instances of Mexican-American homeroom leaders, student council officers, cheer leaders, football heroes, and campus favorites." Nevertheless, just in case, a committee of parents, teachers, and students will review eligibility standards with "the whole idea

... to remove real or imagined obstacles in the way of any worthy child." The superintendent closed by saying Gonzalez's criticisms last May led to

doing a lot of soul searching and hope that the valid criticism leveled at us can be eliminated or at least minimized and constructive suggestions for improvement adopted. Some of your questions, however, are judgment matters and whether we can satisfy all our questioners remains in doubt.[51]

The contents of Downing's letter strike a different tone than do his remarks made five days earlier at a Board of Trustees meeting on September 17, 1970, a Thursday afternoon. The board's agenda routinely included an item listed as "Superintendent's Reports and Recommendations." During this portion of the meeting, Downing introduced a student named Ernest Gamboa, indicating that earlier in the week, Ernest and two classmates from Waco University High School requested that the school set aside two hours on Wednesday for a "workshop to educate Mexican American students on their heritage and culture."[52] Perhaps sensing trouble, Downing stated for the record that he had assembled as many board members as he could that Monday to confer with high school administrators about the request. After conferring, they convinced Ernest Gamboa to present his request to the Board of Trustees that Thursday, September 17, rather than make the decision about the potentially controversial workshop request without the opportunity for the full board to consider the matter.

The minutes of the meeting on September 17, 1970, refer to a reaction by "a number of Mexican American adults" who then presented their opposition to the kind of program Gamboa and his classmates proposed. The minutes do not specify the nature of their concerns, but this very public exposure of the generational divisions within the Waco Mexican American community suggests likely turmoil among family members and friction between friends and neighbors over the students' demands. One might suspect that the solutions Gonzalez outlined months earlier had not gone far enough for the more militant Chicano students. For less politicized members of the Mexican American community, such as local businessman Manuel Sustaita, a dollars and common sense outlook about getting involved in school affairs influenced behavior in this difficult period. Sustaita's political activism took the form of involvement with the newly formed Cen-Tex Hispanic Chamber of Commerce, which promoted business opportunities for Tejanos and

Mexican Americans. Trouble in the schools meant trouble for business, in his view. "We are certainly concerned, just like the Waco business community is concerned about bringing the issue to rest. We are supposed to be bringing new industry to Waco and any time a company looks at Waco and sees we can't seem to find a solution to this problem, they have to wonder whether this is where their employees need to be living."[53]

Sustaita's perspective, along with the reaction of the audience at the Board of Trustee's meeting, suggests a significant level of concern among more conservative members of the Mexican American community that emergent leaders in the Chicano movement did not speak for all. WAMA faced the challenge of keeping a coalition of interests together to remain a viable force in community affairs. The decision by the Waco Board of Trustees to table action on Ernest Gamboa's proposal, "until the Mexican American group could come up with a joint plan for the Board's consideration," shows the board's sense that time favored the institution over the insurgent.[54]

The energies channeled into the alliance continued to build as the school district struggled to confront the backlog of issues left by its segregationist history. WAMA did not wait for Downing to set upon a course of action. In the months prior to Downing's response, the alliance moved ahead with their own strategies to increase the graduation rate among Waco's Mexican American students. By October their representatives met with the city's Human Relations Commission, asking the officials to verify that Waco's "integration system" matched guidelines set by the US Department of Health, Education, and Welfare. They urged the commissioners to fund programs designed to "motivate youths to further their education." Victor Rodriguez spoke on behalf of WAMA, later joined by Robert Garibay, identified by the *Waco Tribune-Herald* the next day as a "local businessman and Mexican American activist." Both men sought to advance bilingual and bicultural understanding. They also raised a new topic, questioning the failure of school or city officials to notify any families about the new attendance boundaries that would be implemented upon the opening of the new Jefferson-Moore High School. The newspaper reported, "the ultimate goal in their argument was to 'prevent a Negro-Mexican school.'"[55] Under pre-Chicano-era constructs of race and ethnicity, LULAC and the GI Forum pressed the case that Mexican heritage entitled one to the privileges of whiteness, setting the stage for school officials to consider meeting court orders based on the black-white binary for grouping minorities.

Whether by coincidence or by design, two guests joined the Waco Human Relations Commission for its next meeting on November 5, 1970. The chair introduced Superintendent Downing and John Faulkner, president of the Waco ISD Board of Education, then declared the floor open for questions. After some give and take with Robert Garibay about the merits of conducting a valid study of the dropout problem, Rabbi N. Podet of the commission suggested the formation of a committee to review the potential merits of such a study; potential sources of funding were also to be reviewed. The minutes of the meeting note a statement by Garibay to the effect that "if a child failed in school, it was the teacher's fault."[56] As it turned out, the suggestion by Podet led to a resolution of the immediate question of how to pay for a proper study of the high school dropout issue.

In March 1971, the Human Relations Commission announced receipt of a grant from the Cooper Foundation to conduct a dropout study focused on Waco ISD students, a step all parties believed necessary. Professor Lawrence G. Felice of the Sociology Department at Baylor University conducted the research. When he submitted his findings, WAMA responded by noting the findings "brought to light the great disparity that exists between the achievement levels of minority groups as opposed to those of the more affluent. It also found that the highest drop-out rate and the lowest achievement level existed among Mexican American students."[57]

The threat of litigation materialized with a lawsuit filed August 12, 1971. Armed with data from the "Drop Out Rates in the City of Waco Public Schools" report, the plaintiffs took their case to the US District Court of Judge Jack Roberts. The case known as *Pete D. Arvizu, et al. v. WISD* (Civil Action #W-71-CA-72) found the judge concentrating on staffing patterns and the administration's use of its power to recruit or transfer teachers in the interest of diversity. His ruling against Waco ISD, handed down July 27, 1973, the fourth intervention by the federal judiciary in Waco public schools since 1963, reflected the power of the testimony of Mexican American students and parents.

Roberts directed Waco ISD officials to file reports with the court on or about January 15 and July 15 of each year that included information about "progress regarding recruitment and assignment of black and Mexican American personnel in the faculty, staff, and administration." Implying the existence of some constraints on the administration's ability to reassign personnel, Judge Roberts stated in Part II of his ruling that "the administration must be given some latitude in assignment of principals and teachers to those schools most drastically affected who are considered especially qualified to facilitate an orderly transition with a minimum of disruption of the school routine."[58] Judge Roberts directed the parties (WAMA leaders and district administrators) to collaborate on the design and implementation of innovative strategies to build tolerance and mutual respect within each school and the community it served.

Highlighting the central role of language in the relationship between Spanish-speaking families and the English-speaking homes of Anglos and African Americans, Roberts ordered the district to "continue to improve and expand its program of bi-lingual and bi-cultural activities." Specifically, the judge stipulated that

efforts will be made to acquire supplemental funding from the emergency school aid program and other areas to develop curricula, continue to seek consultative assistance and involve more participation. The district will also conduct faculty and staff workshops to minimize the effects of any discriminatory practices and/or attitudes.[59]

This judicially mandated collaboration generated complementary grant proposals by WAMA and by Waco ISD to the Department of Health, Education, and Welfare (HEW) for Emergency Supplemental Aid Act (ESAA) funds, a category they qualified for due to the court order. The WAMA application offers significant evidence of a distinctive coalition of left-center interests in the Mexican American community in Waco. The cover sheet lists Pedro D. Arvizu of 1705 South Park Avenue as the contact person and chairman of WAMA, but the sixty-two-page application itself probably involved the work of several other individuals, reflecting the court's expectation for coalition building as part of the grant-writing process.

Fulfillment of the guidelines required the establishment of a citizen advisory group as part of the grant preparation process. Two categories of participants were needed, six students and six adults, each group comprised of two whites, two African Americans, and two Mexican Americans. Selection conferred a degree of recognition for one's contributions or prominence, as well as the individual's acceptability to the selectors. In theory, such a cross section of stakeholders assured that diverse voices and opinions would yield better proposals.

Taken as a whole, the brief profiles submitted by the individuals selected suggest that the process screened out more militant members of the community who would self-identify as Chicanos. As originally envisioned, assurance of grassroots involvement in planning for use of federal funds came in the form of advisory groups comprised of stakeholders. Each of these federally required demonstrations of inclusion represented the potential for building legitimacy for the projects under consideration. The identification of a selection of representatives of stakeholder groups seated at the table—the basic step—involved the exercise of considerable power. By the time of his involvement with this project, Robert Aguilar's experience as a community organizer and his demonstrated credentials as a grant writer proved especially useful.

If these participants were more than token representatives, the group assembled appeared to hold great potential. For example, Neomi Adams, a member of the Cabrera Neighborhood Council, brought over forty years of teaching experience in the rural La Vega and Lorena school districts. "All my work was in segregated schools," she confided on the information sheet advisory council members completed prior to service.[60]

Another member, Chuck Rose, a disabled veteran, represented LULAC on the advisory council. After moving to Waco in 1961, he and his family became active in youth sports programs and scouting. Residing at 1600 Holly Vista, the Rose children attended school at Kendrick Elementary, Sul Ross Elementary, University Junior High, and University High. Rose served as a board member of the Equal Opportunities Advancement Corporation, as he had done for the previous three years. He expressed hope that "by involving the parents in the activities we will get the student's interest. Now we can put some help where it is needed—with the student and the parent."[61]

A seat on the council designated for a "parent at-large" went to Ernest Fajardo of 3417 Wood Street. Membership on the Scholarship Committee for LULAC acquainted him with talented, ambitious students. In addition, Fajardo's work on the local Parent-Teacher Association and volunteer service at the Cabrera Neighborhood Center made him a solid choice. As he stated in his application, "My community involvement has brought me in contact with the school board, city officials and school personnel."[62]

Students like Tracye McDaniel represented the teenage perspective on dropout prevention; her vantage point was as student council secretary and circulation manager of the school newspaper. McDaniel's experience as a tutor for second grade students opened her eyes, as she put it: "the community really does need a tutoring system to help the children that are behind."[63]

To seasoned grant writers now familiar with the mindset of readers at

HEW after almost ten years of Johnson-begotten federal aid to education programs, the advisory group could be perfunctory, however well balanced (or not) its membership. This appears to be the case in Waco. Neomi Adams, Chuck Rose, and Ernest Fajardo may have contributed a one-page information sheet, but none of these three attended either of the two meetings of the committee. The evidence suggests that this ESAA advisory group played no meaningful role in the conception, design, or formulation of the plans to spend the $178,922 grant.

The group WAMA assembled met for the first time on November 12, 1973. The minutes of the meeting show seven of the twelve individuals named to the committee in attendance. As president of WAMA, Robert Aguilar explained the committee members' charge to "review the proposal developed from the defined needs and make comments which would become part of the proposal." The group then brainstormed a list of "Problem Areas." The minutes show a list of nineteen areas of concern, all of which centered on barriers to success adolescents faced at school and in the community at large. As a follow-up activity, the group identified seven needs: dropout prevention, tutorial, cultural awareness, more counselors, school staff sensitizing, parent involvement in school and children, and educational information.

The official minutes of the ESAA Advisory Committee indicate that the task of submitting a proposal for review and comment by the committee on Monday, November 19, 1973, fell to staff members. When the group met as scheduled, the only adult present who had ties to federal programs or to the school district, or both, was Charles Thornal, Waco ISD's director of federal programs. Five students dutifully attended, hearing Mr. Thornal explain how WAMA could best complement the school district's proposal. Then Mr. Thornal excused himself to attend another meeting.

The application materials record November 21—two days later—as the date of preparation. Based on the minutes of the two meetings of the ESAA Advisory Committee and on the twelve pages of Needs, Objectives, Activities, and Evaluation accompanying the application, it appears the committee served as a classic "rubber stamp," not as a vehicle for the people's voice to be heard. The fires of idealism still burned and frustration with the system still bred radicalism, but the body of energy Mexican American organizations expended appears to have been largely attributable to a relatively small group of savvy, pragmatic politicos who knew how to navigate the currents of the Anglo system. They operated in an environment, after all, where Mexican Americans represented just 10 percent of the population.

As historian Marc A. Rodriguez found in his study of the ties between the Chicano movements in South Texas and in Wisconsin in the 1960s and 1970s, pragmatic community leaders did not let ethnicity or gender stand in the way of mutually advantageous alliances.[64] The introduction to the grant cited several local organizations WAMA "has had liaison with over the years," specifically mentioning the Juvenile Achievement Center, the Methodist Home Child Guidance Center, the Neighborhood Centers' Program, the Mexican American Educational Foundation, the Association of Locally Involved Volunteers in Education, and the Friends of the Pablo Bernal Library. Using a War on Poverty–style metaphor, the application described common problems, which "have been significantly handicapped by a lack of facilities, materials, staff, and outreach personnel to substantially mount a frontal attack on the problem at hand."[65] In order to justify the application for $178,922, WAMA needed to demonstrate the shortcomings of the school district. The application asserted:

> The WISD problems are compounded by the fact that many individuals in the community, both students and parents, who, because of prior experiences have gradually perceived, whether correctly or incorrectly, an aura of negativism emanating from the school system and thus are unwilling, at this point, to actively participate in programs conducted by the schools.[66]

Despite its blunt critiques of the Waco school system dating back several years, WAMA's leaders, and Waco ISD officials, recognized their mutual interest in collaborating to obtain federal funding for a number of projects, including the one cited in this research, "Emergency Minority Remediation and Graduation Encouragement." In some respects, the dreams of Great Society liberalism had come true, with more places and faces at the policymaking table determining how to solve local problems with the assistance of federal resources.[67]

The story of the Waco Alliance of Mexican Americans opens a window to an aspect of the political culture from the 1950s into the early 1970s that finds federal aid programs providing leadership opportunities for members of minority groups. Arguably, the advent of significant federal funding for urban renewal and changes in the Brazos River floodplain due to dam improvements at Lake Waco opened doors for representatives of the Mexican American community prior to the emergence of the Chicano movement.

Consequently, dynamic individuals who would later form the core of WAMA gained access to the corridors of power of community politics via programs advanced by Bob Poage and Lyndon Johnson.

Over the course of his career in public affairs in Texas, with formative years in Waco during the Great Society era, Aguilar sought to balance idealism and pragmatism. To a large extent, this final chapter examined the Mexican American experience in Waco with an emphasis on the perspectives of the Chicano generation. These young adults faced an entirely different world from that of those unforgettable children of LBJ's school year in Cotulla. In many ways, the contributions of Robert Aguilar and the Waco Alliance of Mexican Americans to the Central Texas political scene in the 1960s and early 1970s validated Johnson's dream of a better future for Mexican American children.

From their first exposure to each other through the NYA, Bob Poage and LBJ filled slots on advisory councils. As discussed in chapter 2, LBJ argued strenuously with NYA officials in Washington against the integration of the Texas State Advisory Council, but the discussion reflected the demographics of the time. African Americans significantly outnumbered Mexican Americans and Tejanos in Waco and Austin in the 1930s. The gap closed significantly by 1970, but the focus of civil rights discourse remained on relations among blacks and whites.

The social problems did not go away, but Robert Aguilar, Ernest Calderon, and other similar talent and ambition moved into leadership opportunities within the system. For Aguilar, opportunity took the form of the position of executive deputy director for federal programs, which he described as "most of which were all education based. . . . We had another program to train bilingual teachers. . . . And we received money to set up a bilingual program for the migrant. . . . I mean it was really creative . . . beyond its time."

Reflecting on the work he did, and the problems inherent with training predominantly Anglo teachers to work with Hispanic students, Aguilar stated:

> What we did with the Anglo community is we sensitized them to the need of the Hispanic—they had to be working in a predominantly Hispanic school. We made sure we selected people and we recruited in schools where there were Anglo teachers that were working with Hispanics and wanted to learn more about the culture. It wasn't all about

education, but also things like understanding culture, understanding parents, understanding extended families. It was sociology involved with the educational curriculum. . . . So when you have the money and that ability to do things and that power to go in there and change the system. And try to make a permanent change if you can, like Waco . . . here we made a change, and it's been permanent.[68]

One can almost hear LBJ implore his aides, "What the hell is the presidency for?"

Conclusion

OTHER VANTAGE POINTS

CHRISTMAS 1963—what did President Lyndon Baines Johnson have on his mind? Thirty-three days earlier, he aimed to help JFK gain credibility with big money Democrats in Dallas and Houston by teaching the Kennedys how to do political damage control Lone Star style. They would have to carry Texas to win again in 1964—if Johnson were to be on that ticket again. The trip to Dallas, of course, went horribly awry. Johnson biographers concur regarding his utter misery during the vice-presidential years, but as Robert A. Caro's *The Passage of Power* documented, the calm, commanding confidence LBJ exuded upon assuming the presidency struck many of those who knew him well as quite remarkable.[1]

True to form, LBJ made merry with the family at the beloved ranch on that first of seven Christmas holidays he observed there as president, then he made seventeen phone calls. Among those receiving a personal greeting: former president Dwight D. Eisenhower, Secretary of State Dean Rusk, Secretary of Defense Robert McNamara, eminent journalist Walter Lippmann, and Harry Provence, editor in chief of the *Waco Tribune-Herald*.[2] In the four minutes of recorded conversation with Provence, LBJ spoke softly, expressed love, extended warm holiday wishes, and then asked for help with Bob—Bob Poage. The Christmas call to Provence, one of Poage's closest allies in Waco, revealed a fissure in the seamless political partnership that transformed everyday life for Central Texans by bringing federal programs and resources to a part of the country noted for open hostility to Washington, DC. Although Bob Poage retained a New Dealer's view of the proper role of government on a range of policies, even the moderating influence of some of his closest friends in Waco could not budge him from his states' rights stance on race relations. LBJ apparently recognized this early. Evidently agreeing to disagree rather than unleash his full arsenal of persuasive tools on a futile venture, Johnson recognized that his powerful House colleague could make things difficult for him. Provence could talk sense to Bob Poage.

Johnson routinely triangulated conversations, as did his idol, Franklin Roosevelt. He found it effective to arrange opportunities for others to carry his water when getting himself splashed might dampen chances for success. LBJ told Provence that he needed Poage to support substitute language in a bill moving through the House involving US agricultural policy with Africa, or Johnson would face trouble with African nations and with northern states. The tone of voice reflected Johnson's frustration with Poage's apparent refusal to go along with a "strictly symbolic" procedural measure. The reply from Provence can only be interpreted as a slap at the congressman from Waco, hoping for Bob to show some "statesmanship," a quality in short supply in the context of the conversation. A true statesman, in other words, would put country above congressional district and support the president. Provence assured Johnson that he would do what he could, but hardly sounded like someone who thought there might be a chance for success.[3]

Poage could always point to his vote against the Southern Manifesto in 1956 as proof of reasonableness on matters of race, but in politics, one needs a ready reply to the question, "What have you done for me lately?" LBJ held his allies accountable. He kept score. During his years together with LBJ in Congress, 1937–61, Poage scored so well on the former teacher's loyalty tests that in the future many scholars would crop him from the photograph of history. Assessing the dynamics of their relationship, Poage recalled:

> Lyndon was one of those folks who would do for you. He would help you and expect you to do the same thing for him . . . he expected it and demanded it and didn't remain your friend very long [chuckling] if he didn't get it. I think I went along with him a great deal. I know that I supported a good many program that I probably would not have, had it not been for the fact that Lyndon was backing them.[4]

CONCLUSION

LBJ and Poage still used each other, despite the breach in their relationship since 1964. In these photographs from 1966 and 1967, Poage's body language and facial expressions indicate no reluctance to confront the president. *Courtesy Lyndon Baines Johnson Library and Museum.*

Paradoxically, Poage's legacy suffered for being perceived as a Johnson tool, only to suffer again by opposing the most important human rights proposals in modern US history, forever enshrined, unfortunately with Vietnam, as Johnson's legacy. At the time of publication, researchers can access only one recorded telephone conversation between Bob Poage and Lyndon Johnson. They spoke on January 13, 1964, for four minutes about trade issues with Australia; they were exploring ways to encourage Australians to reduce beef imports (presumably because of US competitors) by addressing Australian concerns about US trade policy aimed at stabilizing world sugar prices. When Poage asked LBJ to confirm rumors about administration plans on sugar quotas, he stumped the president, who replied, "Well, I don't know," in a disarmingly matter-of-fact tone. Poage bluntly stated, "I hope not," and launched into a dazzling assessment of the issues, the options, and how he viewed American interests.

The earnest voice LBJ heard on the other end of the phone belonged to one of the most influential figures on US agriculture policy at the time.[5] If posterity has just four minutes of recorded conversation between these giants of Central Texas politics, fortunately most of that brief time captured two policy wonks fully immersed in arcane details of tonnage and previous harvests. These men lived and breathed the details of governing, and while their paths parted over civil rights, they could conduct a richly detailed discussion of trade policy with ease.

Poage confidently presented his reading of the political landscape in the House. The former Master of the Senate asked his old House colleague who would handle the issue in that chamber. First answering, "Harry Byrd," Poage corrected himself just as Johnson started to answer his own question. Russell Long of Louisiana would bring it up in his Senate Finance Committee. LBJ prodded Poage to urge Long "to help his cattlemen," but to not use the president's name.[6] Indeed, LBJ wrapped up the conversation with a story meant to illustrate how sometimes it is best to let someone else be the messenger. He told Poage about his "colored cook, Mary" who, during World War II, could not keep a supply of ration stamps for sugar on hand sufficient to satisfy LBJ's taste for sweetening his coffee, but preferred not to break the news to him herself. Johnson, of course, had a story for every occasion. He punctuated that phone call with his old segregationist friend with a parable featuring a "colored" employee, but to what end? Both men laughed heartily as Johnson recalled the cook's wisdom.[7]

In using that story, did the president signal a fellow white male that he, too, still saw African Americans as part of a servile class? Like Lincoln, Johnson exercised his mastery of storytelling purposefully, but the stories came so frequently, it could be that neither man could help himself in front of an audience of one or more. The context of the story suggests that Johnson brought his cook into the conversation, which represented an effort to connect with a hardliner, but LBJ also told stories of humiliations his African American staff members faced as they encountered Jim Crow exclusions on trips from Texas to Washington, DC, as part of emotional appeals for votes of senators hesitant to embrace federal civil rights legislation.[8] The word "colored" served integrationists and segregationists equally in that time and place in society.[9] The point of telling Poage about his cook's refusal to be the one to notify LBJ that no more sugar stamps could be obtained was to say that he had plenty to deal with already as president, especially when it came to telling people things they did not want to hear. Called foreshadowing in literary circles, Bob Poage would learn secondhand of a significant decision involving Waco several months later that year when LBJ followed his cook's example.

LBJ and Grassroots Federalism documents a political alliance more important to LBJ's power base in Texas than Johnson scholars have previously discussed. After reading dozens of letters and telegrams between Johnson and Poage (including several involving wives Lady Bird and Frances) from 1935 through the vice presidency, which tended toward somewhat flowery expressions of friendship and political fealty, the single recording that captured two professionals doing the nation's business could reasonably be interpreted as proof that their political relationship still existed. The fact they spoke at least once on the phone suggests Poage did not receive the variation of the Johnson treatment Hubert Humphrey called the "freeze" for his stance on civil rights. The freeze meant an indeterminate period of time during which an individual became more or less invisible to Johnson, to remain ignored until the arbitrary sentence of exclusion no longer served a purpose.[10]

Asked directly about whether Johnson punished him for opposition to increased federal involvement on the civil rights front, Poage pointed to funding Waco applied for and received under the Housing and Urban Development Administration's Model Cities program in 1967.[11]

Not in our district he didn't. Of course, it happened that I was one of the first that wanted to be one of these model cities. . . . I was wanting

Waco to be at the head of the list, but, of course, he wanted Austin. And, of course, he put Austin ahead, but I believe we were number five in the state that was given that grant. But Johnson went with us. He didn't turn us down. . . . It was a case where I was anxious to have the federal government—to the extent that they were engaged in a program, I wanted to give Central Texas all the benefits that they'd give to anybody else.[12]

In the parlance of Central Texas, if securing a military base for one's district, as Poage had done earlier in his career by helping to bring the Twelfth Air Force to Waco, counted as a coonskin to hang on the wall, bagging some lesser federal varmint like Model Cities simply did not compare. Interviewed in 1968, with the wound from the Connally Air Force Base closing still raw, Poage offered this analysis of the base closure in the context of a question regarding the impact of LBJ's presidency on his career.

I think it hurt me. In fact, I know it has. Now Lyndon would never admit it, but here in Waco I think it's perfectly clear that he closed James Connally Air Force Base solely because he was from Texas. I didn't fall out with him.[13]

"Solely because he was from Texas?" Since the base stayed in Central Texas but moved one hundred miles to the Tenth Congressional District, Poage's explanation explained nothing. In Austin, an LBJ-mentored representative James Jerrell "Jake" Pickle had earned the president's gratitude as one of five Southern Democrats to vote for the Civil Rights Act of 1964.[14] Poage's explanation of what seemed "perfectly clear" in Waco does not ring true. Circumstances strongly suggest that LBJ determined that the cost of Poage's opposition to the Kennedy/Johnson civil rights agenda should equal one pound of Waco flesh known as the James Connally Air Force Base. With the Southeast Asian "conflict" turning up the burners of the Cold War, no member of Congress would want to face the angry constituents whose livelihoods depended on that military base. The Johnson administration deliberately minimized the budgetary implications of escalation in Vietnam, especially in the early stages when the scope of the engagement promised to be less extensive. LBJ promised fiscal discipline, partially explaining a base closure process underway in the Department of Defense.

The "Waco" entry in the *Handbook of Texas* recounts the impact succinctly: "Connally Air Force Base was closed in 1966, dealing a blow to the

CONCLUSION

city. By 1970 the population had declined to 95,326."[15] Eisenhower's cautionary remarks about the military-industrial complex three years earlier in his
Farewell Address rang true in Waco, and LBJ knew it. Bob Poage knew it,
too. The people of his district paid a price because he placed himself in the
untenable position of being on the wrong side of history and the wrong side
of Lyndon Johnson simultaneously.

Two more conversations between Harry Provence and LBJ recorded the
sound of the other shoe dropping on the base closure. On November 8, 1964,
five days after the most sweeping victory in American political history, Johnson and Provence talked about visits to Waco by Deputy Secretary of Defense Cyrus Vance on November 9, to be followed a few days later by Vance's
chief, Robert McNamara, ostensibly to determine the fate of the Waco base.
Johnson offered no real assurances to Provence, stating, "I hope they don't
close any of yours." He told Provence that he would see if he could arrange
for a meeting with Vance.[16] A few weeks later, Johnson called Provence to
confirm that McNamara agreed to keep the headquarters of the Twelfth Air
Force in Waco for an undetermined amount of time, expressing faith that the
city might actually come out ahead in the long run.[17] Provence wrote about
the episode several years later:

> The closing of James Connally Air Force Base came on the heels of LBJ's
> landslide election in November 1964. We had had a whiff it was coming.
> I made a trip to the LBJ Ranch where Johnson and Defense Secretary
> Robert McNamara gave me the word of what was to come. I managed to
> delay the removal of 12th Air Force Headquarters for a couple of years.
> But the inevitable had arrived.[18]

Provence made no mention of Poage in his recounting of the closure. He
did not refer to telephone conversations with Johnson. The use of the word
"inevitable," given the broader context of Johnson's frustration with Poage,
indicates Provence knew Waco would lose the base to Austin, but why? Did
considerations related to the location of the LBJ ranch play a role in moving the base to Austin? Had changes in aircraft design made Waco's runway
space obsolete? Given the patterns of Lyndon Johnson's life and political
career, it defies the imagination that he just let the process work itself out,
disinterested in a Defense Department decision for or against Waco.

Could LBJ, in the same month of his election, have spent some of his capital within the defense establishment to spare the Eleventh District that loss?

Pundits advised Barack Obama to operate more like LBJ during the negotiations over the Affordable Care Act of 2010, a.k.a. Obamacare; the decision to close Connally Air Force Base in Waco in November 1964 fits the modus operandi the pundits envisioned. Johnson's goals in the area of civil rights stood as lofty as any society could aspire to, but when it came to methods, he remained grounded in the straight razor sharpness of consequence for those who opposed him. There is strength in unity, LBJ had wisely observed in Waco six years before at the groundbreaking ceremony for the dam, but he could have added the corollary that opposition to civil rights severs even the strongest ties that bind. In my reading of the situation, the timing, the motivation, and the opportunity for plausible denial by Johnson combine to strongly suggest that Poage's recalcitrance on federal civil rights legislation, and Jake Pickles's support for it, guaranteed that the base would move to Austin.

This book originated as an inquiry into the workings of federalism in Central Texas from the New Deal through the Great Society, viewed through episodes in the dynamic political partnership of Lyndon Johnson and Bob Poage. Ultimately, however, Bob Poage's opposition to federal civil rights legislation isolated him from Johnson, then from his party, and perhaps, from historians prior to this study. Bob Poage did a great deal for Waco. Without question, many of the votes he cast in the House of Representatives had direct and indirect benefits for people of all backgrounds. Contrasting Poage's record with Johnson's on civil rights in their lifetimes, however, raised the obvious question of how these two New Dealers could see the issue so differently. To answer this, we had to go back to the Central Texas they knew, when the superstructure of segregation underpinned society unevenly, but unshakably.

As shown in the first chapter, the two largest cities in Central Texas during their formative years developed distinctive forms of Jim Crow systems that were reflected in the local political culture, suggesting an explanation for why Lyndon Johnson never asked Bob Poage to vote for the Civil Rights Act of 1964 as a quid pro quo for any previous or future favor. LBJ did not need or pursue Poage's vote in the House, knowing that Waco constituents would punish Poage at the polls at the earliest opportunity.[19] Johnson's Christmas 1963 conversation with Harry Provence might indicate that he was more concerned about the consequences of segregationists using every opportunity to block him, even at the expense of the statesmanship Provence hoped Poage would display.

In 1979, six years after Johnson's death, Poage spoke with evident amusement about Johnson's apparent pragmatic view of Poage's position on civil rights. "No, not in the sense of grabbing me and putting his nose in my face and holding me with one hand as sometimes did [laughing] on some things, but he—Johnson, as I recall it, never—never even discussed with me the civil rights and racial issues."[20] Evidently, LBJ counted noses and did not need Poage's vote, and after the Democratic landslide victory he led in November 1964, LBJ needed it less.

For Bob Poage, the political realities dictated he could safely vote against the Civil Rights Act of 1964, and against "strictly symbolic" procedural matters, and the citizens white enough to vote in the Eleventh District would return him to office. A primary challenge from another local Democrat surely would have ensued had he done otherwise. Harry Provence told LBJ a few days after the 1964 election that the Johnson/Humphrey ticket carried 69.5 percent of the vote in McLennan County, so perhaps Poage's constituency moved faster on the issue than their member of Congress.[21]

Once allied in their strategy to oppose federal interference in race relations in Central Texas, from opposition to federal antilynching legislation in the 1930s to teaming with other key members of the Texas delegation in giving hardline segregationists the brush-off regarding the Southern Manifesto in 1956, Poage and Johnson came to differ substantially about the end of racial segregation over the next decade.[22] In the mid-1950s, each exerted more clout in their respective chambers than ever before. Not surprisingly, Poage specialized in agricultural policy, accumulating seniority on the key House Agriculture Committee that oversaw the federal government's school lunch programs and a host of food assistance initiatives, domestic and international. LBJ could not have found a better legislative partner on those issues while Majority Leader or as president. Bob Poage, however, quite possibly lost the opportunity to serve as John Kennedy's Secretary of Agriculture to Minnesota governor Orville Freeman because of Poage's adherence to traditionalist thinking on matters of race.[23]

The following statement about school desegregation from the oral history recorded near the end of Poage's life epitomizes his consistent effort to downplay the role of race relations in assessing the overall quality of life for Texans:

I don't recall hearing as much complaint as some other people say we heard at the time. I doubt that the district approved of it [the *Brown* decision], but neither did I think that our district was getting up in arms about it.[24]

Analysts of this statement may rightly suggest that the notorious tradition of lynching in the Eleventh District served as what might be termed enforcement terrorism. The active memory of unspeakable acts of violence against innocent members of the African American community in Waco led to a marked population decrease through the establishment of a terrifyingly hostile political culture. The killing of Jesse Washington, decidedly not a consequence of political action on the victim's part, did not represent an isolated incident in McLennan County, whereas the lynching

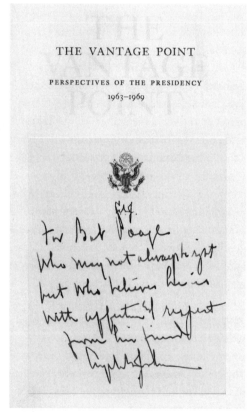

THE VANTAGE POINT

PERSPECTIVES OF THE PRESIDENCY
1963–1969

Poage's copy of LBJ's autobiography, *The Vantage Point*, included a note reading: "For Bob Poage: Who may not always be right but believes he is. With affection and respect from his friend"

culture historian William Carrigan described did not extend into the Hill Country.[25]

This place-based treatment of LBJ and Bob Poage illuminated a substantially unexamined aspect of Johnson's career—his relationship with a congressman from a neighboring district. Poage arguably represented a more conservative constituency in the Eleventh District than LBJ's Tenth District, but Johnson gradually positioned himself further to the right for his second run for the US Senate than during his House career to be more closely aligned with the realities of the broader political climate developing in Texas. Operating in a decidedly conservative atmosphere in the post–World War II era, these one-time New Dealers found ways to bring federal resources to Central Texas in a political culture increasingly hostile to the federal government. The relationship between individuals and Washington, DC, altered considerably during the economic calamity of the 1930s and by the subsequent mobilization for total war. Despite concerns about Uncle Sam's reach, by the 1950s many communities developed effective networks between local, state, and national power brokers to secure their fair share of the newfound imperial wealth.

In the 1950s, Elvis Presley was crowned King of Rock 'n' Roll, Gene Chandler was the self-appointed Duke of Earl, LBJ reigned as the Master of the Senate, and to many farmers, Bob Poage was Mr. Agriculture. Nearly invisible in existing Johnson scholarship and other studies of twentieth-century US political history, and when not ignored, characterized as a wimpy cipher, the career of Bob Poage mattered a great deal, especially to the lives of Central Texans. Poage supported legislation throughout his career that became part of the safety net stitched together from a host of federal programs. He shared enough of FDR's and LBJ's visions of America to support the social welfare system so hated by conservatives.

Obscured by LBJ's bright light, and darkened by his own comfort with status quo race relations when Johnson stepped out of the shadows, Poage's long career exemplified a less defiant form of segregationist thinking than some of his contemporaries. He maintained throughout the 1950s and 1960s that whites and blacks in Waco worked things out adequately without federal interference. Well-intentioned community leaders like Ford dealer Kultgen participated in the Community Relations Committee to relieve the pressure points of segregation when finding that a path to accommodation represented a better alternative than federal intervention. My impression from examining the relationships and records of these men from Waco leads me

Program

Welcome
Representative Dawson Mathis of Georgia
Master of Ceremonies

Invocation
The Reverend Seth R. Brooks, D.D.
*Minister, Universalist National Memorial Church
Washington, D.C.*

The President of the United States, Jimmy Carter
The Former President of the United States, Gerald Ford
The Vice President of the United States, Walter Mondale
Representative Tom Foley
Senator Herman Talmadge
Representative Bill Wampler
Former Secretaries of Agriculture
Charles Brannan
Ezra Taft Benson
Orville Freeman
Clifford Hardin
Earl Butz
Jack Kneble
Secretary of Agriculture Robert Bergland

Presentation of Plaque
E. A. Jaenke, Chairman,
Agriculture Sponsoring Group

Remarks
W. R. "Bob" Poage

Benediction
Dr. Seth Brooks

THE HONORABLE W. R. 'BOB' POAGE
United States House of Representatives

On behalf of American Agriculture, the sponsors listed below wish to express their deep appreciation and admiration for Bob Poage's service in the United States Congress from 1937 through 1978. Some of his major legislative achievements are engraved below. Few who have had the honor of serving in the Congress have attained such an outstanding record.

1949—Rural Telephone Service Act
1954—Watershed Protection & Flood Prevention
1954—Food for Peace Act
1958—Humane Slaughter Act
1960—The Gread Plains Conservation Act
1965—Poage-Aiken Rural Water & Sewer Act
1966—Laboratory Animal Welfare Act
1970—Agricultural Act of 1970
1970—Food Stamp Act Amendments
1971—The Farm Credit Act of 1971
1972—Rural Telephone Bank Act
1972—Rural Development Act
1972—Environmental Pesticide Act
1973—Agriculture and Consumer Protection
1974—Commodity Futures Trading Commission
1977—Food and Agriculture Act of 1977

A program for the tribute to Bob Poage, "Mr. Agriculture," held shortly after his retirement from Congress in 1979. Note the attendance of adversary Ezra Taft Benson, Eisenhower's secretary of Agriculture, and of Orville Freeman, who held the position Poage aide Fowler West suggested may have been Poage's under JFK.

to conclude this key circle of business elites exercised moderating influences on Bob Poage. The unquestionably progressive record of Jack Kultgen, especially for a white business leader in the Old Confederacy, contributed to the effectiveness of their nongovernmental process for reducing tensions and undoubtedly contributed to Bob Poage's vantage point on the racial climate in Waco. Safety valves like the Community Relations Committee encouraged solutions by discouraging confrontations through anticipatory actions. We know that Kultgen worked closely with African American–affiliated Paul Quinn College, but there is much more to be learned about this dimension of race relations in Waco.

LBJ and Grassroots Federalism examined the way our political system assigns some matters for resolution to local decision making, while other matters receive attention at the state or federal level. The problem of flooding on the Brazos system led to a model new for Texas in 1929, a regional body, the Brazos River Authority (BRA). The ubiquitous Jack Kultgen emerged as the vital force for that body. During his years of involvement with the BRA, Jack Kultgen had "been in every place on the Brazos and talked to many people about their problems and through many a congressional hearing. You learn a little as you go along."[26] Every city deserves its own Jack Kultgen. Was he an elite or an everyman? To the real movers and shakers, a car dealer from Waco, Texas, may lean toward nouveau riche rather than the truly privileged, but Kultgen seemed to have the ability to move in all circles. A model of the engaged citizen Johnson hoped to bring forward through advisory councils and similar forms of public involvement, Kultgen deserves a book of his own.

Finding key allies and gaining their loyalty by giving them the sense their voices were heard, Johnson enthusiastically adopted NYA director Aubrey Williams's strategy for citizen engagement to minimize the distance between taxpayers and their government. Immediately upon appointment to his position as state NYA director in 1935, LBJ engaged state senator Poage in the recruitment of an advisory council to determine appropriate projects for McLennan County. Those individuals became key contacts for Johnson.

Along with Poage, Johnson established mutually beneficial connections to key opinion leaders like Jack Kultgen, Harry Provence, and Harlan Fentress. Through the New Deal and World War II, federal programs stimulated participation in the political culture of Waco by traditional elites accustomed to gorging at the public trough as grizzly bears midstream in the thick of a salmon spawning run. The more salient point, however, is the significance of these programs in engineering avenues for engagement by segments of the population previously frozen out by white ice, including future leaders of what would become known as the Chicano movement. The final chapter in *LBJ and Grassroots Federalism* emphasized the power citizens obtained as a result of the policies and processes Johnson put in place. Mexican American community leaders in Waco blended their experiences from organizing *mutualistas* and other support systems with opportunities to engage "the system" that produced strategies to use federal resources to address locally identified needs and to implement locally identified solutions. Johnson's extraordinarily controversial time in politics had come and gone, but the successful engagement between the Waco Alliance of Mexican Americans and the Waco Independent School District, and other bridge-building exercises like it across the country, meant the teacher had not forgotten what his students taught him about the power to be found in honoring simple human dignity.[27]

To build a great society, one needs human capital, and the United States engaged in recalibrating its assets in the 1960s. Recognition of the need to improve the infrastructure of the nation dates back at least as far as George Washington, who surely wished for a bridge to cross the Delaware River. "Internal improvements" policy debates dominated public meetings and tavern talk for decades in the antebellum years, from critical decisions about road building and canals to the routes of rail lines. Farsighted leaders like Henry Clay and Abraham Lincoln built support among their constituents by arguing that when it comes to dealing with transportation of goods, interdependence trumps sovereignty. The Progressive Era response to poor resource management during the rapid industrialization of the late nineteenth century found Teddy Roosevelt asserting a greater federal role than ever. The New Deal stimulated a generation of dam building for hydroelectric power, flood management, and recreational opportunities. The shift in the population of the United States from the Northeast and Midwest to the South and Southwest evident in the post–World War II era presented significant resource management issues, especially with regard to water.

However, public confidence in the federal government, carefully nurtured by schools and the mass culture from the New Deal through World War II and the most intense moments of the Cold War, slowly eroded as policy failures in Vietnam and tip-of-the-iceberg glimpses at corruption in the Watergate era fed resistance to centralization. After the virtual banishment of Lyndon Johnson and the near-conviction of Richard Nixon, both parties successfully tapped this anti-federal mood, from Jimmy Carter's promise of a "government as good as its people," to Ronald Reagan's assertion that "government is the problem."[28] Barack Obama represented a tidal shift, perhaps, back in the direction of federal-state-local government interdependence evident in Waco, especially when it comes to policy matters dealing with the physical environment and the infrastructure we create within it.

Of course, sometimes clumsy things happen when the federal government gets involved, as in the case when Civilian Conservation Corps officials worked with local leaders in 1935 to design and construct Mother Neff State Park along the Leon River near Belton, roughly midway between Waco and Austin.[29] Given isolationist sentiment in the United States in the mid-1930s, few could imagine the need for the sprawling Fort Hood military base. Less than twenty years later, however, the Army Corps of Engineers would flood most of that park with the damming of the Leon to create Lake Belton, largely for the purpose of guaranteeing Fort Hood's supply. For critics of the federal government's ability to plan long term, this example shines brightly.

Before the interruption of the Leon River's free flow, my father, Harold Duke, retreated to its swimming holes with his friends for relief from the endless summer heat. Born in 1915 on a tenant farm south of Waco near the tiny community of Eddy, Texas, where picking cotton and raising turkeys held little appeal, he headed to Chicago during the Depression to find work. Had he stayed in Eddy, perhaps one of those jobs working with the CCC Company 817 would have come his way when they started working on Mother Neff State Park in 1934. Maybe college would have been in reach if the NYA existed a few years earlier. The diploma awarded to him by Bruceville-Eddy High School in May 1932 meant little in the economy of rural Central Texas, long depressed by rock-bottom commodity prices. It would have currency a world away, at Sears, Roebuck, and Company in Chicago.

At the time my father left Falls County, Franklin D. Roosevelt was his president and Bob Poage, a future New Dealer in Congress, his state senator. When my father returned to Central Texas in 1971 upon retirement from Sears, Roebuck, and Company, Poage had won the previous seventeen elections to the US House of Representatives and would serve another three full terms. Lyndon Johnson and Bob Poage gained political power largely from their ability to gain the confidence of men with a worldview like my father. Prior to the Voting Rights Act of 1965, every House and Senate election depended on support from voters committed to maintaining segregation in accordance with local practices. Johnson soon acquired his reputation for bringing federal programs to his home district and to Texas itself. As demonstrated in several examples in this book, Poage also mastered the politics of federalism, as witnessed by changes in the landscape and in the lives of Waco and Wacoans.

Results of city elections on multiple occasions proved voters strongly endorsed Poage's commitment to finding a solution to the blessing and nemesis known as the Brazos River. The chronic problem of "keeping the rain where it falls," as Poage often described the challenge, featuring periods of drought followed by punishing floods, seemed to have a solution in the form of a new dam. When rains forced the forks of the Bosque River over their banks, the convergence into the Brazos just above the city center magnified the problem. Investors and insurers faced an entirely different situation in Waco after the dam expansion. With the official announcement confirming funds in 1958, five years after the utter devastation of many downtown neighborhoods by the monstrous tornado, the neighborhood known as Sandtown could find Waco's most notorious slums replaced by commercial and other interests, notably Baylor University.

The use of advisory bodies in the urban renewal efforts following the Waco tornado of 1953, so effective for NYA director Johnson, proved central to establishing a connection between Washington and community leaders. Johnson's passionate argument against an integrated NYA advisory council in September of 1935 metamorphosed into insistence for appropriate diversity in such bodies by the late 1950s. When Waco embraced federal aid as enthusiastically as city officials did, Majority Leader Johnson had seen to it that a broader representative of affected communities found seats at the table. My research led me to conclude two factors account for Waco standing out at this time as a city so accepting of federal requirements: two decades of skillful nurturing of key relationships by Bob Poage and Lyndon Johnson, and the emergence of white progressives among Waco elites, such as Jack Kultgen, Harry Provence, and Harlan Fentress. The scope of the rebuilding challenge in the aftermath of the tornado combined with the opportunity represented by the promise of relief from the floodwaters of the Brazos constitutes a third factor for Waco's willingness to seat people of color at meetings to decide how to allocate federal funds in the city. Doing so enabled leaders like Robert Aguilar and Ernest Calderon of the Waco Alliance of Mexican Americans to gain invaluable experience for their own development as community leaders, wherein they would serve as role models for others.

Political scientist James McEnteer argued in *Deep in the Heart: The Texas Tendency in American Politics* that dependence on federal support for major infrastructure projects by city officials became a source for leverage for Washington when civil rights issues made some state and local official balk at federal authority.[30] McEnteer made a strong case, but as demonstrated by this study of the broader context in Central Texas, variances in political culture played a major role in how locals perceived federal action. To paraphrase the show tune "New York, New York," if federalism could make it here, it could make it anywhere.[31] For my purposes, Waco proved to be a Model City, just as HUD decided.

With the exceptions of Scarbrough's *Road, River, and Ol' Boy Politics* and Hansen's *Gaining Access*, scholars have not examined the forty-two-year congressional career of this quiet segregationist Democrat who specialized in agricultural policy, but the preceding chapters demonstrated the scope of his impact on Waco. Bob Poage merits more than a footnote or a brush-off in his own right, but the working relationship between Johnson and Poage anchored the policy analysis, infused with the underlying tension, that developed as each reached the pinnacle of his respective career. They had to come to terms with the fact that their political self-interest meant setting aside differences on the proper role of the federal government in matters of civil rights. Having arrived at different conclusions about governmental policies dealing with race relations, as that unhealed sore festered and burst again, and again in the 1950s and 1960s, Johnson and Poage could easily have broken their political alliance over an issue as wrenching as an externally imposed end to racial segregation. Yet LBJ and Poage collaborated to pump federal money into Waco before and after Johnson's public conversion to civil rights. Perhaps the lesson to learn is that whether one is for or against integration, be sure to bring home the bacon.

Bob Poage remained tied the principle of home rule long beyond any political advantage. LBJ could not let go of that school year in Cotulla. Jack Kultgen never forgot his first view of Waco aflood from the swollen Brazos. Children sharing the language and heritage of Robert Aguilar, Ernest Calderon, Margie Citron, and so many others found themselves left behind, however, and the memories of alienation fueled Aguilar and El Movimiento in Waco. We choose sides to fight in the name of tradition or in the name of change.

Ten years after Johnson occupied the White House, his successor was on the way out. It was 1973, the second of three "Watergate summers," and the first summer after LBJ's death. Bob Poage still represented the Eleventh District, retaining a key seat on the House Agriculture Committee, but his longevity started to work against him as seniority-based systems faced challenges from reformers. Johnson would remain a nonperson in the Democratic Party gallery because of Vietnam until his name finally surfaced in the 2008 presidential campaign. Poage's close ties to LBJ assisted him throughout his congressional career—until the war shredded the coalition of conservative and liberal Democrats that enacted so much of the Great Society agenda. Failure to support the Civil Rights Act of 1964, the Voting Rights Act of 1965, or the Open Housing Act of 1968 served to isolate Poage into a dwindling number of Democrats whose effectiveness in Washington fell due to their segregationist leanings.

Longtime associate Fowler West experienced the changes while working alongside the congressman at a time when the Democratic Party's left wing conducted a purge of prowar, anti–civil rights members. By the end of the

1970s, many of these politicians switched their affiliation to the Republican side. Not even the Dixiecrat split of 1948 accomplished that feat. Humiliated by the treatment he received at the hands of fellow party members over chairmanship of the Agriculture Committee, Poage announced he would not seek reelection in 1978.

The conservative movement gained momentum after the 1973 *Roe v. Wade* ruling led to a realignment of priorities for individuals who would soon identify as "prolife" or "prochoice." Conservatives viewed the Supreme Court ruling as a monstrous usurpation of states' rights by the federal government. As historian Gareth Davies asserted in his study of US domestic policy in the 1970s under Nixon and Ford, the intrusiveness of the federal government into state and local affairs increased, despite small-government rhetoric.[32] The emergence of a strong federal presence in everyday life during the New Deal and continuing through the 1960s reflected the high priority that those present for the establishment of the programs initially gave to local input. The passing of that generation of leaders can be seen in the much less pliant bureaucratic systems that now comprise the federal programs that infuriate conservatives today.

Historians hold a mirror up to society, often confronting the question of whether life got "better" or "worse" over some span of time. Progress is a concept some try to measure through mathematical schema, others by citation of the passage or repeal of laws. These methods may be valid and appropriate, depending on the context of and the purpose for their use. This analysis and description did, in fact, draw on such data. Census reports, city plans, maps, and charts offer platforms for interpretation of city life, but even the best paint-by-number rendering cannot capture the wrinkles and creases in the faces and in the clothing of the subjects.

Poage's five decades representing Waco in the Texas legislature and in the House of Representatives, often working closely with Lyndon Johnson as LBJ's career took him from the NYA to the US House and Senate to the White House, provide historians and political scientists with texture more closely resembling the give and take of real politics than very limited scholarly studies of their collaboration have accomplished to date. It would be highly misleading to suggest Poage played a central role in LBJ's career, but Johnson certainly loomed large in the life and times of Bob Poage.

As the first president to advocate affirmative action as a necessary step in maximizing potential, Lyndon Johnson drew upon a lifetime of witnessing people accomplish remarkable things despite inequality. What a great society we could have, he posited, if all citizens were equal under the law. Together, the careers of these two Texans are linked with reshaping the physical and cultural landscape of Waco and Central Texas.

Earlier in his career, Johnson wrote his own public remarks and dictated much of the correspondence issued on NYA or House stationery with his signature. As Senate Majority Leader, with the power and the resources at the disposal of the most powerful legislator in the nation, however, he could delegate the production of speeches to staffers. They knew the tone he tried to achieve and how to match it to the expected audience. During his days at San Marcos State Teachers College, Johnson chose a stilted form of rhetoric for his editorials for the school paper, but one-to-one engagement leveraged Johnson's persuasion, not position papers or rhetoric. Perhaps the teacher in LBJ, a persona he clearly cherished, determined that platitudes about the virtues of civic-mindedness needed reinforcement from public officials.

On a few occasions, Richard Goodwin, Bill Moyers, and others who penned Johnson's public presidential remarks would align the master storyteller's gift with the material. In the address to a joint session of Congress on the voting rights legislation in March 1965, arguably the pinnacle of LBJ's career, the speechwriters found the sweet spot where their words and Johnson's personal convictions melded. Such a phrase launched this book: "strength in unity." The unity Johnson referred to that existed among the local, state, and federal collaborators who planned, funded, and constructed the Waco Dam did not set overnight like poured concrete. Those relationships formed phone call by phone call, favor by favor, and handshake by handshake, bonded together by the never-secret additive of Johnson's ambition. Sometimes people got in the way of building a great society. Sometimes those people were white supremacists whose way of life came to an abrupt halt. During the era of Lyndon Baines Johnson, Central Texas (and the United States, of course) experienced a metamorphosis from institutionalized bigotry to mandatory inclusiveness. Making representative democracy function at the grassroots level required centralized authority—the quintessential irony of the American political culture.

NOTES

ACKNOWLEDGMENTS

1. Dan K. Utley and Cynthia J. Beeman, *History Ahead: Stories beyond the Texas Roadside Markers* (College Station: Texas A&M University Press, 2010); Utley and Beeman, *History along the Way: Stories beyond the Texas Roadside Markers* (College Station: Texas A&M University Press, 2013).

2. Wayne J. Urban, *Gender, Race, and the National Education Association* (New York: RoutledgeFalmer, 2000).

INTRODUCTION

1. Then a state senator, Poage lost to incumbent Otto Cox in the 1934 primary, but went on to win the Democratic primary in 1936 against a local attorney, Frank Tirey. Poage wrote in his memoir, *My First 85 Years* (Waco, TX: Baylor University Press, 1985): "Each candidate praising the reforms of the Roosevelt Administration, which we all supported without much understanding of the economics involved" (57).

2. "Waco Wires Ike to Get Federal Aid in Disaster," *Big Spring Daily Herald*, May 14, 1953, *GenDisasters*, accessed June 21, 2013, at http://www3.gendisasters .com/texas/12464/waco-tx-tornado-may-1953-disaster-aid.

3. For insights about Johnson's collaborations with speechwriters, see Robert Hardesty, "The LBJ the Nation Rarely Saw," August 27, 1983, accessed June 24, 2013, http://www.lbjlibrary.org/lyndon-baines-johnson/perspectives-and-essays/the-lbj-the-nation-seldom-saw. Hardesty recalled Johnson setting strict four-hundred-word limits on public statements. Despite Rebekah Johnson's best efforts, he rarely seemed comfortable behind a lectern, regardless of the quality of the prepared text.

4. W. R. Poage, "Speech at Groundbreaking for Waco Dam," July 5, 1958, Box #1489, File 22, Poage Legislative Library, Baylor University, Waco, Texas.

5. Robert A. Caro, *The Years of Lyndon Johnson: Master of the Senate* (New York: Knopf, 2002).

6. Critics of Clinton's observations, as well as supporters, would be very interested in the relationship between these men and the landmark acts portrayed by Nick Kotz in *Judgment Days: Lyndon Baines Johnson, Martin Luther King, Jr., and the Laws That Changed America* (Boston: Houghton Mifflin, 2005).

7. Eleanor Clift, "Obama's LBJ Moment," *The Daily Beast*, July 9, 2009, accessed June 24, 2013, http://www.thedailybeast.com/newsweek/2009/07/09/obama-s-lbj-moment.html.

8. LBJ expressed the desire that his Presidential Library in Austin should offer scholars and the public the ability to examine the full record of his public life, "with the bark off." For the full text of his remarks at the dedication ceremony for the library on May 22, 1971, see http://www.lbjlib.utexas.edu/johnson/archives.hom/speeches.hom/710522.asp, accessed June 24, 2013.

9. For the full text of Humphrey's remarks on July 14, 1948, see his autobiography, *The Education of a Public Man: My Life and Politics* (Garden City, NY: Doubleday, 1976), 458–59. The famous sentence, "The time has arrived for the Democratic Party to get out of the shadows of human rights and step forthrightly into the bright sunshine of human rights," appears on page 459. Humphrey won his first US Senate race later that fall. He trumpeted liberal causes through his nomination and election as Johnson's vice president in 1964.

10. This was, of course, the "Johnson treatment" in practice—physical, emotional, humorous, and highly localized.

11. Transcripts of interviews with Poage reveal him to be convinced that local remedies to issues of race were best, and that the situation in Waco did not require federal intervention in any way. LBJ, in his view, had gone too far.

12. Robert Dallek, *Lone Star Rising: Lyndon Johnson and His Times, 1908–1960* (New York: Oxford University Press, 1991), 161. Johnson was sworn in as a member of Congress on May 13, 1937.

13. Transcript of W. R. Poage Oral History Interview by Joe B. Frantz, recorded

on November 11, 1968. File William R. Poage, AC74–235, pp. 2–4, LBJ Library, Austin, Texas.

14. Linda Scarbrough, *Road, River, and Ol' Boy Politics* (Austin: Texas State Historical Association, 2005).

15. Brown and Root, later Kellogg, Brown, and Root, eventually became a subsidiary of Halliburton, one of the most controversial of the corporations awarded billions of dollars of business by the US government during the Iraq War (2003–11).

16. The second volume of Caro's Johnson biographies, *The Means of Ascent* (New York: Knopf, 1990), takes on the relationship between Johnson and George Brown of Brown and Root in great detail. The result is a withering critique of the unseemly ties between the federal government and influential players within Texas political culture. Johnson distributed Brown's money among Democrats. Caro does not name Poage as one of the players in this high stakes game, but one could reasonably surmise that campaign funds were available to Poage via Johnson, though Poage's safe Waco district demanded few expenditures.

17. Poage, *My First 85 Years*, v.

18. Ibid., 157–59.

19. "Poage, William Robert," *Handbook of Texas Online*, accessed June 27, 2011, http://www.tshaonline.org/handbook/online/articles/fp050.

20. Poage, *My First 85 Years*, 137.

21. John Mark Hansen, *Gaining Access: Congress and the Farm Lobby, 1919–1981* (Chicago: University of Chicago Press, 1991), 209n.

22. Thomas Stephen Foley and Poage, by all accounts, including this *New York Times* article, demonstrated extraordinary grace in this awkward situation. David Rosenbaum, "Man in the News," *New York Times Online*, accessed June 20, 2013, http://www.nytimes.com/1989/06/02/us/man-in-the-news-thomas-stephen -foley-a-politician-outside-the-mold.html?pagewanted=all&src=pm.

23. Perhaps the greatest rift between the two men came when Johnson approved the closing of James Connally Air Force Base, located at Waco, in favor of Bergstrom Airfield outside of Austin, as discussed further in the conclusion.

24. Robert A. Caro, *The Years of Lyndon Johnson: The Path to Power* (New York: Knopf, 1982). The references to Poage are on pages 533 and 553. My investigations of Poage's papers suggest that virtually no one referred to him as anything other than Bob or W. R. Use of the middle name here indicates a lack of familiarity with Poage's relationship with LBJ, akin to referring to Tom O'Neill instead of Tip. See page 130 of Caro's *Means of Ascent* (1990) for a reminder that above all else, apparently, Poage is "unassertive."

25. Robert A. Caro, *The Years of Lyndon Johnson: The Passage of Power* (New York: Knopf, 2012).

26. Robert Dallek, *Flawed Giant: Lyndon Johnson and His Times, 1961–1973* (New York: Oxford University Press, 1998). Caro, to date, needed three volumes totaling 2,500 pages to get Johnson through his Senate career, while Dallek managed to tell LBJ's story through his passing in two volumes of 1,000 pages each.

27. Hansen, *Gaining Access*, 205.

28. Fowler West, *He Ain't No Lawyer: Memories of My Years with Congressman Bob Poage* (Waco, TX: Baylor University Press, 2009). This volume was published by Baylor University Press for the thirtieth anniversary observation of the W. R. Poage Legislative Library located on the Baylor campus in the heart of Waco along the Brazos River.

29. Ibid., 1.

30. LBJ took great satisfaction humiliating Bobby Kennedy when JFK moved faster on the invitation to the ticket than his brother had realized. This tale from the 1960 convention is found in varying degrees of detail in just about any book on the subject. Dallek, Caro, and Doris Kearns Goodwin do a good job with it in their respective biographies, and Theodore White's *The Making of the President: 1960* recounting makes for good political theater. Robert McNamara recounted his appointment as secretary of defense in the superb documentary film by Errol Morris, *The Fog of War*. Stitched together, these accounts of assembling the Kennedy cabinet do not bring to mind a well-oiled machine. Johnson noticed.

31. West, *He Ain't No Lawyer*, 31.

32. Transcript W. R. Poage Oral History Interview, June 20, 1977, by James B. Rhoads, File William R. (Bob) Poage, AC79–77, LBJ Library.

33. Transcript, W. R. Poage Oral History Interview, November 11, 1968, by Joe B. Frantz, LBJ Library. William Robert Poage, File AC74–235, LBJ Library. Poage's wife disliked LBJ's frequent criticism that her husband lacked ambition, but she exchanged warm letters with Lady Bird about visits to the ranch on the Pedernales and Lyndon's health.

34. Edward L. Schapsmeier and Frederick H. Schapsmeier, *Encyclopedia of American Agricultural History* (Westport, CT: Greenwood Press, 1975), 271–72. As Eisenhower's secretary of agriculture, Benson struggled to get his free market agricultural policies enacted by Congress, where members like Poage insisted on maintaining federal price supports.

35. Neil Foley, *The White Scourge: Mexicans, Blacks, and Poor Whites in Texas Cotton Culture* (Berkeley: University of California Press, 1997).

36. Tony Badger, "Southerners Who Refused to Sign the Southern Manifesto," *Historical Journal* 42 (June 1999): 520–23.

37. Ibid., 522.

38. For more insights about the functioning of the Texas delegation in the post-Rayburn era, see Barbara Deckard's "State Party Delegations in the U.S House of

Representatives—A Comparative Study of Group Cohesion," *Journal of Politics* 34 (February 1972): 199–222.

39. Caro, *The Years of Lyndon Johnson: The Path to Power*, xix.

40. L. Patrick Hughes, "Working within the System: Lyndon Johnson and Tom Miller, 1937–1939," *Southwestern Historical Quarterly* 96 (October 1992): 199.

41. Randall B. Woods, *LBJ: Architect of American Ambition* (New York: Free Press, 2006).

42. James T. Patterson, *Freedom Is Not Enough* (New York: Basic Books, 2010).

43. See Doris Kearns Goodwin's *Lyndon Johnson and the American Dream*, 8th ed. (New York: St. Martin's Press, 1991) for Johnson's recounting of nightmares and similarly dark visions for the future of his programs.

44. The satirists had plenty of material to work with, and the backdrop of the Vietnam disaster gave resonance to the *MacBeth* parody created in 1967 by Barbara Garson. See "She Hopes 'MacBird' Flies in a New Era," *Washington Post*, http://www.washingtonpost.com/wp-dyn/content/article/2006/09/04/AR200609 0400993.html, accessed June 24, 2013.

45. Nick Kotz, *Judgment Days: Lyndon Baines Johnson, Martin Luther King, Jr., and the Laws That Changed America* (Boston: Houghton Mifflin, 2005).

46. Ira Katznelson, *When Affirmative Action Was White* (New York: Norton, 2005). Katznelson did not focus on the NYA, and although the book is subtitled *An Untold History of Racial Inequality in Twentieth-Century America*, he mentioned Mexican Americans just once. Perhaps the regional nature of the issue with Mexican Americans explains that decision.

47. Gareth Davies, "Towards Big-Government Conservatism: Conservatives and Federal Aid to Education in the 1970s," *Journal of Contemporary History* 43 (October 2008): 624.

48. Philip Funigiello, *The Challenge to Urban Liberalism* (Knoxville: University of Tennessee Press, 1978).

49. Mitchell Lerner, "'To Be Shot At by the Whites and Dodged by the Negroes': Lyndon Johnson and the Texas NYA," *Presidential Studies Quarterly* 39 (June 2009): 245–74.

50. Richard Flanagan, "Lyndon Johnson, Community Action, and Management of the Administrative State," *Presidential Studies Quarterly* 31 (December 2001): 588.

51. Lerner, "To Be Shot at by the Whites and Dodged by the Negroes," 245–74.

52. Sidney M. Milkis and Jerome M. Mileur, eds., *The Great Society and the High Tide of Liberalism* (Amherst: University of Massachusetts Press, 2005).

53. James McEnteer, *Deep in the Heart: The Texas Tendency in American Politics* (Westport, CT: Praeger, 2004), 129–34.

54. Ibid., 2–5.

55. See Patricia Bernstein's *The First Waco Horror: The Lynching of Jesse Washington and the Rise of the NAACP* (College Station: Texas A&M University Press, 2005). At least three new historical treatments of Waco have followed *The First Waco Horror* in the past two years, perhaps in an attempt to appease those with local ties hoping to provide a less disturbing overview of the city once referred to by boosters as the "Athens of Texas." Each of these new books draws extensively, as my project does, on the Texas Collection and the Institute for Oral History at Baylor University. Eric S. Ames, a member of the Waco Landmark Preservation Commission, recently applied his skills in digital preservation of rare and fragile materials to produce *Waco*, a volume in the *Images of America* series by Arcadia Publishing. A landmark anniversary celebration of the dedication of Waco's William Cameron Park, located where the Bosque River enters the Brazos, led local historical societies and Baylor University to produce *Waco, Texas' William Cameron Park, A Centennial History, 1910–2010*. The aforementioned local histories, such as *Our Land, Our Lives*, the tribute to McLennan County, typically refer to Poage as Mr. Agriculture, due to his long service on that committee. A prolific writer, Poage contributed substantially to local history by publishing several books on Waco and McLennan County, as well as his memoirs, during an active retirement.

56. Bernstein, *The First Waco Horror*, 110. Bernstein's wrenching description of the event uses contemporaneous sources to estimate the crowd at between ten and fifteen thousand people. See "In Waco, a Push to Atone for the Region's Lynch-Mob Past," http://www.washingtonpost.com/wp-dyn/content/article/2006/04/25/AR2006042502306.html, for an article on how various Waco citizens regard this episode from the vantage point of almost a century later (accessed October 17, 2013).

57. Bradley T. Turner, *Lust, Violence, Religion: Life in Historic Waco* (Waco, TX: TSTC Publishing, 2010), 55. The title of Turner's fascinating collection of stories, which the boosters seldom emphasize, indicates his focus is not on federalism, but he also points to how deeply these events imprinted on the general public's awareness of the city and its culture.

58. Goodwin, *Lyndon Johnson and the American Dream*, 160–209.

59. Nick Bryant, *The Bystander: John F. Kennedy and the Struggle for Black Equality* (New York: Basic Books, 2006).

60. Charles Peters, *Lyndon B. Johnson* (New York: Times Books, 2010), 159.

61. Kevin Fernlund, *Lyndon B. Johnson and Modern America* (Norman: University of Oklahoma Press, 2009).

62. See Nancy Gibbs and Michael Duffy, *The President's Club* (New York: Simon and Schuster, 2012), for a rather unsettling recounting of the last weeks of the 1968 campaign and the ongoing quest for peace in Vietnam.

63. Goodwin, *Lyndon Johnson and the American Dream*.

1. Transcript of Edward Joseph Oral History Interview, File AC81-3, LBJ Library.

2. "Texas Legislature," *Handbook of Texas Online*, accessed January 23, 2004, www.tsha.utexas.edu/handbook/online/articles/view/TTmkt2.html. Reapportionment in 1921 increased the size of the House to a maximum of 150.

3. "W. R. Poage," *Handbook of Texas Online*, accessed June 22, 2011. Bob Poage had not yet completed Baylor Law School when he ran for the state House in 1924, four years after his father's passing.

4. "Texas Legislature," *Handbook of Texas Online*.

5. "Sam E. Johnson." Results of Inquiry by Walter Jenkins dated August 14, 1964 re: Sam E. Johnson's legislative record. Family Correspondence Box #2, LBJ Library.

6. Lyndon attended summer school in San Marcos in 1922 to work on his German, as documented in a letter from his mother to his teacher. Rebekah Johnson, letter to Flora Eckert, July 11, 1922. Papers of Rebekah Johnson, Box 8, LBJ Library. None of his biographers are specific about the dates he was on the House floor in Austin, but since school was not in session during the month-long special call, it is certainly a possibility.

7. Transcript of Juanita Roberts Oral History Interview recorded April 28, 1965, LBJ Library.

8. Transcript of Kittie Leonard Oral History Interview, LBJ Library.

9. This localized political dynasty pales in comparison to the Dingells of Michigan, where father and son have served uninterrupted congressional terms since 1933. John D. Dingell Jr. set the record in June 2013 for the longest uninterrupted service in the House of Representatives. He took over his father's seat in December 1953.

10. Randall B. Woods, *LBJ: Architect of American Ambition* (New York: Free Press, 2006), 75.

11. Bob Poage, more than eight and a half years older, saw the war from a different vantage point than LBJ, but both men reached adulthood in those years between World War I and the onset of the Great Depression.

12. Arthur Waskow, *From Race Riot to Sit-In, 1919 and the 1960s: A Study in the Connection between Conflict and Violence* (Garden City, NY: Doubleday, 1966), 16–18.

13. "Longview Race Riot of 1919," *Handbook of Texas Online*, accessed June 26, 2013, http://www.tshaonline.org/handbook/online/articles/jc102.

14. *Austin American*, August 3, 1919. Austin File Chronological, Austin History Center. Jason John McDonald's study indicates the Austin police typically had one African American on the force. As the migration from Mexico increased,

hiring a Mexican American "boosted" departmental diversity ("Race Relations in Austin, Texas, c. 1917–1929" [PhD diss., University of Southampton, 1992]).

15. Ben Heber Johnson, *Revolution in Texas* (New Haven, CT: Yale University Press, 2003).

16. Lewis Gould's *Progressives and Prohibitionists* (Austin: Texas State Historical Association, 1992) captured the Austin/Washington axis of the Wilson years quite effectively. James McEnteer's work, discussed in the introduction, speaks to the disproportionate influence of Texas and Texans in national affairs.

17. See Godfrey Hodgson, *Woodrow Wilson's Right Hand: The Life of Edward M. House* (New Haven, CT: Yale University Press, 2011).

18. For more insights regarding Du Bois's change in thinking on the future of race relations in the United States, see "NAACP History: William Edward Burghardt Du Bois," accessed June 25, 2013, http://www.naacp.org/pages/naacp-history-w.e.b.-dubois.

19. John Hope Franklin and Alfred Moss Jr., *From Slavery to Freedom: A History of African Americans*, 8th ed. (New York: Knopf, 2000), 384.

20. Ibid.

21. Pioneers of using artifacts from popular culture to explain patterns of racism in the United States, historians Lewis Carlson and George Colburn compiled post–World War I advertisements for lakefront and other desirable properties across Michigan, complete with overt racist language and associated restrictions. See *In Their Place: White America Defines Her Minorities, 1850–1950* (New York: Wiley, 1971).

22. Of these two leaders, Reverend L. L. Campbell fits more closely with the well-established role of the clergy in reflecting and mobilizing public opinion in the African American community. From his dental office in East Austin, Givens's approach to engagement with whites in civic affairs fit the times very well in the 1920s, and from that experience he came to be known to most, if not all, of the key figures in the white Democratic establishment as someone they could work with among the African American community.

23. William D. Carrigan, *The Making of a Lynching Culture* (Urbana: University of Illinois Press, 2004), 198–202.

24. A. C. Greene, *Sketches from the Five States of Texas* (College Station: Texas A&M University Press, 1998).

25. Neil Foley, *The White Scourge: Mexicans, Blacks, and Poor Whites in Texas Cotton Culture* (Berkeley: University of California Press, 1997), 16.

26. In addition to Greene, an outstanding source on the appeal of the Hill Country region is Verne Huser's pictorial *Rivers of Texas*, which draws heavily from the writings of Texas environmentalist John Graves, whose *Death of a River* reads like a letter from a heartbroken lover who is coming to terms with the appeal

of engineers who could, like so many Supermen, change the course of mighty rivers, seemingly with their bare hands. Huser connected the stunning beauty of the Hill Country landscape with the historic movement of people. Surely it was land the likes of which neither European nor Appalachian migrant's eyes had ever seen.

27. D. W. Meinig, *Imperial Texas* (Austin: University of Texas Press, 1969), 123.

28. African Americans played many roles in the Texas agricultural economy however, from cowboys to ranch hands and general farm laborers. In *White Scourge*, Foley documents that almost 100,000 farms and ranches were owned, or farmed on a tenant or sharecropper basis, by African Americans in 1920, with one out of eight such operations in the state owned by families of former slaves. He discusses African American ownership on pages 83–84 and on 241n.

29. V. O. Key, *Southern Politics in State and Nation* (Knoxville: University of Tennessee Press, 1984).

30. Dale Baum, "Pinpointing Apparent Fraud in the 1861 Texas Secession Referendum," *Journal of Interdisciplinary History* 22 (Autumn 1991): 210.

31. Lewis L. Gould, *Progressives and Prohibitionists* (Austin: Texas State Historical Association, 1992), 228.

32. Robert A. Caro, *Years of Lyndon Johnson: The Path to Power* (New York: Knopf, 1982).

33. Carlos Kevin Blanton, *The Strange Career of Bilingual Education in Texas, 1836–1981* (College Station: Texas A&M University Press, 2007), 83–84.

34. Johnson taught at Sam Houston High School in Houston in the 1929–30 school year.

35. Michael Harrington, *The Other America: Poverty in the United States* (New York: Macmillan, 1997).

36. To distinguish between references to tribal groups and Anglos who came to Texas from southern states such as Tennessee, Kentucky, and Virginia, "Native Americans" is the phrase used for the former and "native" Texans for the latter.

37. "Throckmorton County," *Handbook of Texas Online*, http://www.tsha online.org/handbook/online/articles/hcto5, accessed October 18, 2013. Throckmorton County in the early 1900s, like Gillespie and Blanco Counties, knew few African Americans as residents. The census of 1900 recorded zero "colored" individuals.

38. Caro, *Path to Power*, 68.

39. Helen Conger Poage, Bob's mother, lacked the journalist's training that informed Rebekah Johnson's writing through her adult life. Caro's first volume, *The Path to Power* portrays LBJ's mother as a gifted individual trapped in a situation wherein she knew her potential could never be reached.

40. Completed in the scant four years between Johnson's presidency and his death in 1973, LBJ's official memoir fell flat in terms of sales and critical reception.

Goodwin addressed Johnson's refusal to let his lengthening hair down in *LBJ and the American Dream*, knowing that the "presidential" voice he insisted upon would not seem genuine.

41. Caro, *Path to Power*, 74.

42. Census Image, *Heritage Quest Online*, accessed June 26, 2013, http://persi .heritagequestonline.com.ezproxy.emich.edu/hqoweb/library/do/census/results /image?surname=Poage&series=12&state=7&countyid=1814&hitcount=2&p=1& urn=urn%3Aproquest%3AUS%3Bcensus%3B17791122%3B109670138%3B12%3B7& searchtype=1&offset=1.

43. W. R. Poage, *My First 85 Years* (Waco, TX: Baylor University Press, 1985), 2.

44. Ibid., 1.

45. Walter Prescott Webb, *The Great Plains* (Lincoln: University of Nebraska Press, 1981). Webb theorized that life west of the 98th meridian required significant adaptations for anyone raised east of there.

46. "William Allen Poage," *Handbook of Texas Online*, accessed June 25, 2013, http://www.tshaonline.org/handbook/online/articles/fpo58.

47. Ibid.

48. Throckmorton County in the early 1900s, like Gillespie and Blanco Counties, knew few African Americans as residents. The census of 1900 recorded zero "colored" individuals.

49. Ten years Johnson's senior, Poage would find success in school and was engaged in law practice in Waco at the time LBJ began teaching.

50. Carrigan, *The Making of a Lynching Culture*.

51. Cynthia Skove Nevels, *Lynching to Belong* (College Station: Texas A&M University Press, 2007). Nevels devotes a few paragraphs to the depiction of the monstrous treatment of Jesse Washington in Waco as a means of illustrating Carrigan's thesis of a "lynching culture" in Central Texas. Rather than examine the issue of ethnicity in McLennan County, however, she understandably concentrated on a county downstream along the Brazos with richer veins to mine.

52. In *The First Waco Horror*, Patricia Bernstein does an excellent job of documenting the aftermath of the incident on a national and local level. The letter from Dean Kesler of Baylor is discussed on page 168. The faculty letter is addressed in pages 146–48 (*The First Waco Horror: The Lynching of Jesse Washington and the Rise of the NAACP* [College Station: Texas A&M University Press, 2005]). She also tells of Kesler's unfortunate fate: People in the city he defended when it earned the reputation for barbarism, which Carrigan detailed so graphically in *Making of a Lynching Culture*, condemned him after US entry into World War I for his German heritage.

53. Baum, "Pinpointing Apparent Fraud in the 1861 Texas Secession Referendum," 210.

54. Carrigan provides the data and the case histories substantiating the terror in appendixes A and B beginning on page 275 in *Making of a Lynching Culture*.

55. Carrigan, *Making of a Lynching Culture*, 170–74.

56. As reported in US census data, Austin's population grew by 52.3 percent between 1920 and 1930, from 34,876 residents to 53,120. Waco's population, which would approximate Austin's through the Johnson era before falling far behind in the late twentieth century, followed a similar trajectory, though less steep, growing from 38,500 in 1920 to 52,848 in 1930.

57. T. R. Fehrenbach, *Lone Star: A History of Texas and the Texans* (New York: Da Capo Press, 1998), 687–88.

58. Austin Chamber of Commerce Annual Report for 1919 (Austin, 1920), 4.

59. Jason John McDonald's 1992 dissertation, "Race Relations in Austin, Texas, c. 1917–1929," remains the most comprehensive treatment of the Mexican American experience in Austin during the 1920s. There is no parallel study of Waco. McDonald's analysis relies mainly on statistical groupings rather than by providing descriptions of individual experiences via oral histories or diaries. McDonald portrays a city transitioning from a biracial to a triracial society. He points to the need for further investigation that would add texture and dimension to the representation of the daily lives of Mexican Americans as their prominence in Austin and Waco political affairs grew.

60. Transcript of Emmette S. Redford Oral History Interview, File AC85-19, LBJ Library.

61. Emilio Zamora, *Mexican Labor Activity in South Texas, 1900–1920* (Austin: University of Texas Press, 1983), 93–94.

62. Ibid., 90.

63. Transcript of Carl Phinney Oral History Interview, recorded October 11, 1968, AC74-233, LBJ Library.

64. Transcript of Wright Patman Oral History Interview, recorded August 11, 1972, File AC74-97, LBJ Library.

65. Carol Kilpatrick. *Washington Post*, April 1, 1965.

66. Transcript of Welly K. Hopkins Oral History Interview, recorded May 11, 1965, AC94-26, LBJ Library.

67. Redford Transcript.

68. *Austin Statesman*, August 31, 1921, vol. 50, no. 89, AHC Collection 2:46, Austin History Center, Austin, Texas.

69. Patman Transcript.

70. *Austin Statesman*, September 3, 1921, vol. 50, no. 93, AHC Collection 2:47, Austin History Center, Austin, Texas.

71. Ibid., 2:48

72. *Religious Bodies 1926*, US Department of Commerce Bureau of the Census

(Washington, DC: US Government Printing Office, 1930), 369. This volume contains information based on the 1920 census. It is difficult to overestimate the role of religion as a normative force in the maintenance of a segregated society. Sabbath called for community members to gather at places of worship. In 1920, 24,652 of Austin's 34,876 residents claimed membership in a church or synagogue. African Americans and Mexican Americans each had their own Roman Catholic church, as did the white Catholics, of course. Dozens of Baptist churches and a host of other Protestant denominations, as well as the two aforementioned synagogues, tallied seventy-nine designated places of worship. The majority of Mexican Americans were Catholic, some worshipped in Presbyterian, Pentecostal, Methodist, or Episcopal churches. African Americans attended various "Negro Baptist" services in the greatest numbers. Almost five thousand were in attendance at twenty-four different Baptist churches, while hundreds more used the hymnals at the five African Methodist Episcopal sites.

73. Hopkins Transcript.

74. Bernstein, *The First Waco Horror*, 179.

75. Ibid., 100.

76. Poage, *My First 85 Years*, 43.

77. McDonald, "Race Relations in Austin, Texas, c. 1917–1929," 326. Indications of Klan pressure on the Mexican American community can be seen by their recognition of Shelton for his efforts at a civic function in September 1922.

78. *Austin Statesman*, November 2, 1921, vol. 50, no. 154, AHC Collection, p. 2:61, Austin History Center, Austin, Texas.

79. *Austin Statesman*, December 11, 1921, vol. 50, no. 193, AHC Collection 2:71, Austin History Center, Austin, Texas.

80. McDonald, "Race Relations in Austin, Texas, c. 1917–1929," 305.

81. M. M. Crane correspondence to Judge Victor Brooks, August 12, 1924, Gubernatorial Campaign Correspondence August 1–30, 1924, Center for American History, University of Texas.

82. M. M. Crane correspondence to F. W. Hill, August 13, 1924, Gubernatorial Campaign Correspondence, August 10–30, 1924, Center for American History, University of Texas.

83. "The Unveiling of the Ku Klux Klan," promotional flyer, Papers of Rebekah Johnson, Box 26, LBJ Library.

84. Emmette Redford Transcript of Interview conducted October 2, 1968, AC74-238, LBJ Library.

85. Transcript of John F. Koeninger Oral History Interview, Recorded November 1981, AC83-6.

86. Tera W. Hunter, *To 'Joy My Freedom: Southern Black Women's Lives and Labors after the Civil War* (Cambridge, MA: Harvard University Press, 1997), 69.

87. McDonald, "Race Relations in Austin, Texas, c. 1917–1929," 218.

88. Ibid., 62.

89. Anthony M. Orum, *Power, Money, and the People* (Austin: Texas Monthly Press, 1987), 191.

90. McDonald, "Race Relations in Austin, Texas, c. 1917–1929," 304.

91. *Austin Statesman*, September 1, 1919. Austin Chronological File, Austin History Center.

92. "NAACP," *Handbook of Texas Online*, accessed June 26, 2013, www.tsha .utexas.edu/handbook/online/articles/view/NN/ven1.html.

93. James Weldon Johnson, *Along This Way* (New York: Viking Press, 1933), 339–44. McDonald's dissertation put the number at seventy-five by the end of 1918 (301). The difference may suggest rapid growth during the early life of the organization.

94. David C. Humphrey, *Austin: A History of the Capital City* (Austin: Texas State Historical Association, 1997), 35 and 39.

95. Hunter, *To 'Joy My Freedom.*

96. *Austin American*, February 3, 1922, Austin History Center Collection 1:1.

97. McDonald, "Race Relations in Austin, Texas, c. 1917–1929," 305.

98. J. Mason Brewer, *Historical Outline of the Negro in Travis County* (Austin: Samuel Huston College, 1941), 54.

99. Ibid., 54.

100. Ibid., 34.

101. R. L. Polk and Co., *Austin City Directories* (editions published in 1920 and 1930–31); Morrison and Fourmy Directory Company (Austin, 1931). Also, McDonald, "Race Relations in Austin, Texas, c. 1917–1929," 387. The first elementary school serving Mexican American children was only established on West Avenue in 1916. Growth in East Austin led to the construction of the Comal Avenue school in 1925. McDonald reported high illiteracy rates, transience, and numerous social factors as major barriers to Mexican American students even attempting the "white" schools as fourth graders.

102. McDonald, "Race Relations in Austin, Texas, c. 1917–1929," 387.

103. Chrystine Shackles, *Reminiscences of Huston-Tillotson College* (Austin: Best Printing, 1973), 9–15.

104. Ibid., 15.

105. *Austin City Directory 1930–31*, and McDonald, "Race Relations in Austin, Texas, c. 1917–1929," 431.

106. McDonald, "Race Relations in Austin, Texas, c. 1917–1929," 161.

107. "A Trip into the Past," *Austin American-Statesman*, April 7, 1974.

108. Ibid.

109. Obituary program for Eunice Lyons Prescott, AF-BIOG, Edward G. Carrington, Austin History Center.

110. Orum, *Power, Money, and the People*, 178.

111. Brewer, *Historical Outline of the Negro in Travis County*, 34.

112. Humphrey, *Austin: A History of the Capital City*, 40.

113. Brewer, *Historical Outline of the Negro in Travis County*, 34.

114. *Austin American-Statesman*, December 1, 1961, AF-BIOG Givens, E. H. AHC Collection, 1–2, Austin History Center, Austin, Texas.

115. Caro, *Path to Power*.

116. *Austin American*, July 1927.

117. Connelly-Yerwood Nomination to the US Department of the Interior by Texas State Historical Commission, May 3, 2002, 14.

118. Humphrey, *Austin: A History of the Capital City*, 36.

119. Koch and Fowler, *A City Plan for Austin*, January 14, 1928, 66–67, AHC Collection, Austin History Center, Austin, Texas.

120. As discussed in the introduction, Nick Kotz's *Judgment Days* brilliantly illuminates the realities of the summit by probing the interactions between LBJ and Dr. Martin Luther King Jr. In many ways, the negotiations over the Austin City Plan in the 1920s create the same need for local VIPs from their respective communities to strike a bargain, although King had considerably more leverage than Givens.

121. W. E. B. Du Bois, *The Souls of Black Folk and Other Writings* (New York: Barnes and Noble, 2003), 47.

122. Orum, *Power, Money, and the People*, 178.

CHAPTER TWO

1. The author served as a K–12 school superintendent in Michigan from 1994 to 2003, hired by locally elected trustees of the Boards of Education of two districts, Mendon (1994–2000) and Gull Lake (2001–3). Seven individuals served on each board, generally under four-year terms. Certainly there are issues better handled at a higher level, but these officials tend to guard the sovereignty of their districts with the territorial instincts of nesting geese.

2. In Mitchell Lerner, "'To Be Shot at by the Whites and Dodged by the Negroes': Lyndon Johnson and the Texas NYA," *Presidential Studies Quarterly* 39 (June 2009): 269. Lerner's article does an exemplary job of putting LBJ's stint as NYA director in the broader context of the South and how African Americans fared in other states. Comparisons with Mexican Americans are not part of the discussion, due to the very limited sample away from the US-Mexico border.

3. Christie Bourgeois, "Stepping Over Lines: Lyndon Johnson, Black Texans, and the National Youth Administration, 1935–1937," *Southwestern Historical Quarterly* 91 (October 1987): 171.

4. John Kincaid, "From Cooperative to Coercive Federalism," *Annals of the American Academy of Political and Social Science* 509, American Federalism: The Third Century (May 1990): 139. Kincaid goes on to describe "pragmatic federalism" as the consequence of some conservative backlash and success at the polls in the late 1970s and early 1980s. His article does not offer a label for the period from 1933 to 1954, which I would argue had many elements of all three forms of federalism he identifies: cooperative, coercive, and pragmatic.

5. Aubrey Williams, charged with implementing the NYA program, deserves enormous credit for the role he played in defining the parameters of the NYA; he balanced structure with trial and error, like others did in so many New Deal programs. See Carol Whiteside Weisenberger, "The National Youth Administration in Texas, 1935–1943: A Case Study" (PhD diss., Texas A&M University, 1988), for a discussion of Williams's skeletal framework for the program (60–73).

6. Kincaid, "From Cooperative to Coercive Federalism," 141–43.

7. Lerner, "To Be Shot at by the Whites and Dodged by the Negroes." 253.

8. Neil Maher, *Nature's New Deal: The Civilian Conservation Corps and the Roots of the American Environmental Movement* (New York: Oxford University Press, 2009). Maher profiles CCC inductees and discusses the transformative effects, physical and otherwise, it had on the participants.

9. Weisenberger, "The National Youth Administration in Texas, 1935–1943," 164.

10. Johnson's performance as Texas NYA director from July 1935 to March 1937 put him in contact with virtually every significant Democratic player in Texas, at least among elected officials at the local and state level. His network would expand into the big-money boys after his election to the House of Representatives. Virtually every Johnson biographer addresses this vital upturn in the arc of his career, with Caro's treatment in *The Years of Lyndon Johnson: The Path to Power* and Dallek's *Lone Star Rising* as outstanding examples.

11. Weisenberger, "The National Youth Administration in Texas, 1935–1943," 61.

12. "Thomas Connally," *Handbook of Texas Online*, accessed June 27, 2013, http://www.tsha.utexas.edu/handbook/online/articles/CC/fco36.html, describes Senator Connally as "seldom differing form the administration" during the first Roosevelt term, but growing disillusioned by the time of the "court-packing" debacle of 1937. Randall Woods, in *LBJ: Architect of American Ambition*, portrayed Connally on page 106 as "not exactly excited about the New Deal and its myriad agencies."

13. Neil Foley, *The White Scourge: Mexicans, Blacks, and Poor Whites in Texas Cotton Culture* (Berkeley: University of California Press, 1997). Foley brought together elements of whiteness studies and labor history into an analysis of contesting forces among Central Texas farmers. As evidenced by the *Waco Farm and Labor Journal*, Poage's state senate and congressional districts represented fertile ground for union organizers. The willingness of many of these activists to recruit

nonwhite members drove a wedge into the movement, but it also represented the existence of integrationist thinking among some whites.

14. See John Mark Hansen, *Gaining Access: Congress and the Farm Lobby, 1919–1981* (Chicago: University of Chicago Press, 1991) for an overview of agriculture policy and the farm lobby during the time Poage earned the name "Mr. Agriculture."

15. LBJ letter to Dan Rose dated June 3, 1939. Pedernales Electric Cooperative NYA Building Project at J.C. File, Box 191, Papers of Lyndon B. Johnson House of Representatives, 1937–1949. LBJ Library.

16. Transcript of Sherman Birdwell Oral History Interview, accessed June 27, 2013, http://webstorage4.mcpa.virginia.edu/lbj/oralhistory/birdwell_w_1970_1021 .pdf. Pages 17–21 concentrate on Birdwell's discussion of the NYA years, taken from an interview conducted thirty-three years after Johnson left the agency to run for the Tenth Congressional District seat vacated by the sudden death of Representative James "Buck" Buchanan in late February. See Randall Woods's discussion of Johnson's decision to run in *LBJ: Architect of American Ambition* (New York: Free Press, 2006), 116.

17. Franklin D. Roosevelt, Second Inaugural Address, January 20, 1937.

18. Weisenberger, "The National Youth Administration in Texas, 1935–1943," 31.

19. Ibid., iii.

20. Ibid., 35.

21. Weisenberger referred to an agreement reached in June 1935 that called for the US Office of Education to oversee programs providing "off the job" training, while NYA would continue to oversee "on the job" education. This territorial skirmishing eased but did not go away entirely, at least on the national level.

22. For more on this rivalry, see Marjorie Murphy, *Blackboard Unions* (Ithaca, NY: Cornell University Press, 1990), and Wayne J. Urban, *Gender, Race, and the National Education Association* (New York: RoutledgeFalmer, 2000).

23. Murphy, *Blackboard Unions*, 37.

24. Ibid., 275.

25. Weisenberger, "The National Youth Administration in Texas, 1935–1943," 40.

26. Urban's fascinating study of the NEA devotes considerable attention to the quest for cabinet-level status. Urban does not attempt to address AFT concerns at any length. See Marjorie Murphy's *Blackboard Unions* for a discussion of AFT's opposition.

27. The NEA included administrators and teachers in its membership until its focus shifted strongly to collective bargaining in the 1960s.

28. Joe K. Skiles Letter to W. R. Poage, W. R. Poage Papers, BCPM, Baylor University, Waco, Texas.

29. In a situation somewhat analogous to that presented by online shopping

today, "mom and pop" stores across Texas were dealing with regional or even national chain stores. One legislative remedy was a tax on the chain store, which would theoretically make their goods more expensive, thereby rescuing the smaller retailer.

30. W. R. Poage Letter to NYA nominees Ben S. Peek, Box #5, File #39, W. R. Poage Papers, BCPM, Baylor University, Waco, Texas.

31. Letter from George O. Jones to W. R. Poage dated October 19, 1935, Box #5, File #39, W. R. Poage Papers, BCPM, Baylor University, Waco, Texas. Jones's is the only letter of acceptance on file, suggesting others may have replied by telephone or in person.

32. "Outline of 4-Point Program of National Youth Administration," Box #5, File #39, W. R. Poage Papers, BCPM, Baylor University, Waco, Texas.

33. Poage for Congress 1936 Campaign Flier, Box #6, File 41, Senate Correspondence 1936, W. R. Poage Papers, BCPM, Baylor University, Waco, Texas.

34. *Waco Farm and Labor Journal*, January 25, 1935, Box #5, File #31, 1936 Newsclippings, W. R. Poage Papers, BCPM, Baylor University, Waco, Texas.

35. Ibid.

36. Letter from Joe Skiles, Director, NYA District No. 1, to Hon. W. R. Poage, State Senator dated October 5, 1935, Box #5, File #39, W. R. Poage Papers, BCPM, Baylor University, Waco, Texas.

37. Weisenberger, "The National Youth Administration in Texas, 1935–1943," 142.

38. Teresa Palomo Acosta and Ruthe Winegarten, *Las Tejanas: 300 Years of History* (Austin: University of Texas Press, 2003), 103 and 327.

39. Julie Leininger Pycior, *LBJ and Mexican Americans: The Paradox of Power* (Austin: University of Texas Press, 1997).

40. Ibid., 149.

41. Ibid., 147–48.

42. LBJ letter to John Corson, September 22, 1935, LBJ US Gov't Records/NYA, LBJ Library, Austin, Texas.

43. Ibid.

44. Ibid.

45. Ibid.

46. Weisenberger, "The National Youth Administration in Texas, 1935–1943," 135.

47. Ibid.

48. Bourgeois, "Stepping Over Lines," 157–58.

49. Ibid., 159.

50. Ibid., 160.

51. Report of NYA Projects on Which Negro Youths Are Employed, NYA

Projects Division. Special Report of Negro Activities of NYA in Texas, March 16, 1936, LBJ US Gov't Records NYA. LBJ Library.

52. Weisenberger, "The National Youth Administration in Texas, 1935–1943," 66.

53. Ibid., 66.

54. Ibid., 76.

55. Ibid. Letters to NYA nominees found in Poage's papers, all four prepared by the same individual (initials l.b.) contain this spelling. Letters are on file for nominees from the areas of education, industry, labor, and agriculture, but not for a representative of "youth." Poage nominated the principal of South Junior High School in Waco, Ben S. Peek, for the education representative and may have worked through Peek to identify the student nominee.

56. Ibid. W. R. Poage letter to Ben S. Peek et al., as described above.

57. Available at http://webstorage4.mcpa.virginia.edu/lbj/oralhistory/birdwell_w_1970_1021.pdf, accessed October 20, 2013.

58. A member of the Texas delegation, Fritz Lanham, would guide landmark legislation through Congress in the autumn on 1941, when mobilization for engagement with Germany and Japan disrupted housing patterns, and therefore school enrollment all across the nation. The Lanham Act aimed to mitigate the impact of massive increases in student population. This issue is addressed in the form of a case study of the impact of the doubling of the size of Fort Custer near Battle Creek, Michigan, had on the nearby village of fewer than one thousand residents. "Fort Custer and the Village of Augusta, 1939–1941," *International Journal of Regional and Local History* (December 2005).

59. Weisenberger, "The National Youth Administration in Texas, 1935–1943," 66.

60. Ibid., 66. This "hybrid" example of a partnership involving a federal agency, a Baptist university, and Waco public schoolchildren made sense politically, but given that there was no public college in Waco to partner with, Johnson made a pragmatic decision.

61. Austin's Huston-Tillotson College did not host a Freshman Center, surprisingly.

62. Bourgeois, "Stepping Over Lines," 162. Significantly, Bourgeois found, "Although blacks in Texas composed 14.7% of the total population and 27.8% of the youth population, in November 1936 they received on 9.8% of the school aid" (165).

63. Bourgeois, "Stepping Over Lines," 163

64. Ibid., 76.

65. Report of NYA Projects on Which Negro Youths Are Employed, NYA Projects Division, Special Report of Negro Activities of NYA in Texas, March 16, 1936, LBJ US Gov't Records NYA, LBJ Library.

66. Letter to Professor H. R. Brentzel from W. R. Poage dated November 30, 1935, Box #6, File #40, W. R. Poage Papers, BCPM, Baylor University, Waco, Texas.

67. Letter to W. R. Poage from John Griswell dated January 11, 1936, Box #6, File #43, W. R. Poage Papers, BCPM, Baylor University, Waco, Texas.

68. Texas NYA Form A-155, "Information Concerning the College Aide Program," Box #3, File #14, W. R. Poage Papers, BCPM, Baylor University, Waco, Texas.

69. Ibid.

70. Raleigh Moses, letter to W. R. Poage, April 6, 1935, Box #6, File #44, Senate Correspondence 1936, W. R. Poage Papers, BCPM, Baylor University, Waco, Texas.

71. W. R. Poage, letter to Raleigh Moses, April 7, 1936, Box #6, File #44, Senate Correspondence 1936, W. R. Poage Papers, BCPM, Baylor University, Waco, Texas

72. V. I. Moore, letter to University of Texas students, July 6, 1936, Box #6, File #45, Senate Correspondence, W. R. Poage Papers, BCPM, Baylor University, Waco, Texas.

73. The University of Texas Federal Student Employment Application Form, enclosure with letter from V. I. Moore, ibid.

74. W. R. Poage, letter to V. I. Moore dated August 5, 1936, Box #6, File #45, Senate Correspondence 1936, W. R. Poage Papers, BCPM, Baylor University, Waco, Texas.

75. Ibid.

76. W. R. Poage, letter to V. I. Moore, August 14, 1936, Box #6, File #45 Senate Correspondence 1936, W. R. Poage Papers, BCPM, Baylor University, Waco Texas.

77. Patterns of what resembled psychological abuse of aides emerge from reading about the workplace environment he created for his subordinates. This is observable in his NYA assignment and continues throughout his career. Outstanding constituent service gains votes, and Johnson's strong sense of public service led him to demand immediate feedback. See Robert A. Caro's first two volumes of *The Years of Lyndon Johnson: The Path to Power* (New York: Knopf, 1982), and *The Means of Ascent* (New York: Knopf, 1990). Robert Dallek's *Lone Star Rising* covers this phase of LBJ's career brilliantly, though somewhat less hard-hitting on the darker side of fund-raising.

78. Charles Stevenson, letter to LBJ, May 23, 1939, Papers of Lyndon B. Johnson House of Representatives, 1937–1949, Box 191, Pedernales Electric Cooperative NYA Building Project at J.C. LBJ Library.

79. Ibid.

80. "Suggested Labor Supervisory Requirements for Johnson City NYA-REA Building," Papers of Lyndon B. Johnson House of Representatives, 1937–1949, Box 191, Pedernales Electric Cooperative NYA Building Project at J.C. LBJ Library. Weisenberger discussed pay at various points throughout her study of the NYA in Texas. Maher's *Nature's New Deal* discusses compensation and working conditions at some length, but the most commonly noted aspect of the pay

arrangement by historians is the provision that $25 of the $30 earned would be sent home. No similar requirement accompanied these NYA jobs.

81. LBJ letter to Charles Stevenson, May 27, 1939, Papers of Lyndon B. Johnson House of Representatives, 1937–1949, Box 191, Pedernales Electric Cooperative NYA Building Project at J.C. LBJ Library.

82. LBJ letter to Dan Rose, June 3, 1939, Papers of Lyndon B. Johnson House of Representatives, 1937–1949, Box 191, Pedernales Electric Cooperative NYA Building Project at J.C. LBJ Library.

83. Ibid.

84. Ibid.

85. Dan Rose, letter to LBJ, June 5, 1939, Papers of Lyndon B. Johnson House of Representatives, 1937–1949, Box 191, Pedernales Electric Cooperative NYA Building Project at J.C. LBJ Library.

CHAPTER THREE

1. Rayburn served continuously in the House of Representatives from 1913 until his death in 1961.

2. Transcript of J. H. Kultgen Oral History Interview, transcript of recording June 27, 1974, by Thomas Charlton, 109, Texas Collection, Baylor Institute for Oral History, Waco, Texas.

3. Referenced in the introduction, LBJ used this phrase at the dedication ceremony for his presidential library in Austin in 1971. It is Texan for today's preferred term, "transparency."

4. Transcript of J. H. Kultgen Oral History Interview, 108–9.

5. "Brazos de Dios," the name given by Spanish explorers, translates into English as "Arms of God." Over time, maps came to use the shortened version—Brazos River. Locally, it is pronounced BRAZ-us, instead of the Spanish BRA-sohs. Similarly, the pronunciation of the tributaries is Anglicized, so locals say BOS-key, rather than the Spanish BOHS-kay.

6. The first dam, sometimes referred to as the "old" dam, was dedicated in 1930, while the "new" dam, planned in the 1950s and dedicated in 1965, is the much larger "modern" dam.

7. Devotees of historian Walter P. Webb's work on the settlement of the Great Plains, which highlighted the marginal chances of successful settlement west of the 98th meridian, should note the coordinates for expansion proposed for a new dam that would end repeated flooding of Waco and farmland far downstream: lat 31°35′N, long 97°12′W.

8. Neil Foley considers the social and economic implications of the soil

composition of Central Texas in *The White Scourge* (Berkeley: University of California Press, 1997), noting in his introduction that "in the ethnoracial borderlands of central Texas, the South, with its dyadic racial categories, first encountered the Southwest, where whiteness fractured along class lines and Mexicans moved in to fill the racial space between whiteness and blackness" (11).

9. Named for William Cameron, an early settler whose descendants bestowed the acreage for a park to the city of Waco in two installments in 1910 and 1920.

10. "Waco," *Handbook of Texas Online*, accessed June 5, 2009, http://www.tsha online.org/handbook/online/articles/hdw01.

11. Transcript of J. H. Kultgen Oral History Interview by Thomas Charlton, recorded June 27, 1974, 109, Texas Collection, Baylor Institute for Oral History, Waco, Texas. For further information about Congressman Henry, a summary of his career in public service and in the practice of law is available at http://bioguide.congress .gov/scripts/biodisplay.pl?index=H000516, accessed October 22, 2013.

12. John Graves, *Goodbye to a River: A Narrative* (New York: Vintage Departures, 1988), 265.

13. Neither of the two dams, the original or its successor, used turbines or other means of converting the energy of flowing water into electric power.

14. *Waco Tribune-Herald*, October 26, 1965. George Washington Goethals was the first and only chief engineer for the canal project, serving from 1907 to 1914. The damming of the Chagres River to create Lake Gatun proved to be one of the key engineering feats of the endeavor. After leaving the military in 1919, Goethals established a consulting firm in New York, which he led until his death in 1928. Assessing the flood control options for Waco, then, proved to be one of the last projects of his storied career. See http://www.pancanal.com/eng/history/bio graphies/goethals.html, accessed February 25, 2012.

15. J. B. Smith, "Lake Waco," *Waco History Project*, accessed June 9, 2011, http:// wacohistoryproject.org/Places/LakeWaco.htm. To clarify the issue of two or three forks of the Bosque, the middle fork of the Bosque joins the south fork prior to the convergence with the North fork.

16. *Waco Tribune-Herald*, May 25, 1930.

17. At http://www.brazos.org/ourMission.asp, accessed May 17, 2009.

18. *Waco Farm and Labor Journal*, January 25, 1935, Box 5, File 31, W. R. Poage Papers, W. R. Poage Legislative Library, Baylor University, Waco, Texas.

19. At http://www.brazos.org/brazosHistory.asp, viewed May 17, 2009.

20. Dan K. Utley and James W. Steely, *Guided with a Steady Hand* (Waco, TX: Baylor University Press, 1998), 145.

21. Robert A. Caro, *The Years of Lyndon Johnson: The Path to Power* (New York: Knopf, 1982), 378–79. The Marshall Ford Dam project on the Lower Colorado

River was getting underway as Johnson moved into his first term as congressman from the Eleventh District.

22. Randall B. Woods, *LBJ: Architect of American Ambition* (New York: Free Press, 2006), 110. Twenty of these Freshman Centers were established in Texas, the first of their kind in the nation and clearly an indication of the influence LBJ's own experiences as a teacher and as a student had on his sense of what the federal government could do. In this case, implementing a bridging program between high school and college for students from low-income families.

23. J. H. Kultgen, Interview by Thomas Charlton, transcript of recording made June 27, 1974, 109–10, Texas Collection, Baylor Institute for Oral History, Waco, Texas.

24. This terminology refers to good corporate citizenship during wartime in the form of executive personnel assigned to government jobs "on loan" for the symbolic and patriotic amount of $1.

25. Kultgen interview, 57–65.

26. James McEnteer, *Deep in the Heart: The Texas Tendency in American Politics* (Westport, CT: Praeger, 2004), 81–82.

27. Agnes Meyer, *America's Home Front* (New York: Harcourt, Brace, 1943). Housing shortages, price controls, overcrowded schools, and a host of conditions brought about by wartime migration of millions of Americans in search of job opportunities.

28. Kultgen interview, 69.

29. Credit to the screenwriters for *Star Trek II: The Wrath of Khan* for giving a very similar line to actor Leonard Nimoy's character, Spock.

30. Smith, "Lake Waco," *Waco History Project*. Jack Kultgen probably included subsequent trips to Washington, DC (after 1956, that is), when he cited "an actual count of 42 trips to Washington in connection with these various dams, helping appear before legislative committee." Downplaying his own role, he added, "It was more or less routine because I suppose it would have come anyway."

31. Ibid.

32. J. H. Kultgen Interview by Thomas Charlton, transcript of recording made August 9, 1974, 151, Interview #3, Texas Collection, Baylor Institute for Oral History, Waco, Texas.

33. Ibid.

34. Ibid., 157.

35. Ibid., 86.

36. Ibid., 89.

37. Ibid., 99.

38. For the Merchant Marine issue: Letter from LBJ to J. H. Kultgen, June 11, 1953. Highway: Letter from LBJ to J. H. Kultgen dated July 8, 1953. Waco visit: LBJ

to J. H. Kultgen, September 29, Box 107, File Ku-Ky 151, 1953, Papers of Lyndon Baines Johnson United States Senate, 1949–61, Master File Index Kr-Laa-Lam. All of these letters were exchanged in the summer following the devastating tornado that destroyed downtown Waco, but the heart of the damage was in the heart of the city along the riverfront. The Bird-Kultgen Ford Dealership, located south of the city center by a mile, did not suffer extensive damage. Given Kultgen's role in civic affairs, however, it is highly likely that the September visit included many conversations about federal assistance for disaster relief, as discussed in the next chapter.

39. Letter from J. Carroll Wood to Poage dated March 15, 1954, Box 715, File 1, Project Waco Dam (Bosque River), W. R. Poage Papers, W. R. Poage Legislative Library, Baylor University, Waco, Texas.

40. Letter from W. R. Poage to J. Carroll Wood dated March 18, 1954, Box 715, File 1, Project Waco Dam, W. R. Poage Papers, W. R. Poage Legislative Library, Baylor University, Waco, Texas.

41. Ibid.

42. Letter from Poage to E. Price Bauman dated May 12, 1954, Box 715, File 1, Project Waco Dam, W. R. Poage Papers, W. R. Poage Legislative Library, Baylor University, Waco, Texas.

43. Letter from W. R. Poage to Robert. W. Brown dated May 11, 1954, Box 715, File 1, Project Waco Dam (Bosque River), W. R. Poage Papers, W. R. Poage Legislative Library, Baylor University, Waco Texas.

44. Letter from W. R. Poage to Sidney Dobbins dated May 1, 1954, Box 715, File 1, Project Waco Dam (Bosque River), W. R. Poage Papers, W. R. Poage Legislative Library, Baylor University, Waco Texas.

45. Transcript of W. R. Poage Oral History Interview, recorded November 8–9, 1979, volume 2: 50.

46. Telegram from W. R. Poage to Fentress, Dobbins, etc., dated June 30, 1954, Box 715, File 1, Project Waco Dam (Bosque River), W. R. Poage Papers, W. R. Poage Legislative Library, Baylor University, Waco, Texas.

47. Undated *Waco Herald-Tribune* article by "Mr. Foster," Poage Papers, Box 715, File 1.

48. Letter from LBJ to J. H. Kultgen, July 31, 1954, Box 107, File Ku-Ky 151, 1954, Papers of Lyndon Baines Johnson United States Senate, 1949–61, Master File Index Kr-Laa-Lam.

49. *Waco Tribune-Herald*, November 16, 1954, Poage Papers, Box 715, File 1.

50. Box 715, File 1, of the Poage Papers contains notes from a meeting on December 7, 1954, with Poage, Walter Lacy Jr., Jack Kultgen, Sidney Dobbins, Ralph Russell, and Stanton Brown Jr.

51. W. R. Poage letter to Sidney Dobbins dated April 13, 1955, Poage Papers, Box 715, File 1.

52. Petition found in Poage Papers, Box 715, File 1.

53. Letter from W. R. Poage to Sidney Dobbins dated May 1, 1954, Box 715, File 1, Waco Dam Project, W. R. Poage Papers, W. R Poage Legislative Library, Baylor University, Waco, Texas.

54. Letter from LBJ to J. H. Kultgen, May 21, 1955, Box 107, File Ku-Ky 151, 1955, Papers of Lyndon Baines Johnson United States Senate, 1949–61, Master File Index Kr-Laa-Lam.

55. Transcript of Interview with J. H. Kultgen.

56. See Robert Dallek, *Lone Star Rising: Lyndon Johnson and His Times, 1908–1960* (New York: Oxford University Press, 1991), 463–64.

57. Extension of Remarks by Lyndon B. Johnson, *Congressional Record*, May 24, 1955, A3600, US Government Printing Office, Washington, DC.

58. Letter from Representative W. R. Poage to Representative John E. Fogarty, May 24, 1955, Poage Papers, Box 715, File 3.

59. Letter from Representative T. Millet Hand to W. R. Poage, May 27, 1955, Poage Papers, Box 715, File 1.

60. Letter from Sam McCracken to W. R. Poage dated June 1955, Poage Papers, Box 715, File 1.

61. Letter from Lady Bird Johnson to Jack Kultgen, August 4, 1955, Box 107, File Ku-Ky 151, 1955, Papers of Lyndon Baines Johnson United States Senate, 1949–61, Master File Index Kr-Laa-Lam.

62. Letter from LBJ to J. H. Kultgen, November 24, 1955, Box 107, File Ku-Ky 151, 1955, Papers of Lyndon Baines Johnson United States Senate, 1949–61, Master File Index Kr-Laa-Lam.

63. Letter from LBJ to J. H. Kultgen, November 27, 1955, Box 107, File Ku-Ky 151, 1955, Papers of Lyndon Baines Johnson United States Senate, 1949–61, Master File Index Kr-Laa-Lam.

64. Letter from LBJ to J. H. Kultgen, December 20, 1955, Box 107, File Ku-Ky 151, 1955, Papers of Lyndon Baines Johnson United States Senate, 1949–61, Master File Index Kr-Laa-Lam.

65. Letter from W. R. Poage to Edith Scott, September 10, 1955, Poage Papers, Box 715, File 1.

66. Letter from Colonel Harry Fisher to W. R Poage dated November 30, 1955, Poage Papers, Box 715, File 1.

67. Letter from Sam McCracken to W. R. Poage dated January 14, 1956, Poage Papers, Box 715, File 1. The Benson referred to in the letter is mostly likely Ezra Taft Benson, Eisenhower's secretary of agriculture at the time.

68. Ibid.

69. Letter from W. R. Poage to W. P. Lester dated February 13, 1956, Poage Papers, Box 715, File 1.

70. Letter from L. Fulton to W. R. Poage dated February 27, 1956, Poage Papers, Box 715, File 1. The pamphlet uses the friendliest approach possible for readying the property owner for the inevitable loss. The Corps of Engineers revealed its empathetic capacity in addressing these questions. Topics addressed in the pamphlet: How will real estate needs for a project by determined? Will you be contacted by the Corps of Engineers should your land be needed? Will all lands be acquired at once? How much will you be paid for your property? How will the value of your property be determined? When will you learn what the government estimates your property to be worth? What is an option contract? What happens if you don't agree to accept the appraised value? What is a condemnation proceeding? When will you get your money? What if your title isn't clear? What happens when the government takes only part of your land? How long will you be allowed to remain on the property after the government acquires title? Will you be paid for the cost of moving off your property? Can buildings, fences, and improvements be salvaged and retained? What about growing crops? How may acquired reservoir lands be leased by the government? What disposal is made of lease revenues? Will the money I receive from the sale of my property to the government be subject to the federal income tax? Are oral agreements made by government representatives binding?

71. Letter from E. F. Grimes to W. R. Poage dated February 24, 1956. Poage Papers, Box 715, File 1.

72. This reference is to Price Daniel, the other senator from Texas.

73. Letter from W. R. Poage to Harlan Fentress and Sidney Dobbins dated January 21, 1956, Poage Papers, Box 715, File 1.

74. Letter from Walter Jenkins to J. H. Kultgen, March 2, 1956, Box 107, File Ku-Ky 151, 1956, Papers of Lyndon Baines Johnson United States Senate, 1949–61, Master File Index Kr-Laa-Lam.

75. Telegram from W. R. Poage to Sidney Dobbins dated March 6, 1956, Poage Papers, Box 715, File 1.

76. Letter from Walter Jenkins to Jack Kultgen, April 5, 1956, Box 107, File Ku-Ky 151, 1956, Papers of Lyndon Baines Johnson United States Senate, 1949–61, Master File Index Kr-Laa-Lam.

77. Letter from LBJ to Jack H. Kultgen, May 15, 1956, Box 107, File Ku-Ky 151, 1956, Papers of Lyndon Baines Johnson United States Senate, 1949–61, Master File Index Kr-Laa-Lam.

78. Telegram from Lyndon B. Johnson to W. R. Poage et al., dated June 8, 1956, Poage Papers, Box 715, File 1.

79. J. H. Kultgen, interview by Thomas Charlton, transcript of recording made June 27, 1974, 106, Texas Collection, Baylor Institute for Oral History, Waco, Texas.

80. Letter from John D. McCall to Jack Kultgen dated June 13, 1956, Poage

Papers, Box 715, File 1. McCall headed the law firm of McCall, Parkhurst, and Crowe at 1501 Mercantile and Securities Exchange Building, Dallas Texas.

81. *Waco News-Tribune*, September 25, 1956.

82. Letter from LBJ to J. H. Kultgen, August 28, 1956, Box 107, File Ku-Ky 151, 1956, Papers of Lyndon Baines Johnson United States Senate, 1949–61, Master File Index Kr-Laa-Lam.

83. Colonel Harry Fisher, remarks in *Waco News-Tribune*, October 9, 1956.

84. Notes dated October 10, 1956, from unnamed office assistant (initials RL) for W. R. Poage. Poage Papers, Box 715, File 1.

85. Ibid.

86. W. R. Poage letter to Leon Dollens dated October 19, 1956, Poage Papers, Box 715, File 1.

87. Box 715, File 3, Waco Dam Project, W. R. Poage Papers, W. R. Poage Legislative Library, Baylor University, Waco, Texas.

88. Letter from W. R. Poage to Sam Rayburn dated April 12, 1957, Poage Papers, Box 715, File 3.

89. Correspondence between Kultgen and the senator (or his designees) addressed the concerns of small business at least five times from February 21, 1957, through January 15, 1958, with the Small Business Administration a source of mutual frustration. Box 107, File Ku-Ky 151, 1957 and 1958, Papers of Lyndon Baines Johnson United States Senate, 1949–61, Master File Index Kr-Laa-Lam.

90. "Brief Information on Waco Dam," document appears to be a set of talking points used in promoting funding for the dam during the 1957–58 congressional hearings. Poage Papers, Box 715, File 1.

91. Graves, *Goodbye to a River*, 64–65.

92. Letter from Arthur C. Perry to Jack Kultgen, April 16, 1957, Box 107, File Ku-Ky 151, 1957, Papers of Lyndon Baines Johnson United States Senate, 1949–61, Master File Index Kr-Laa-Lam.

93. Smith, "Lake Waco," *Waco History Project*.

94. "Brief Information on Waco Dam," Poage Papers, Box 715, File 1, Waco Dam Project.

95. Letter from L. R. Holze to W. R. Poage dated May 1, 1957, Box 715, File 3, Waco Dam Project.

96. Letter from W. R. Poage to L. H. Holze dated May 3, 1957, Box 715, File 3, Waco Dam Project, 1957, W. R. Poage Papers, W. R. Poage Legislative Library, Baylor University, Waco, Texas.

97. Letter from LBJ to Jack Kultgen, November 4, 1957, Box 107, File Ku-Ky 151, 1957, Papers of Lyndon Baines Johnson United States Senate, 1949–61, Master File Index Kr-Laa-Lam.

98. Telegram from LBJ to W. R. Poage, January 13, 1958. Box 715, File 1, W. R. Poage Papers.

99. *Waco Tribune-Herald*, January 19, 1958.

100. This exchange, totaling four letters, initiated by McSwain on July 8, 1957, finds a confident Poage taking on an archconservative and defining what old New Deal Democrats of the South stood for in the 1950s. Box 715, File 3, Waco Dam Project, 1957, W. R. Poage Papers, W. R. Poage Legislative Library, Baylor University, Waco, Texas.

101. *Waco Tribune-Herald*, January 26, 1958.

102. Transcript of interview with J. H. Kultgen.

103. *Waco Tribune-Herald*, February 18, 1958.

104. *Report of the Comptroller General of the United States*, November 3, 1965.

105. Ibid., 101. Despite his new assignment, Kultgen remained engaged in lobbying in areas of more direct interest to the business of selling Ford products. When the Small Business Administration (SBA) denied an application by Bird-Kultgen Ford, Inc., Kultgen turned to Senator Johnson for assistance. Walter Jenkins replied on LBJ's behalf, stating the SBA showed "very little change in their thinking," because their Waco dealership was one of thirty-eight in the United States to have sales exceeding $2,000,000. At the time there were 41,407 car dealers.

106. Ibid., 101.

107. Ibid., 103.

108. Letter from Walter Jenkins to J. H. Kultgen, January 15, 1958, Box 107, File Ku-Ky 151 1958, Papers of Lyndon Baines Johnson United States Senate, 1949–61, Master File Index Kr-Laa-Lam.

109. Letter from W. R. Poage to Harlan Fentress, May 12, 1958, Poage Papers, Box 715, File 1.

110. LBJ telegram to W. R. Poage, H. Fentress, et al. on July 3, 1958, W. R. Poage Papers, Box 715, File 1.

111. Letter to Colonel Walter Wells from Lieutenant Colonel J. H. Hottenroth dated May 7, 1958, W. R. Poage Papers, Box 715, File 1.

112. Letter from Lieutenant Colonel J. H. Hottenroth to W. R. Poage dated May 28, 1958, W. R. Poage Papers, Box 715, File 1.

113. *Waco Tribune-Herald*, July 6, 1958.

114. Telegram from W. R. Poage and Lyndon Johnson to Jack Kultgen et al., dated January 19, 1959.

115. Telegram from Colonel Walter Wells to W. R. Poage dated August 28, 1959, W. R. Poage Papers, Box 715, File 1.

116. Telegram from W. R. Poage to Harry Provence dated January 6, 1960, W. R. Poage Papers, Box 715, File 1.

117. *Waco Times-Herald*, November 7, 1959.

118. Note to W. R. Poage from the city of Waco, undated, Poage Papers, Box 715, File 1, Waco Dam Project.

119. Poage and Johnson both dealt with this kind of eminent domain issue related to US military base demands for acreage and the consequences for local school districts. See "Ft. Custer and the Village of Augusta, 1939–1941," *International Journal of Regional and Local Studies* for a study I did of a community in Michigan that experienced base expansion.

120. Letter from W. R. Poage to Harlan Fentress, Poage Papers, Box 715, File 1, Waco Dam Project.

121. *Waco News-Tribune*, April 20, 1960.

122. *Lariat*, November 30, 1961.

123. *Waco News-Tribune*, November 20, 1962.

124. *Waco Times-Herald*, November 20, 1962.

125. Letter from W. R. Poage to Bill Moyers dated February 10, 1965.

126. Five months passed between Poage's "no vote" on the Civil Rights Act of 1964 and the notification by LBJ to Harry Provence in Waco of the base closing. The situation is addressed in much greater detail in the conclusion.

CHAPTER FOUR

1. The NYA remained in operation into 1943. Like the CCC, terminated the year before, it faced both supply and demand issues as a result of the US mobilization for World War II. Upon entry into the war, nationalism prevailed, and while discussions about appropriate use of federal power continued, the context had changed significantly.

2. Transcript of J. H. Kultgen Oral History Interview by Thomas Charlton, recorded June 27, 1974, 163.

3. Kincaid's concept of cooperative versus coercive federalism is addressed in chapter 2.

4. Julie Leininger Pycior, *LBJ and Mexican Americans: The Paradox of Power* (Austin: University of Texas Press, 1997), 245.

5. Correspondence between Kultgen and Johnson addresses economic conditions, along with some concerns by Kultgen that his Ford dealership is too large to be eligible for federal assistance from the Small Business Administration. See note 105 in chapter 3.

6. W. F. Soule and Associates, "Strategy for Regional Planning and Policy Guidelines Waco-McLennan County Region," October 1967, Waco, Texas, Vertical File, Texas Collection, Baylor University, Waco, Texas.

7. A report from the engineering firm contracted by the city of Waco, Soule and Associates, indicated that plans made in 1958 comprised the basis of projects undertaken in 1960. Ibid.

8. Transcript of W. R. Poage Oral History Interview by Thomas Charlton, Volume 3, Interview 13, recorded April 2, 1981, 1014, Texas Collection, Baylor University Institute for Oral History, Waco, Texas.

9. Transcript of Tomas Arroyo Oral History Interview by Rebecca Jimenez, recorded June 2, 1983, 14, Texas Collection, Baylor University Institute for Oral History, Waco, Texas.

10. Nick Kotz, *Judgment Days: Lyndon Baines Johnson, Martin Luther King, Jr., and the Laws That Changed America* (Boston: Houghton Mifflin, 2005), 313.

11. Mandates came later, after the US Supreme Court *Lau v. Nichols* ruling in 1974 interpreted bilingual education in the context of civil rights and held local schools responsible for providing programming whenever twenty or more English-language learners would benefit from some kind of transitional service.

12. Transcript of Robert Aguilar Oral History Interview with Thomas Charlton recorded October 17, 2005, 13, Texas Collection, Baylor University Institute for Oral History, Waco, Texas.

13. Ibid., 11–12.

14. Ibid., 43.

15. Ibid., 46–48.

16. Ibid., 7.

17. Transcript of Ernest Calderon Oral History Interview by Tom South recorded March 27, 1973, 45–52, Texas Collection, Baylor University Institute for Oral History, Waco, Texas.

18. Transcript of Robert Aguilar Oral History Interview recorded by Thomas Charlton, #3, 25, and Aguilar interview #4, 14.

19. Calderon transcript, 82.

20. Ibid., 82.

21. Antonio Quiroz, *Claiming Citizenship: Mexican Americans in Victoria, Texas* (College Station: Texas A&M University Press, 2005).

22. Aguilar interview.

23. Calderon transcript.

24. Pycior, *LBJ and Mexican Americans*, 244–45.

25. The Texas Secretary of State's office issued Charter #265478 on August 22, 1969.

26. Aguilar, introduction to application for assistance from the Campaign of Human Development, Waco Organizations, Box 21169, Waco Alliance of Mexican Americans File, Texas Collection, Baylor Institute for Oral History, Waco, Texas.

27. Bradley T. Turner, ed., *Lust, Violence, Religion: Life in Historic Waco* (Waco, TX: TSTC Publishing, 2010), 141.

28. Transcript of Mardell Armstrong Oral History Interview by Mrs. Clifton Robinson recorded November 1, 1976, Texas Collection, Baylor University Institute for Oral History, Waco, Texas.

29. Transcript of Almarie Bulloch Blaine Oral History Interview by Jerrie Callan recorded November 13, 1975, 46, Texas Collection, Baylor Institute for Oral History, Waco, Texas.

30. Transcript of Margie Lopez Cintron Oral History Interview by Elinor Maze recorded November 2006, Texas Collection, Baylor University Institute for Oral History, Waco, Texas.

31. Transcript of Robert Gamboa Oral History Interview by Ali Clark, Mark Ruth, Amber West, and Stephen Aston recorded March 4, 2006, 2, Texas Collection, Baylor University Institute for Oral History, Waco, Texas.

32. Transcript of Carol Duron Oral History Interview by Elinor Maze recorded November 11, 2006, Texas Collection, Baylor Institute for Oral History, Waco, Texas.

33. Blaine transcript, 46.

34. Transcript Robert Aguilar Oral History Interview by Thomas Charlton recorded September 19, 2005, #1, Texas Collection, Baylor University Institute for Oral History, Waco, Texas.

35. The dropout data come from an application Aguilar prepared for the Campaign for Human Development referenced previously.

36. Aguilar transcript, #8.

37. Margie Lopez Cintron, interview by Elinor Maze, transcript of recording made November 11, 2006, Texas Collection, Baylor Institute for Oral History, Waco, Texas.

38. Aguilar transcript, #15.

39. M. M. McRae, letter dated December 5, 1973. It is page 8 of an application for ESAA funds dated November 21, 1973. Waco Organization Box 2L169. [Waco] Alliance of Mexican Americans File, Baylor University Institute for Oral History, Waco, Texas.

40. Samuel W. Newman, ed., *History of the Waco Public Schools* (Waco, TX: Waco Independent School District, 1976), Texas Collection, Baylor University, Waco, Texas.

41. As Kevin Carlos Blanton explained in *Strange Career of Bilingual Education in Texas, 1836–1981* (College Station: Texas A&M University Press, 2004), 114–16, the Texas State Department of Education allowed schools to use the "Inter-American Test in Oral English" to segregate students through first grade until a successful court challenge by LULAC and the GI Forum in *Hernandez v. Driscoll* in

1957, but the federal district court ruling by former Texas governor James V. Allred did allow Spanish-speaking children to be tracked into different groupings based on "scientific" testing of individual students. For a summary of the *Delgado* ruling, see *Handbook of Texas Online*, available at http://www.tshaonline.org/handbook/online/articles/jrho2, accessed October 24, 2013.

42. Transcript of Wilbur Allen Ball Oral History Interview by Thomas Charlton recorded June 5, 1974, 9, Texas Collection, Baylor University Institute for Oral History, Waco, Texas.

43. Elizabeth Cruce Alvarez, *Texas Almanac 2006–2007* (Dallas: Dallas Morning News, 2006), 227. For a more detailed discussion of the make-up of the population of Goliad before and after Texas independence from Mexico, see the *Handbook of Texas Online*, http://www.tshaonline.org/handbook/online/articles/hj go5, accessed October 24, 2013.

44. Robert Gamboa, interview by Thomas Charlton. Transcript of recording made November 11, 2006, #2, 6–9 (elementary school); 46–50 (junior high incident), Texas Collection, Baylor Institute for Oral History, Waco, Texas.

45. Newman, *History of the Waco Public Schools*, 79.

46. Charles Gonzalez, letter to Waco Board of Education dated May 23, 1970, Waco Organizations, Box 2L169, [Waco] Alliance of Mexican Americans File, Texas Collection, Baylor University Institute for Oral History, Waco, Texas.

47. Waco Independent School District, Minutes of the Board of Trustees, May 21, 1970. Document obtained by FOIA request to Waco ISD, Waco, Texas, as are all subsequent references to minutes of the Waco ISD Board of Education meetings, which are kept at the district's administrative offices in Waco.

48. Gonzalez letter to Waco ISD board.

49. Ibid.

50. Waco Independent School District, Minutes of Board of Trustees meeting on May 21, 1970.

51. Avery R. Downing, letter to Charles Gonzalez dated September 22, 1970, Waco Organization, Box 2L169, [Waco] Alliance of Mexican Americans File, Texas Collection, Baylor University Institute for Oral History, Waco, Texas.

52. Waco Independent School District, Minutes of Board of Trustees Meeting September 17, 1970.

53. Ibid.

54. Ibid.

55. *Waco Herald-Tribune*, October 16, 1970. "Mexican Americans Request Review of Integration Plan," Vertical File, Texas Collection, Baylor University, Waco, Texas.

56. Minutes of the Human Relations Commission, November 5, 1970, Waco Organizations, Box 2L169, [Waco] Alliance of Mexican Americans File, Texas Collection, Baylor University Institute for Oral History, Waco, Texas.

57. Waco Alliance of Mexican Americans, from "Introduction and Philosophy" (Section 4, 9) of application for ESAA funds. Application dated November 21, 1973, Waco Organizations, Box 2L169, [Waco] Alliance of Mexican Americans File, Texas Collection, Baylor University Institute for Oral History, Waco, Texas.

58. Ruling by Judge Jack Roberts in *Pete D. Arizu, et al. v. WISD*, US District Court Western District of Texas Division Civil Action No. W-71-CA-56, 4, Waco Organizations, Box 2L169, [Waco] Alliance of Mexican Americans File, Texas Collection, Baylor University Institute for Oral History, Waco, Texas.

59. Ibid.

60. Neomi Adams, information sheet for advisory committee members contained with ESAA application by WAMA. Waco Organizations, Box 2L169, (Waco) Alliance of Mexican Americans, Texas Collection, Baylor Institute of Oral History, Waco, Texas.

61. Chuck Rose, information sheet for advisory committee members contained with ESAA application by WAMA. Waco Organizations, Box 2L169, (Waco) Alliance of Mexican Americans, Texas Collection, Baylor Institute of Oral History, Waco, Texas.

62. Ernest Fajardo, information sheet for advisory committee members contained with ESAA application by WAMA. Waco Organizations, Box 2L169, (Waco) Alliance of Mexican Americans, Texas Collection, Baylor Institute of Oral History, Waco, Texas.

63. Tracye McDaniel, information sheet for advisory committee members contained with ESAA application by WAMA. Waco Organizations, Box 2L169, (Waco) Alliance of Mexican Americans, Texas Collection, Baylor Institute of Oral History, Waco, Texas.

64. Marc A. Rodriguez, "A Movement Made of 'Young Mexican Americans Seeking Change': Critical Change, Migration, and the Chicano Movement in Texas and Wisconsin, 1960–1975," *Western Historical Quarterly* 34 (Autumn 2003).

65. WAMA application, "Introduction and Philosophy," 15.

66. Ibid., 16.

67. Ibid., 17.

68. Aguilar transcript #2, interview by Thomas Charlton, transcript of recording made October 3, 2005, Texas Collection, Baylor Institute of Oral History, Waco, Texas.

CONCLUSION

1. Robert A. Caro. *The Years of Lyndon Johnson: The Passage of Power* (New York: Knopf, 2012).

2. Perhaps more than seventeen calls were made, but that is the tally of the recordings released to the public by the LBJ Library through the outstanding Miller Center website at the University of Virginia, where recordings of presidential conversations from Franklin Roosevelt through Richard Nixon can be accessed. Presidents after Nixon have not recorded calls, as far as the public knows.

3. Recording of telephone conversation between LBJ and Harry Provence, December 25, 1963, Miller Center.

4. Transcript of W. R. Poage Oral History Interview by Thomas Charlton, Volume 4, Interview 23, recorded July 16, 1982, 1150, Texas Collection, Baylor University Institute for Oral History, Waco, Texas.

5. The program for a retirement event for Poage in 1978 tells the story of his influence (photograph of program on p. 186) and features presidents Carter, Ford, and all living secretaries of agriculture, including Poage's nemesis from the Eisenhower administration, Ezra Taft Benson. Poage's party unceremoniously stripped him of his role as chair of the House Agriculture Committee, but his successor, Tom Foley of Washington, relied heavily on Poage.

6. Recording of telephone conversation between LBJ and W. R. Poage, January 13, 1964, Miller Center.

7. Ibid.

8. The heart-wrenching examples of denial of basic human decencies LBJ used to underline the realities of the Jim Crow practices in the South may or may not have been dramatized for effect, but they were certainly plausible. Caro, Dallek, and most other Johnson scholars refer to this tactic as the Johnson Treatment during the civil rights debate in 1964.

9. Johnson often used the word "negro," pronounced in his Hill Country drawl as "nigra." When he believed the language fit the circumstances and the audience, he used the word "nigger," as well. His public remarks as president trace the evolution of the language of race in political discourse in the 1960s. A white person in Texas in Johnson's time would not have referred to a Mexican American as "colored," but simply as a Mexican. The Chicano movement embraced the use of the color "brown" to distinguish their agenda and interests from those of "blacks," although they would find much in common. The phrase "people of color" was not widely used in Central Texas in Johnson and Poage's time.

10. Hubert H. Humphrey, *The Education of a Public Man: My Life and Politics* (Garden City, NY: Doubleday, 1973).

11. The Model Cities program came to an abrupt end when the Nixon administration took over. The plan to offer grants to fifty cities, one for each state, quickly proved untenable; funding for the program moved through Congress, where it all became watered down by adding cities faster than funds were added. Model Cities became, if anything, a model for what went wrong with several Great Society

initiatives. The seeds of ideas grew in a hothouse environment but struggled when planted in the fields because of too little attention.

12. W. R . Poage Interview by Thomas Charlton, Volume 4, Interview 24, transcript of recording made February 23, 1983, Texas Collection, Baylor University Institute for Oral History, Waco, Texas.

13. W. R. Poage Interview by Joe Frantz, Transcript of recording made November 11, 1968, LBJ Library.

14. Pickle took office on December 24, 1963, after a special election in the Tenth Congressional District that had LBJ's fingerprints all over it. At Johnson's recommendation, Kennedy had named Congressman Homer Thornberry, an LBJ man since college, to a federal judgeship. Pickle, a former NYA staffer (he started after Johnson went to Congress), considered his vote in favor of the Civil Rights Act to be the most difficult one of his sixteen terms in the House. At http://www.tsha online.org/handbook/online/articles/fpi47, accessed June 20, 2013.

15. At http://www.tshaonline.org/handbook/online/articles/hdw01, accessed June 17, 2013. The population of Waco in 1960 was 97,808, more than 2.5 percent above the figure ten years later.

16. Recording of LBJ telephone conversation with Harry Provence, November 8, 1964.

17. The base closed in 1966. Johnson may have been correct in the long run, given the thousands of individuals who received valuable training at facilities established on the site of the base, including the Texas State Technical Institute.

18. At http://wacohistoryproject.org/firstperson/harryprovence.html, accessed June 19, 2013.

19. Poage addressed this point during interviews with Thomas Charlton of Baylor University, although he did not do so in the context of the construction of the dam. He indicated during his reflections on his relationship with LBJ that there was no effort to get him to vote "yes" on that landmark legislation, despite the president's legendary arm-twisting tactics.

20. W. R. Poage Interview by Thomas Charlton, Volume 4, Interview 23, transcript of recording made July 16, 1982, 1239, Texas Collection, Baylor University Institute for Oral History, Waco, Texas.

21. Recording of LBJ telephone conversation with Harry Provence, November 8, 1964.

22. Tony Badger, "Southerners Who Refused to Sign the Manifesto," *Historical Journal* 42 (June 1999): 517–34.

23. Fowler West, Poage's legislative aide, is the only source of a rumored cabinet appointment by JFK, but given the efforts by the Kennedy administration to signal African Americans of future intentions, naming someone opposed to their

agenda, even for the secretary of agriculture, would have created unnecessary complications for little gain.

24. Badger, "Southerners Who Refused to Sign the Manifesto," 525.

25. The statement used in Tony Badger's article about the Southern Manifesto is found in Volume 3 of Poage's oral history. Poage's observation of the racial climate certainly suggests either ignorance or indifference, but these statements were made when he was well into his eighties. One of the sadder aspects of reading these extensive interviews (the quote on race relations in Waco is found on p. 815) is the very evident loss of memory. Poage frequently acknowledged in that last round of questions and answers that he had trouble remembering. Nevertheless, his characterization of race relations certainly fits the mold of "conservative" thought in Texas and across the South, which viewed the notion of racial unrest as the result of instigation by troublemakers from the North.

26. Transcript of interview with J. H. Kultgen.

27. As president, Johnson favored the use of task forces comprised of elites from academia, corporate foundations, and key interest groups to formulate policy recommendations. Political scientists Richard L. Schott and Dagmar S. Hamilton provide an overview of how Johnson approached the formation and charging of dozens of these bodies in *People, Positions, and Power: The Political Appointments of Lyndon Johnson* (Chicago: University of Chicago Press, 1983).

28. Carter campaign speeches from 1976 and Ronald Reagan's 1981 inaugural speech.

29. Named after the wife of Governor Pat Neff. See Dan K. Utley and James W. Steely, *Guided with a Steady Hand: The Cultural Landscape of a Rural Texas Park* (Waco, TX: Baylor University Press, 1998).

30. James McEnteer, *Deep in the Heart: The Texas Tendency in American Politics* (Westport, CT: Praeger, 2004). Lewis Gould develops the Wilson administration's ties to Texas in *Progressives and Prohibitionists* (Austin: Texas State Historical Association, 1992).

31. The line from the song referenced here, popularized by Liza Minnelli and by Frank Sinatra, is, "If I can make it here, I can make it anywhere—New York, New York!"

32. Gareth Davies, "The Great Society after Johnson: The Case of Bilingual Education," *Journal of American History* (2010): 1405–29.

BIBLIOGRAPHY

GOVERNMENT REPORTS AND DOCUMENTS

Austin Chamber of Commerce Annual Report for 1919. Austin, Texas, 1920. Koch and Fowler, *A City Plan for Austin*, January 14, 1928.

National Youth Administration. United States Government. "Report of NYA Projects on Which Negro Youths Are Employed: Special Report of Negro Activities of NYA in Texas," March 16, 1936.

Soule, W. F., and Associates. "Strategy for Regional Planning and Policy Guidelines Waco–McLennan County Region," October 1967. Waco, Texas.

US Department of Commerce Bureau of the Census. *Religious Bodies: 1926.* Washington, DC: US Government Printing Office, 1930.

US Government. *Report of the Comptroller General of the United States.* November 3, 1965.

Waco Independent School District Board Minutes. Waco, Texas.

LIBRARIES AND ARCHIVES

Austin History Center, Austin Public Library, Austin, Texas.
Baylor Institute for Oral History, Baylor University, Waco, Texas.

Lyndon Baines Johnson Presidential Library, Austin, Texas.

W. R. Poage Legislative Library, Baylor University, Waco, Texas.

Texas Collection, Baylor University, Waco, Texas.

Texas Historical Commission, Austin, Texas.

BOOKS AND ARTICLES

Alvarez, Elizabeth Cruce. *Texas Almanac, 2006–2007*. Dallas: Dallas Morning News, 2006.

Amers, Eric S. *Waco*. Images of America. Charleston, SC: Arcadia Publishing, 2009.

Badger, Tony. "Southerners Who Refused to Sign the Southern Manifesto." *Historical Journal* 42 (June 1999): 517–34.

Baum, Dale. "Pinpointing Apparent Fraud in the 1861 Texas Secession Referendum." *Journal of Interdisciplinary History* 22 (Autumn 1991): 201–21.

Bernstein, Patricia. *The First Waco Horror: The Lynching of Jesse Washington and the Rise of the NAACP*. College Station: Texas A&M University Press, 2005.

Blanton, Carlos Kevin. *The Strange Career of Bilingual Education in Texas, 1836–1981*. College Station: Texas A&M University Press, 2004.

Bourgeois, Christie. "Stepping Over Lines: Lyndon Johnson, Black Texans, and the National Youth Administration, 1935–1937." *Southwestern Historical Quarterly* 91 (October 1987): 149–72.

Brewer, J. Mason. *Historical Outline of the Negro in Travis County*. Austin: Samuel Huston College, 1941.

Bryant, Nick. *The Bystander: John F. Kennedy and the Struggle for Black Equality*. New York: Basic Books, 2006.

Carlson, Lewis, and George Colburn. *In Their Place: White America Defines Her Minorities*. New York: Wiley, 1971.

Caro, Robert A. *The Years of Lyndon Johnson: Master of the Senate*. New York: Knopf, 2002.

———. *The Years of Lyndon Johnson: Means of Ascent*. New York: Knopf, 1990.

———. *The Years of Lyndon Johnson: The Passage of Power*. New York: Knopf, 2012.

———. *The Years of Lyndon Johnson: The Path to Power*. New York: Knopf, 1982.

Carrigan, William D. *The Making of a Lynching Culture: Violence and Vigilantism in Central Texas, 1836–1916*. Urbana: University of Illinois Press, 2004.

Dallek, Robert A. *Flawed Giant: Lyndon Johnson and His Times, 1961–1973*. New York: Oxford University Press, 1998.

———. *Lone Star Rising: Lyndon Johnson and His Times, 1908–1960*. New York: Oxford University Press, 1991.

Davies, Gareth. "The Great Society after Johnson: The Case of Bilingual Education." *Journal of American History* (June 2002): 1405–29.

———. "Towards Big-Government Conservatism: Conservatives and Federal Aid to Education in the 1970s." *Journal of Contemporary History* 43 (October 2008): 621–35.

Deckard, Barbara. "State Party Delegations in the U.S House of Representatives—A Comparative Study of Group Cohesion." *Journal of Politics* 34 (February 1972): 199–222.

Du Bois, W. E. B. *The Souls of Black Folk and Other Writings.* New York: Barnes and Noble, 2003.

Duke, Robert Harold. "Fort Custer and the Village of Augusta, 1939–1941." *International Journal of Regional and Local History* (December 2005): 21–39.

Fehrenbach, T. R. *Lone Star: A History of Texas and the Texans.* New York: Da Capo Press, 1998.

Fernlund, Kevin. *Lyndon B. Johnson and Modern America.* Norman: University of Oklahoma Press, 2009.

Firmin, Mark E. *Waco, Texas' William Cameron Park, A Centennial History, 1910–2010: A Long Love Affair with Nature's Splendor.* Waco, TX: Baylor University Press, 2010.

Flanagan, Richard. "Lyndon Johnson, Community Action, and Management of the Administrative State." *Presidential Studies Quarterly* 31 (December 2001): 585–608.

Foley, Neil. *The White Scourge: Mexicans, Blacks, and Poor Whites in the Texas Cotton Culture.* Berkeley: University of California Press, 1997.

Franklin, John Hope, and Alfred Moss Jr. *From Slavery to Freedom.* 8th ed. New York: Knopf, 2000.

Funigiello, Philip. *The Challenge to Urban Liberalism.* Knoxville: University of Tennessee Press, 1997.

Goodwin, Doris Kearns. *Lyndon Johnson and the American Dream.* 2nd ed. New York: St. Martin's Press, 1991.

Gould, Lewis. *Progressives and Prohibitionists.* Austin: Texas State Historical Association, 1992.

Graves, John. *Goodbye to a River: A Narrative.* New York: Vintage Departures, 1988.

Greene, A. C. *Sketches from the Five States of Texas.* College Station: Texas A&M University Press, 1998.

Hansen, John Mark. *Gaining Access: Congress and the Farm Lobby, 1919–1981.* Chicago: University of Chicago Press, 1991.

Harrington, Michael. *The Other America: Poverty in the United States.* New York: Macmillan, 1997.

Hodgson, Godfrey. *Woodrow Wilson's Right Hand: The Life of Colonel Edward M. House.* New Haven, CT: Yale University Press, 2011.

Hughes, L. Patrick. "Working within the System: Lyndon Johnson and Tom Miller, 1937–1939." *Southwestern Historical Quarterly* 96 (October 1992): 179–212.

Humphrey, David C. *Austin: A History of the Capital City.* Austin: Texas State Historical Association, 1997.

Humphrey, Hubert H. *The Education of a Public Man: My Life and Politics.* Garden City, NY: Doubleday, 1973.

Hunter, Tera W. *To 'Joy My Freedom: Southern Black Women's Lives and Labors after the Civil War.* Cambridge, MA: Harvard University Press, 1998.

Huser, Verne. *Rivers of Texas.* College Station: Texas A&M University Press, 2000.

Johnson, Ben Heber. *Revolution in Texas.* New Haven, CT: Yale University Press, 2005.

Johnson, James Weldon. *Along This Way.* New York: Viking Press, 1933.

Katznelson, Ira. *When Affirmative Action Was White: An Untold History of Racial Inequality in Twentieth-Century America.* New York: Norton, 2005.

Key, V. O. *Southern Politics in State and Nation.* Knoxville: University of Tennessee Press, 1984.

Kincaid, John. "From Cooperative to Coercive Federalism." *Annals of the American Academy of Political and Social Science* 509, American Federalism: The Third Century (May 1990): 139–52.

Kotz, Nick. *Judgment Days: Lyndon Baines Johnson, Martin Luther King, Jr., and the Laws That Changed America.* Boston: Houghton Mifflin, 2005.

Lerner, Mitchell. "'To Be Shot at by the Whites and Dodged by the Negroes': Lyndon Johnson and the Texas NYA." *Presidential Studies Quarterly* 39 (June 2009): 245–74.

Maher, Neil M. *Nature's New Deal: The Civilian Conservation Corps and the Roots of the American Environmental Movement.* New York: Oxford University Press, 2009.

McEnteer, James. *Deep in the Heart: The Texas Tendency in American Politics.* Westport, CT: Praeger, 2004.

Meinig, D. W. *Imperial Texas.* Austin: University of Texas Press, 1969.

Meyer, Agnes. *America's Home Front.* New York: Harcourt, Brace, 1943.

Milkis, Sidney M., and Jerome M. Mileur. *The Great Society and the High Tide of Liberalism.* Amherst: University of Massachusetts Press, 2005.

Murphy, Marjorie. *Blackboard Unions.* Ithaca, NY: Cornell University Press, 1990.

Nevels, Cynthia Skove. *Lynching to Belong.* College Station: Texas A&M University Press, 2007.

Newman, Samuel W., ed. *History of the Waco Public Schools.* Waco, TX: Waco Independent School District, 1976.

Orum, Anthony M. *Power, Money, and the People: The Making of Modern Austin.* Austin: Texas Monthly Press, 1987.

Patterson, James T. *Freedom Is Not Enough: The Moynihan Report and America's Struggle over Black Family Life from LBJ to Obama.* New York: Basic Books, 2010.

Peters, Charles. *Lyndon B. Johnson.* The American Presidents. New York: Times Books, 2010.

Poage, W. R. *My First 85 Years.* Waco, TX: Baylor University Press, 1985.

Polk, R. L., and Co. *Austin City Directories,* 1920 and 1930–31 editions. Austin: Morrison and Fourmy Directory Company.

Pycior, Julie Leininger. *LBJ and Mexican Americans: The Paradox of Power.* Austin: University of Texas Press, 1997.

Quiroz, Antonio. *Claiming Citizenship: Mexican Americans in Victoria, Texas.* College Station: Texas A&M University Press, 2005.

Rodriguez, Marc A. "A Movement Made of 'Young Mexican Americans Seeking Change': Critical Change, Migration, and the Chicano Movement in Texas and Wisconsin, 1960–1975." *Western Historical Quarterly* 34 (Autumn 2003): 275–99.

Scarbrough, Linda. *Road, River, and Ol' Boy Politics.* Austin: Texas State Historical Association, 2005.

Schapsmeier, Edward L., and Frederick H. Schapsmeier. *Encyclopedia of American Agricultural History.* Westport, CT: Greenwood Press, 1975.

Schott, Richard L., and Dagmar S. Hamilton. *People, Positions, and Power: The Political Appointments of Lyndon Johnson.* Chicago: University of Chicago Press, 1983.

Shackles, Chrystine. *Reminiscences of Huston-Tillotson College.* Austin: Best Printing, 1973.

Turner, Bradley T., ed. *Lust, Violence, Religion: Life in Historic Waco.* Waco, TX: TSTC Publishing, 2010.

Urban, Wayne J. *Gender, Race, and the National Education Association.* New York: RoutledgeFalmer, 2000.

Utley, Dan K., and Cynthia J. Beeman. *History Ahead: Stories beyond the Texas Roadside Markers.* College Station: Texas A&M University Press, 2010.

———. *History along the Way: Stories beyond the Texas Roadside Markers.* College Station: Texas A&M University Press, 2013.

Utley, Dan K., and James W. Steely. *Guided with a Steady Hand: The Cultural Landscape of a Rural Texas Park.* Waco, TX: Baylor University Press, 1998.

Waskow, Arthur. *From Race Riot to Sit-In, 1919 and the 1960s: A Study in the Connection between Conflict and Violence.* Garden City, NY: Doubleday, 1966.

Webb, Walter Prescott. *The Great Plains.* Lincoln: University of Nebraska Press, 1981.

West, Fowler. *He Ain't No Lawyer.* Waco, TX: Baylor University Press, 2009.

White, Theodore. *The Making of the President: 1960.* New York: Harper Perennial, 2009.

Woods, Randall B. *LBJ: Architect of American Ambition.* New York: Free Press, 2006.

Zamora, Emilio. *Mexican Labor Activity in South Texas, 1900–1920.* Austin: University of Texas Press, 1983.

DISSERTATIONS

Duke, Robert Harold. "Bilingual Education, Federalism, and the Political Culture of American Public Education, 1964–1980." PhD diss., Western Michigan University, 2008.

McDonald, Jason John. "Race Relations in Austin, Texas, c. 1917–1929." PhD diss., University of Southampton, 1992.

Weisenberger, Carol Whiteside. "The National Youth Administration in Texas, 1935—1943: A Case Study." PhD diss., Texas A&M University, 1988.

INDEX

Carter, Jimmy, 82, 188
Cen-Tex Hispanic Chamber of Commerce, 166
Central Texas political culture, 23, 30, 31, 111, 112, 185; African Americans, 4, 27, 41, 48, 146; anti-federal sentiments, 6, 8, 22, 23, 25, 33, 34, 44, 45, 70, 148, 151, 185, 187, 188; Democratic party factions, 78; distinctions between Hill Country and blackland prairie, 17, 22, 25, 31, 37, 49; effects of KKK, 35, 46, 49–56, 59, 63; emergence of non-Anglo influence, 21, 41, 47; growth of military-industrial interests, 113, 114; increased tolerance among Anglo males, 116, 117; influence of German immigrants, 41, 50; influence of New Deal, 56, 71, 111, 136, 145, 187, 192; lynching, 22, 23, 31, 45, 184, 185; Mexican Americans, 33, 67, 92, 146, 151–156, 160, 166; opposition to New Deal, 20; public schools, 152, 163; organized labor, 13–15, 85–87; secession vote, 22; segregation 149; urban renewal, 149–151
Chapin, Joe, 85
Chicano movement, 49, 154, 167, 170, 172, 187
Cintron, Margie, generational issues, 163, growing up in Waco, 158, 160, 163; political engagement, 160
Circle Development Company, 121
Civil Rights Act of 1957, 6
Civil Rights Act of 1964, Hillary Clinton, 3; LBJ and MLK, 18; Poage opposition, 7, 12, 15,19
Civilian Conservation Corps (CCC), see New Deal

Clarksville, African American housing patterns in Austin, 48
Clinton, Hillary, 3
Colorado River, 21, 37
Colored Welfare Board (Austin), 57, 148
Community Action Program (CAP), 19, 20, 74
Community Welfare Association (Austin), 60; NYA, 60, 66
Connally, James Air Force Base—see Twelfth Air Force base
Connally, Tom, 77, 78
constituent letters (Johnson), expectations of staff, 121; importance, 7; NYA, 71, 72, Pedernales Electric Cooperative project, 99-102
constituent letters (Poage), expectation of staff, 121; importance, 7; new Bosque River dam, 119-121, 125–129, 132, 134–136, 141; tone, 123; NYA, 95–103
Cooper Foundation, 168
Corson, John, and LBJ on segregated advisory councils, 88–90, 103
Cotulla, Texas, LBJ's teaching experience, xi, 41, 76, 83, 102, 151, 173, 164, 191; NYA program, 88; student poverty, 40, 41, 76, 102, 182
Crane, Marian McNulty, 54, 55
Crawford, W.H., 57
Crisis, Du Bois report of "Waco Horror," 22
Cross, Otto, 70, 87, 112
Crystal City, 156
Cruz, Ted, 22

Daniel, Price, 146, 156
Davis, W.L., 89
Delgado v. Bastrop ISD, 161

Pace, Lula, 142

Patman, Wright, 49–51

Pedernales Electric Cooperative project, 99–102

Peek, Ben S., 84–85

Pete D. Arizu, et al. v. WISD, 168

Perry, Rick, 22

Persons, General, 161

Pickle, J. J. ("Jake"), support for Civil Rights Act of 1964, 6, 217; location of Twelfth Air Force base, 7, 180

Poage, Frances, 17; friendship with Lady Bird Johnson, 126

Poage, Helen Conger, 42, domestics in household, 42, 87; family background, 42; influence on Bob Poage, 87, 107; *p. 42*

Poage, William Allen, 42, career in Texas legislature, 29, 106; death, 53; Lazy "Leven Ranch, 42; response to anti-German hysteria, 39; return to Waco, 42; support for federal action on drought relief, 44

Poage, W. R. ("Bob"), agriculture policy, 10, 13, 16, 17, 20; Army Corps of Engineers, 127, 132; boyhood, 10, 42, 45; Bosque Dam groundbreaking, 1, 169; brothers, 42; campaign of 1960, 3; civil rights, 12, 13, 15–17, 19, 156, 183, 184; college education, 44, 70; clout in House of Representatives, 10, 11, 13, 140, 150, 163, 177, 180; constituents, *see* constituent letters (Poage); construction bids for Bosque Dam project, 137, 139, 140; dam dedication, 143; delay in dam construction, 173; effect of dam project delays on reputation, 134; Eisenhower, 150; election victory in 1936, 8, 69–71; failed congressional

campaign 1934, 1, 70, 87, 112; federal aid, 25, 179–180; House Agriculture Committee, 12, *118*, 182, 193; influence of father's career, 29–31, 42, 53; influence of New Deal on philosophy, 11, 12, 14, 16, 62, 75, 132, 179; interest groups, 9, 10, 12, 14, 16, 136; JFK, 3, 13, 221; KKK "anti-masking bill," 52; Mexican Americans, 156, 160; "Mr. Agriculture," 185, *186*; Model Cities, 153, 179, 180; new Bosque River dam project, 115–143; NYA appointees, 8, 20, 75, 84–87, 92, 149, 173; opposition to Dixiecrats, 5, 15; political philosophy, 13, 14, 45, 75, 80, 86; relationship with Harlan Fentress, 1, 106, 120–123, 129, 138, 142–144; relationship with LBJ, 2, 7, 8, 10, 12, 13, 15, 17, 23, 26, 27, 30, 32, 33, 37, 69, 70, 92, 93, 103, 115–123, 126, 138, 140, 143, 144, 145, 149, 173, 175–179, 182–193; relationship with Jack Kultgen, 1, 106, 115-123, 140, 143, 144; relationship with Harry Provence, 1, 106, 130–135, 175, 176,, 181–183, 187; refusal to sign Southern Manifesto, 15, 16; REA, 9; RTA, 9; state legislature, 8, 29, 44, 106, 189; Twelfth Air Force base, 7, 113, 143, 180–182; urban renewal, 149, 150; views on labor, 13, 14, 78, 86; Waco NYA programs, 13-14, Waco tornado relief, 2

Poage-Aiken Act, intergovernmental cooperation, 148

Podet, Rabbi N., 168

Political Association of Spanish Speaking Organizations (PASSO), Waco chapter, 154-156

Populists, 38

Posey, Mrs. Ollie, 164
Possum Kingdom Lake, BRA project, 112, 117
Prairie View State Normal and Industrial College (Prairie View), NYA programs for African Americans, 89, 90; representation on NYA advisory council, 89
Prescott, Eunice Lyons, 77, 78
Prohibition, 38
Provence, Harry, dam dedication, 142; efforts for secure funding for Bosque Dam project, 106, 115, 130, 135, 143; LBJ, 175, 181-183, 190; notification by Poage of bid outcomes, 140; relationship with Poage, 106, 115, 130, 130-135, 143, 175, 176, 181-183

Quinn, Paul College, NYA programs, 81, 94, 113; hosts NYA African American advisory council meeting, 90; role of Jack Kultgen, 146, 186

Rayburn, Sam, characterization by Everett Givens, 64, 65; communication with Poage about Bosque Dam project, 133; LBJ mentor, 10; legislative prowess, 180; oil industry, 22; urban renewal, 150; tutelage of Texas delegation, 15–18, 78, 106
Reagan, Ronald, 188
Rhoads, Joseph J., 89
Rice, Ben, 161
Roberts, Jack, 168, 169
Robertson, Felix D., 54, 55, 59
Rodriguez, Victor, 167
Roosevelt, Eleanor, 87
Roosevelt, Franklin Delano, NYA, 69, 81, 83, 85, 86; LBJ mentor, 12;

support for Mansfield Dam (Colorado River), 1, 2; Texas political network, 77, 78; Triangulation, 176
Roosevelt Hotel (Waco), 120, 126, 135, 136
Rose, Chuck, ESAA advisory council, 170, 171
Rountree, Gordon, 165
Rural Electrification Act, 9
Rural Electrification Administration, 99-102
Rural Telephone Act, 9
Rusk, Dean, 175
Russell, Richard, 10

Samuelson, Agnes, 83
San Gabriel River, 9, 10
Sandtown (Waco), descriptions, 157, 158; effect of tornado, 157, 158; Mexican American community leadership 26; increase of Mexican American population, 48
Secession referendum (1861), 22
Segovia, Crecesenciano, 68
Senate Appropriations Committee, 130, 138
Senate Finance Committee, 178
Senate Public Works Committee, 124, 142
Shackles, Chrystine, 62
Shelton, John, Austin KKK investigation, 53
Shillady, John, 58
Shivers, Alan, 142
Skiles, Joe K., 84
Smith-Hughes Act, 100
Smith, Truett, 136
Soule, W.F. and Associates, 179
Southeast Asia, see Vietnam
Southern Manifesto, 15, 16, 176
Southern Tenant Farmers' Union, 14, 78